Praise for *The Sea in the Metro*

'This is a book like sheet lightning: sudden, illuminating and sometimes terrifying. *The Sea in the Metro* tells the story of falling out of love with a city and back in love with life, the perfect denouement to Jayne Tuttle's Paris trilogy. Frank. Devastating. Hilarious.'
—**Tegan Bennett-Daylight, author of *The Details***

'A whirlwind of longing – mother-longing, lover-longing, artist-longing – this book will sweep you off your feet.' —**Siang Lu, author of *Ghost Cities***

'Epic, fearless and compellingly honest … Tuttle's writing rings with authenticity while facing the darker, utterly real moments of motherhood, desire and the beautiful, infuriating pursuit of art.'
—**Katherine Brabon, author of *Body Friend***

'Living intersections of bodies and wit, there is an addictive element about it – memory, consciousness, motherhood. It is a truly sweeping account of viscera. Not giving fucks. Birth – poking thoughts.'
—**Misha Honcharenko, author of *Trap Unfolds Me Greedily***

'Lyrical, fierce and often funny, *The Sea in the Metro* is a wonderfully vivid self-portrait of a young woman navigating the entanglements of love and loss, mortality and motherhood, creativity and paying the bills. It's also a profound meditation on the idea of home. I loved it.'
—**Jennifer Higgie, author of *The Other Side, A Journey into Women, Art and the Spirit World***

Praise for *Paris or Die* and *My Sweet Guillotine*

'Jayne Tuttle's two linked actor-in-Paris memoirs, *Paris or Die* and *My Sweet Guillotine*, start merrily and step off the edge into calamity, in writing that is joltingly alive, beautiful and terrifying.'
—**Helen Garner**, *The Age*

'By turns madcap and heartbreaking, a witty and wise reflection on the power of cities to help us become ourselves. I devoured it and I can't wait to read more from my new favourite writer.'
—**Lauren Elkin, author of** *Scaffolding, Art Monsters*

'Jayne Tuttle is all nerve endings and astute noticing. We don't have anyone else in this country writing memoir quite like Jayne.'
—**Claire Thomas, author of** *The Performance*

'A subtle mix of escapist writing that will appeal to any person feeling any affinity with Paris, but that also engages with deeper questions of trauma and survival. The author's literary talent is undeniable.'
—*The French Australian Review*

'Jayne Tuttle's writing is irresistible – at once totally enchanting and gripping. A writer who has perfected her craft.' —**Ceridwen Dovey, author of** *Mothertongues*

'Pitch-perfect and pacy – very, very funny at times, and raw and affecting at others.

An exquisite study of what happens to the wild force of attraction when it crashes into the hard structures of societal, class and cultural difference.' —**Linda Jaivin, author of** *Eat Me*

'Jayne Tuttle's writing is a delicious delight.' —**Christos Tsiolkas, author of** *The In-Between*

'Stunning.' —*Marie Claire*

The Sea in the Metro

Also by Jayne Tuttle

Paris or Die
My Sweet Guillotine

The Sea in the Metro

Jayne Tuttle

Hardie Grant

BOOKS

Published in 2025 by Hardie Grant Books, an imprint of Hardie Grant Publishing

Hardie Grant Books (Melbourne)
Wurundjeri Country
Level 11, 36 Wellington Street
Collingwood, Victoria 3066

Hardie Grant North America
2912 Telegraph Ave
Berkeley, California 94705

hardiegrant.com/books

Hardie Grant acknowledges the Traditional Owners of the Country on which we work, the Wurundjeri People of the Kulin Nation and the Gadigal People of the Eora Nation, and recognises their continuing connection to the land, waters and culture. We pay our respects to their Elders past and present.

All rights reserved. No part of this publication may be reproduced, stored in a retrieval system or transmitted in any form by any means, electronic, mechanical, photocopying, recording or otherwise, without the prior written permission of the publishers and copyright holders. No part of this book may be used or reproduced in any manner for the purpose of training artificial intelligence technologies or systems.

The moral rights of the author have been asserted.

Copyright text © Jayne Tuttle 2025

 A catalogue record for this book is available from the National Library of Australia

The Sea in the Metro
ISBN 978 1 74379 786 0
ISBN 978 1 76144 024 3 (ebook)

10 9 8 7 6 5 4 3 2 1

Publishing Director: Pam Brewster
Head of Editorial: Jasmin Chua
Commissioning Editor: Claire Davis
Editor: Kimberley Davis
Creative Director: Kristin Thomas
Cover Designer: Jo Thomson
Cover photo by Matt Davis
Typesetter: Cannon Typesetting
Head of Production: Todd Rechner
Production Controller: Elly Cridland

Printed in Australia by Griffin Press, an Accredited ISO AS/NZS 14001 Environmental Management System printer.

 The paper this book is printed on is certified against the Forest Stewardship Council® Standards. Griffin Press holds FSC® chain of custody certification SCS-COC-001185. FSC® promotes environmentally responsible, socially beneficial and economically viable management of the world's forests.

For Libby, Mary, Matt and Frankie

Car rien qui bestialise un être comme le goût du bonheur éternel, la recherche à tout prix du bonheur éternel, et mademoiselle Lucifer est cette pute qui n'a jamais voulu quitter le bonheur éternel.

For nothing bestialises like the taste for eternal happiness, the search for eternal happiness at any price, and mademoiselle Lucifer is that slut who never wanted to abandon eternal happiness.

– Antonin Artaud, *Sûppots et Suppliciations*

Bien

It's August: high summer in the Faubourg-Saint-Denis. I'm sitting with Francine and the Chunk in the window of the Napoléon, where there's no air, but it's too smoky out on the terrasse and, besides, there's no air there either. Through the open doorway comes a steady draught of baked trash, smoke and sweat, or is it my own sweat, the clamour of bikes and cars and shouting deliverymen. Our window position is the perfect vantage point from which to view the bustling intersection of the rues du Château d'Eau, Faubourg-Saint-Denis and Petites Écuries, the weight of the day's heat seeming to sag the bodies and buildings, the shuttered papeteries and bars and butchers and boulangers, the tired balconies and overflowing bins.

Francine is telling a story about how she moved to the countryside for six months when she was a teenager in the '60s. Hated it, she says, never lived outside Paris again. As she describes her horreur, horreur de la province, the Chunk turns and reaches into my tank top, grabs my tit and tries to swipe it out and towards her mouth like a hot dog. Francine turns to look out the window, as if giving me permission to feed, which I doubt – in public, and a toddler? As I swipe the Chunk's hand away and she clambers to the floor, Francine takes a deep breath, and says, gazing with adoration at the honking, filthy street:

Et on n'est pas bien là?

Literal translation: And one is not well here? 'Well' meaning happy, fine, joyful, healthy, fulfilled, exultant. 'Here' meaning Paris, a city, this city, the 10th arrondissement, this corner, in this age, this era, early twenty-teens, today, this evening, now, Monday. Yes, Monday.

Who would want to be anywhere else, is what she really means. A statement, not a question. We sit looking out. People kiss, people ride, people smoke against a pole, people empty a van *PARIS NORD BOISSONS* ... too busy or poor or preoccupied to escape the city and put their feet in a nice cool stream.

I ask Francine if she's heard of Paris Syndrome, the meltdown that happens to certain tourists who, on arriving in Paris, are so shocked by the reality they have a psychotic break and have to be airlifted home. I remember experiencing something similar the first time I walked down this street. But in a good way. Returning to Paris after my mother died, and knowing the city only from my time as an au pair in the pristine Parc Monceau area, my mind exploded at the door to the Lecoq Theatre School on the rue du Faubourg-Saint-Denis. But instead of being airlifted home I wanted to stay inside that feeling forever.

Francine hasn't heard of Paris Syndrome. She is too blissed out by the scene before her, her soon-to-be neighbourhood. Hard to imagine a sixty-something Marguerite Duras like her living here amongst the noise, the traffic, the throng. The cosy, hidden place she's rented forever in the quiet, orderly building in the Marais is being sold, and in September she'll move to a soot-stained Haussmannien on the Boulevard de Strasbourg, next to the ever-pumping Château d'Eau métro station. She's fine with it, she says, she's ready for a change. And she likes this area, it's authentique. Her grandparents lived here, and when her grandchildren are back from the States she'll be closer to them. Life changes, she says. Il faut faire avec.

Best to roll with it.

The Chunk muddles beneath the table with a bunch of old sugar wrappers. Francine hands her a clean pack as the bartender arrives with a bowl of ice cubes to add to our wine, and puts one in the Chunk's spare hand, to her delight. Music plays and Francine looks around the bar, readjusting her heavy glasses. She looks sweaty and alive, the armholes of her summer dress low enough not to expose her sweat, unlike my tank top, which I can feel is soaked in rings.

She asks if I've seen the Godard film *Une Femme Est Une Femme*, with Anna Karina and Jean-Paul Belmondo. The film is set here, she tells me, in this bar, and up in the apartment on the top floor. He really filmed it up there, she says. This bar was called Le Napoléon, even back then. I'll like the film, she tells me, Anna K plays a stripper, she sings, she wants a baby … She'll lend it to me, she has it on DVD.

I wonder for a moment why Francine thinks I'll like it. Because I'm a certain type of person? I have no clue how she sees me. Whatever her impression, the idea that she thinks she knows me sends a warm feeling through my body.

Fuck. Think that's my period. Franprix shuts early in August. Pharmacy too. Doublefuck. Try to stop it with my mind, suck it up and away from my small black shorts. Francine asks what M is doing in Amsterdam, and I tell her about the recording, my stomach still in a knot over the way he left, as well as the cramping, about to release a gush. She confirms the Chunk and I are still coming to Saint-Malo on the weekend and I say yes with as much calm as I can, though I'm so excited to get out of the city I could cry.

We finish our drinks and she offers to pay but I insist, then she puts out her hand to the Chunk, who takes it grubbily and they hobble together out onto the corner of the street. She points to the top floor of the building, where the characters lived in the movie. Two ramshackle balconies, one with a flowerpot attached crudely to it. I move away and follow them around the corner, down the rue des Petites Écuries. Francine is so short she doesn't have to bend over to the Chunk, and it occurs to me this might be why the Chunk feels so close to her. It hurts my heart, her doughy arm reaching up to Francine. The grandmotherly ease. They totter along in front of me, two small people taking up the entire footpath's breadth, looking in doorways and up at the buildings – Où est ta maison? Ça ma maison! – in their own world, their French world. At number eighteen, Francine passes the tiny hand back to me, at which the Chunk starts crying. Francine kisses me on both cheeks, says she'll see me at the station in Saint-Malo on Friday, and leaves.

We begin the walk up the four flights of stairs, the Chunk begging me to carry her. My thighs are slick with sweat and perhaps blood. Baba walk, I say, but she says, Non Maman kawee. At the top of the first flight she wriggles down and goes to crouch in the usual corner for her inexplicable minute-long ritual of staring silently into space. On the third floor she opens the old electric box to pull out the broken piece of concrete. Pizza! We play the pizza game, yum, yum, then I grab her, walk up one more flight to our door, push it open, drop her and the bags. Mama! Yoyo! Mama! Yoyo! I get her the yoghurt, go to the bathroom, pull down the sticky knickers, sigh.

Yes, one is bien here. One has always been bien here. Since one first set foot in this neighbourhood nine years ago, despite the Paris Syndrome. Since one pushed open the door to the theatre school and spent two years writhing in a scrum of bodies, writhing with Adrien, the Frenchman who one almost married. Since one returned after surviving an ultra-Parisian elevator accident, M in tow with his guitars and his amps, dragging them on a makeshift trolley down the hill to the Studio Bleu, right across from here. Since one returned once more, this time with small child, ending up in the same neighbourhood, as though there never was anywhere else.

Face in the doorway, smeared in yoyo.

Tuck! Viens, Maman!

She grabs my pointer finger and drags it towards the windows as I pull up my shorts with my other hand, trailing the wad of paper I was fashioning into a stopgap. The garbage trucks, her favourite moment of the day – or every other day right now, the garbage men on summer rotation. The ballet of limbs and heads plays out from pavement to truck. Hoorah! – we applaud from our balcony seats – Encore! – as the bins are swung into the great steel buckets that crunch and grind amidst the mounting chorus of furious cyclists and motorists blocked in the one-way street. My forearm ledges the Chunk's sticky butt as we lean against the closed window – too scary to have it open, though there's really no chance of her falling. My forehead gets a red dot from the leaning and the Chunk smacks her palm on it, giggling, which sends a lightning bolt behind my eyes and I have to blink to recover my balance.

Of course one is bien. M's making music, we're together, our kid is healthy, we just paid this month's rent, we live in one of the most beautiful cities in the world. Look, our windows have a view in both directions of the forever-theatre of the rue des Petites Écuries. Little Stables Street. M doesn't work at the track anymore but it still tickles him we live on Stables Street, where I guess horses were kept when this was all fields. He dresses her in little green gumboots and takes her out, to Auteuil, Vincennes, Longchamp …

What does a cow say? *Meuhh!*

What does a cat say? *Riaow!*

What does a horsey say? *GO GO GO!*

Look. There are curtains and window boxes, one, two, three. We've planted mint and basil and flowers, and in the far window I've hung the embroidered one-euro curtain I bought with my first friend in Paris, Kiki the painter, at the Montreuil market back when I was a student. It looks weird next to Sido's chic beige ones but it makes the place more ours.

Look. Built-in bookshelves in the salon next to the dining table, heaving with Jacques and Sido's academic texts and novels and books on philosophy, history, art, cinema, with their talcum-white spines. So much stuff my softened brain won't let me read. All the Bs: Balzac, Breton, Barthes, Baudelaire, Benjamin, Bataille, de Beauvoir ... medical texts and dry sociology, Dante, Deleuze, Debord, de Lautréamont's *Maldoror*, which I occasionally attempt. A theatre section: Genet, Ionesco, Artaud ... Many books on Artaud actually, my theatre-school pin-up. *Là où ça sent la merde, ça sent l'être*. Where it smells of shit, it smells of being. My Danish classmate made a strangely hot piece about that. I think of it every time I change a nappy.

On the bottom shelf are movie box sets, and loose ripped DVDs that M has managed to operate despite their various regional settings. Tarantino, bad '80s stuff, *Betty Blue*, Tarkovsky, Kusturica, stacks of old New Wave films, most of which I've never seen. A complete Godard collection: *À Bout de Souffle*, *Masculin Féminin* ... ah voilà, *Une Femme Est Une Femme*. On the cover Anna Karina in a sailor suit, balancing two men on her fingertips. I put it on the small pile I've been gathering: *Le Bonheur*, *Vivre Sa Vie*, *Jeanne Dielman*, *Love in the Afternoon*, Haneke's *Amour*. That was the last real movie M and I watched together, about the old married couple, the woman's slow descent into dementia. We didn't make it to the end. I can't remember if it was that M got tired or it was just too, too sad. It doesn't bother him not to have seen the end, but I need to, and I don't want to watch it on my own. Though of course there's only one way it can go.

Look, my old red velvet chair, retrieved once again from my Paris sister Nadine after my moving back and forth, back and forth from Australia. Beside it, the record player. Symbolic, that record player. M always wanted a record player, but we've always been in short-term places and he said we should wait until we moved somewhere permanent. Stables Street isn't permanent, but Paris is, and this will be the longest we've ever lived in one apartment together.

There's a real oven. Not one of the sandwich ones that short out the electricity if you put the kettle on, like when I lived as a student in the once-monastery up the road, the Récollets. Parquet floors that creak, which I love, and gratefully old René below seems deaf to the tiny thunderous footfalls up and down the hall. The ceilings are high and moulded for chandeliers, but Sido and Jacques have put in cool modernist lights with dimmers. Imagine owning a place like this. Any place. I never cared about it before. But having to move five times since the Chunk was born, I'm getting to understand why it is such a popular calling.

There's a bath. The Chunk in it now, lining up ducks on its edge, with great concentration. Her father's daughter. My stomach clenches again at the thought of him, his orderliness, his patience. I am a terrible, horrible person. I am the worst person in the world. Bad wife. Bad lover. Bad mother. Bad woman. Bad daughter. Bad sister. Bad cook. Bad tidier. Bad writer. Good copywriter. Bad actor. Bad friend. Bad French-imitator. Bad Australian. Bad duck-sitter. Bad splasher.

Bad towel-wrapper.

Bad raspberry-blower.

If we do things in order, she's not too hard to get into bed. Tonight, because of our date with Francine, things are out of order. I feed her with my drained chest, stroke her head and lay her down. We sing Les Petits Poissons. She wants Le Loup but it's too scary, and then she wants Meunier, Tu Dors, but that one has a fast part at the end when the windmill speeds up and it will excite her. I sing her the Irish song Will Ye Go, Lassie, Go, and she looks like she's falling asleep, then her eyes spring open like the devil just as I move away. Fuck. Dodo, Bébé do, the song my theatre-school best friend Marie-France taught me before I gave birth. The Chunk is still wide awake but I leave her and go back into the living room. Protest cry, not a real cry. Still haven't mastered which is which. M can tell.

I pour some wine. Put on a record, take it off. Time to work, my mind is everywhere, open my computer, social posts for a new range of teenage skincare. If I get it done tonight, I won't be backed up tomorrow if new work comes in. If I start behind, I won't be able to catch up, especially without M here. And if I get the work done and no more comes in, I may even have time to work on the book.

MAMA!

Look, in my phone, a picture from our window yesterday, the sun casting its final ray down the narrow street, creating a red ring of refraction that makes the faded buildings look like a dream. Look, the Chunk in the Récollets park, on top of the castle, pigtails and friends. My old window up there looking over the park, ghost on the second floor, hello single me! Student me, naked with Frenchman, not a care in the world.

Maaamaaaaaa!

Eggs on toast. Can't work when she's crying. Can't work when I'm near her at all. Cotton brain, fluff brain. DADDA! DADDEEEE! He's in Hamsterdam, remember? DODO NOW. Steam burn. Eggs undercooked. Send a photo of the dribbly mess to M: *dinner is served.*

He doesn't respond. I go to the window and watch the family opposite at their dinner table. If I hadn't ordered the champagne before he left, it would have been fine. Why did I order the champagne? Dying to smoke. These windows are made for smoking. Sido does, and she's a doctor. It's the city that smokes, not us. We just live in the smoking city. Three children over there. They look fine, bien, happy, sitting together, the older kid, a teenager, on a computer at the table. It's theatre, I know. They are in deepest hell. If the mother could see me over here, lone figure with wine, she'd probably think, *heaven.*

The Chunk goes quiet. I feel guilty at her quietness, want to wake her up, remind her I love her.

Laptop. Couch. The job takes hours, but I get it done and sent.

Wired. I put *Une Femme Est Une Femme* in my computer and get into bed with it, trying to hear the movie over the men fucking in the apartment above. Anna Karina is standing at the bar in the Napoléon, the walls yellow and grainy rather than tartan wallpaper. She abandons her coffee and walks out onto the rue du Faubourg-Saint-Denis. The corner of the rue des Petites Écuries looks exactly as it is now, only with street sellers and produce carts. She goes into a papeterie – I think where the Corsican wine joint is now – and leadingly opens a magazine on pregnancy in front of her boyfriend, who works there. He is Émile. She is Angela. Night is falling, my favourite time of day in the wintry street. She leaves the paper shop and walks out into the evening sky, down towards the arch, in that dreamy anonymous way I remember from when I was alone. Past the buzzing shops and the old men talking and the people buying groceries. Past the boxing hall at number fifty-seven, which in ten years will become a theatre school and in forty-three have me in it and in fifty-two have me walking past it with a little chunk of love. And it will all look basically the same, the pigeons, the Petit Pot bistrot on the corner, the evening traffic bumper to bumper on the boulevard.

A bang from upstairs. If it wasn't for the moans, mounting, I'd think the men were moving house. Chairs dragging, cupboards closing, something rolling. The building is alive with the fucking, and all of us inside. Old René, the Dutch couple on the second floor, Patrice and Adèle on the first, with their seventeen-year-old Bastien, babysitter divine. Even the partying assholes on the sixth floor must feel it despite their oblivion to noise, M yelling up through the breezeway, FERMEZ LA FENÊTRE, or me standing furious in their doorway, screaming child in arms.

Still going. Manu and his methodical moan, taking such a long time to mount. They live in the fucking. I don't think their fucking is why M and I don't do much in bed together anymore. If we manage to get in at the same time, we just want to watch stuff. Not artful stuff like we used to, entertaining stuff like *Mad Men* or *The Colbert Report* or movies like *This Is 40*. How we loved *This Is 40*. We never wanted it to end.

I would like to hear the Godard better but don't want to wake the Chunk or try to find my earphones, so I give up and roll over, pull the covers above my ears, don't bother to wash my face. As I'm falling asleep my phone wakes me up: *yummy*. A love heart appears beneath the photo I sent him of the sleeping Chunk. Not sure if it's the photo he's love-hearting, or me.

Paradise City

It's not so bad, solo parenting. You just have to be organised. Which I'm not, but when you're on your own you have no choice. It's a relief somehow. Your role is set, you have to step up, there's no fallback, no confusion about whose responsibility it is to do what, who is doing more, who's making dinner tonight, who's taking her, collecting her, bathing her, doing the sleep routine, who's getting up in the night when she wakes, who's working harder, compromising more. Keeping her alive is your one job. Anything extraneous to work, love and food, such as working on a novel, is redundant. But when she's got daycare, and you happened to get all your work done last night and nothing is due until at least eleven, a window might open up that you could use for creative purposes.

Look at her, in her little shorts and T-shirt with the apple on it. *A is for … ?* Pomme, she says.

Her shoes are on. She is usually pleased to set off in the morning, though recently she's been mimicking another kid and pouting up her lips to say, Je veux PAS! Wanna stay with MAMAN, but I can tell it's an act.

Come on, you little Gavroche!

I wonder what a Gavroche is. Don't tell me, I'm not asking. I am just saying I wonder. The more I learn French, the more I lose that space of wonder, that gap where non-understood words and expressions fill my mind like a dream. The Chunk's garderie – holdery? – is called Le Club des Petits Gavroches. The Club of Little Grommets? Little Bad Boys. Little Gavins climbing rocks. I will break the person who tells me what a Gavroche actually is. The Chunk is a Little Gavroche and I call her that as I tickle and growl her out the door, which makes her laugh, probably because she knows what a Gavroche is.

Strange to have a two-year-old be better at something than you. The way she pronounces pink. *Rrrose*. Worse for M – at the supermarket he has to ask her the words for things.

She calls it Club. Cup, actually. A small space composed of six rooms, each with its own activity: painting, mixing, cooking, singing, playing, eating/sleeping. Three sessions a week with attentive, enthusiastic, exhausted women who pay special attention to each child, at a small, subsidised cost, vive la France. At the start of the school year in September, la rentrée, we've also got her into the municipal holdery here in Petites Écuries – another nine hours of work time – and that one is completely free of charge.

The pram got stolen, so I have to carry her this morning, strapped to my front in the tired old baby carrier, though she's way too big for it. She loves it, curls up like a baby, which suits me fine – she's too dreamy at walking, and we're already late. It's not that far: up Little Stables to the rue du Faubourg-Saint-Denis, and up Fidélité to the polluted and clamorous carrefour of the boulevards de Magenta and Strasbourg. I remember bumping into Sido at this deafening grey intersection. I was single then, she had newborn Jojo in a carrier like this. How can you bring up a baby in this environment, I remember thinking. Cut to me, four years later, bringing up my baby in this environment. In her apartment.

Down Magenta, left at Vinaigriers and up the canal to Club, a narrow building that juts out like a ship's hull on the angle of the rues de Marseille and Beaurepaire. She runs in, snot wiped across her cheek. I put her things in the casier, say bonjour to Maude and the ladies, and wiggle my way out of the tiny space, though there's hardly anyone here today. Holidays. Summer. No clim – aircon – of course. Maude has a tiny handheld fan blowing in her face. Thank god they work through August.

Quick coffee Chez Prune. Omar is working, bises, he brings my coffee to the table that faces Club, asks how she's doing, laughs at my staring, hoping for a glimpse of her in the window, though I could just go and get her any time. Omar has seen many versions of me in this spot over nine years. Alone, reading, crying, drunk with theatre students, fighting with Adrien, huddling with M, mutilating pastries with Nadine, assiettes mixtes and wine with Marie-France, Kiki, my sister, my dad, his girlfriend, a thousand visitors, a thousand friends, we always come here, we've always been coming here since the beginning of time. Until the Chunk, I never once noticed there was a child holdery across the road, in that prominent corner shop with the kiddy pictures stuck up glaringly in the windows. Twenty years it's been there but, like some kind of portal, it became visible only when we needed it.

The first time we dropped her at Club for a trial, we sat in this window, watching across the street and trying not to sob. We were sure she would be distressed, missing us, crying, but when we picked her up they said she hadn't noticed we were gone.

I found this dream recently when reading through my old notes. It was from a year before I became pregnant:

13 AUGUST
I am pregnant with a girl.
When I give birth to her she simply steps out of me.
She doesn't need me. She is independent already. I feel anxious about the fact she is not reliant on me, but also relieved.

I go to work and come back to the house, afraid I am going to find her dead, but I pull aside a giant theatre curtain and there she is, playing merrily, barely aware of my presence.
I am sad, but happy, as I can keep my independence.
I go to breastfeed with my tiny nipples, the right one dripping with milk.
Being sucked feels ecstatic.
The baby looks up at me and says:
'Nice little titty.'

When I showed the dream to M, he wasn't as gobsmacked as I'd expected. Not by the detail that she was a girl, or that I had predicted such a large part of her character. He's generally unfazed by dreams. But the sense that I could have programmed her prior to her existence haunts me, and makes me wonder what else I could have transmitted to her unaware, what subconscious desires and perversions may have leaked from the deep regions of me into her.

A bear-like urge to run across and grab her comes over me, to steal us away into the forest, bury us deep, but I fight it and head out into the already-baking day.

The canal streets are quiet back to Magenta, and I take the rue de la Fidélité towards the office, which becomes the rue de Paradis. Fidelity leads to paradise. It's funny it's named Paradise Street, with its plain residential buildings and banal concrete office blocks, though in a few fortuitous moments, through some of the open portes cochères I've seen gardens and old hôtel particuliers and ateliers I'd never have imagined. And of course there's the iconic Boulenger faïence building with its decorative arches and graceful mosaics, which perplexingly now houses horror nights: fireballs blown from up high at regular intervals as teenagers wait, trembling, in queues. We can hear the fire and screams from the Chunk's bedroom window.

Aside from the glimpses of magic that you're never quite sure you've seen and can never find again, the rue de Paradis is one of the blander streets in the neighbourhood, and the one I find myself on most often, as it's the most direct route from the canal to the office. I wanted to live here instead of its parallel rue des Petites Écuries, because paradise. *Where do you live? Paradise Street!* In the current draft of my novel, Greta, the main character, lives on Paradise Street, in a chambre de bonne. She's an au pair, like I was, but instead of living in the elegant 17th arrondissement, she lives here in the 10th, and goes to the theatre school. Combining the two periods of my own life feels like a good idea, except there aren't many fancy apartment blocks on the rue de Paradis, if any, and I can't quite feel the kind of people living in the 10th would work for tobacco giants and have real Tamara de Lempickas on the wall. I might have to change them to advertising executives or something. The real Marcel and Marie Florent would never have set foot in the 10th, and certainly not Paradise Street.

The rue de Paradis doesn't curve like the rue des Petites Écuries, nor for some reason does it get the same lovely light. It does have a short row of trees that blossom pink in spring, but they look uncomfortable in their concrete beds. This is the street you walk down without noticing because in your mind you're already at your destination. Today I'm trying to notice it for the book, pay attention, note down details. Also I'm procrastinating, as for the first time in months I have a few hours to actually sit down and write, which I have been dreaming of, shouting about, and, now it's here, it's making me gnash my teeth.

Internet cafés, employment agencies, haberdashery warehouses but not romantic ones – dusty, messy spaces that look like they've been deserted in a hurry. Copy centres, car parks, a shop selling glass objects, Baccarat, Lalique, Christofle ... this was once the factory area for crystal and porcelain and also newspapers like *France-Soir*, where Francine's grandfather worked.

Two caryatids at number forty-four above an old shoe shop, the female sculptures covered in spikes to stop the pigeons shitting on them, though the spikes look worse than shit ever could. It makes the caryatids seem doubly punished: Grecian beauties standing tall in the facade, holding up the whole fucking building with their heads. The one on the left has her right breast exposed, the nipple erect, spiked. They each stand above their own plaque:

TRAVAIL

COMMERCE

Alright, alright, I'm on my way.

It was Francine who pointed out the ladies holding up Paris to me. Near her place, on the rue de Turbigo, there is a giant angel that astonished me not only for its size – almost the whole building high – but for the amount of times I'd passed it without ever noticing.

Now I see them everywhere. Like children and holderies. Everywhere I look, women holding up buildings, in the rue Lafayette and the rue d'Abbeville, the boulevard de Strasbourg, the rue de Provence. Occasionally men – they're called atlantes, and their faces are strained as they do their hard man's work of keeping things standing.

The women don't show their effort. Like Mum, lifting mountains, always with a smile. The caryatids, Francine told me, were women from Caryae who barracked for the wrong team during the Greco-Persian Wars and were punished forevermore. I'm not sure who the men were. I must ask Francine. The men represent power and force, the women submission and grace. During the French Revolution, Francine said, the statues took on the ideals of industry, capitalism, social reform. *WORK. COMMERCE.*

THE SEA IN THE METRO

When she saw I was interested, Francine told me to watch Agnès Varda's documentary *Les Dites Cariatides*. In it, people wash the huge angel-caryatid on rue de Turbigo with brooms from their windows. A man walks naked down the street. In voiceover, Baudelaire laments sleeping with Madame Sabatier, his white venus, who yesterday he saw as a divinity, but alas, now, just a woman.

Outside the Cité Paradis, a group of young guys are smoking. I stop by the gates and think of asking for one, to see if I exist. A woman asks me for directions to the Service des Impôts and I point her past the guys into Paradise City. Poor soul. Paradise City is the place you go to bury your dreams. Glum buildings, greyed with pollution and tedium, the reality of actual life in Paris, tax on tax on tax on forms on paper on grumpy fonctionnaires stamping envelopes and telling you to come back next Tuesday for eternity.

There was a time I thought I'd never leave Paradise City. Each time I pass it I hustle by, afraid it will suck me back into its infinite void. Today I lean on a pole and make some notes in my phone, in view of the boys who don't notice me at all.

Move along. Organic shop. Bank. Sad little second-hand toy shop, all the cheap little things I've gathered in there on my hurry home, guilty for neglecting her in favour of work work work. *TRAVAIL. COMMERCE.* Scaffolding and bins. Franprix. Xerox. Nanashi.

Nanashi is where, a year ago, M announced he was going to stop trying to work in film and television here, and start a new band instead. We seem so young now, sitting there, hunched over our bento boxes. I think that's where the rupture began. For the first time we weren't on the same page, and I didn't have a clue how to communicate it.

I get the urge to call him now but send a message instead: *how is it?*

He responds straight away: *good, all set up. recording early 2moro, great vibe.*

He seems clear and uncompromised, no sign of anger or resentment in his tone, but who knows by text.

It's going to be great, I write to him. I'm sure it is. Adversity makes for better work. Heartbreak. I've broken his heart so many times lately, my only solace is that it could make for good art.

Sudden urge to get the hell off Paradise Street. I rush down to the rue du Faubourg-Poissonnière, turn left, almost knock a kid off his trottinette, pardon, power into the rue Ambroise Thomas, click open the porte to the building, clack the heavy door to our office, lean my hot body against the cool door, slink down it like someone in a TV melodrama.

His space is silent. I fight the urge to go and sit in his chair, touch his guitar and amp, notepaper, keyboard, feel what it is to be him. He loves this place. We both do. Where work is delineated from home, where writing and copywriting and music composition are defined as work. After falling over each other and the kid in the flat for as long as we could, we agreed we needed an office. We couldn't afford it, but by then we couldn't afford not to, tripping at home over leads and cables, playdough in M's amp. We found two places: one to the left of the apartment, one to the right, both five minutes' walk away. To the left, a stinking shoebox above the Monop' on the rue du Faubourg-Saint-Denis with bloodstains on the carpet, or this place, double the price, with tall windows, on the ground floor of an old workshop on the lovely rue Ambroise Thomas, where rue des Petites Écuries becomes rue Richer. *Richer* was what we needed to be, so we chose right. And Ambroise Thomas was a composer from the romantic era, so we knew it was meant to be.

M took the window side, as there's a ledge that's perfect for his instruments and leads. We put a table between our desks in the middle of the room, so our spaces felt separate but we could still see each other, help each other, arrange who'd do the pick-up or the shopping. On the separating table are the mock-ups of artwork for the album he has been finalising, different designs in mostly bright shapes, words in caps and blocks of colour. Sheets of butcher's paper with the words MIXER / AMSTERDAM / BE / PART written in texta, which the band held up in front of the camera in the video for the funding drive. I think of the champagne again and my chest constricts.

The night before he left we went to see an apartment that was coming up for rent, a friend's place in rue Tiquetonne. It's far too early for us to be looking but we went anyway, for a drink and to see the place in the daylight, which we only knew from parties and in the light of day revealed itself as a total child death zone, from balcony to bookshelves to mini kitchenette.

Afterwards we had at least an hour left on the babysitter, so we decided to meander like we used to through the summer-thick night air, follow our noses, which led us to lovely old Chez Georges. It was so hot we weren't hungry, so we shared rillettes and the cheapest plat we could see. At the last minute I called the waiter and ordered two glasses of champagne, even though we never order champagne in restaurants – it's hors de prix, you can buy a whole bottle at the Franprix for the same as two glasses. But he'd done it! Achieved his goal, raised the money, they were recording an EP in Amsterdam with a renowned producer. We would celebrate.

When the champagne arrived we held up our flutes and looked into each other's eyes. I wasn't prepared. My throat choked and my eyes flooded. Not in a good way. It took me by surprise – I hadn't realised how incongruous my inner world had become with the outer – and in that moment he saw what was in there. He saw too much.

I had no way of explaining the clot of emotions. The jealousy that he was going, that he was doing what he loved. The fatigue from working, the stress of our livelihood being dependent on one frail ability of mine. The fear that deep down I wasn't capable of parenting alone right now, my neck sore from typing, my body drained.

As the copywriting work had picked up, M had been cooking the meals, taking responsibility for the Chunk. I had become reliant on this as if it were my own mother in the house, providing that constant sense of stability. Alone, I felt unreliable, scattered, like a child, worried I'd make a mistake, hurt her, lose her in the street.

Of course I wanted him to go. I wanted him to succeed and be happy. I wanted to be the rock'n'roll wife, go get 'em, like before.

Damn.

Who can't look into their husband's eyes?

We walked home in silence, hearts leaden.

I tried to make up for it the next morning, walking him to the Gare du Nord. We stood over a high table, drinking coffee. I was upbeat. Hurting him like that had shaken me awake, my act was back, I was good again. I told him how sorry I was about Chez Georges. I was just tired but now I was fine, it would be fine, I would love the time with the Chunk, it was only a week! It was amazing what he'd done, how far he'd come. What an achievement.

It will all be better when he gets home.

It will. It will be better. I will be better. I will make it better.

A pigeon lands on the window ledge, reminding me of the unexpected pocket of time right now to write. *TRAVAIL*. The more I work on the book the calmer and less resentful I feel. My phone beeps. *COMMERCE*. I dig the vibrating object out of my bag, but it isn't work. It's Marie-France, sending a photo of today's *Libération* with a line-up of the French football team with their dicks out, full shot, double-page spread.

I love this country, I write back to her.

She sends an eggplant emoji.

Still no work emails.

Come on. *TRAVAIL*.

Open the file: Final Draft August FINAL FINAL FINAL.

Write a sentence as clean as a bone, says Baldwin from a Post-it.

Duende, says Lorca.

The chambre de bonne was at 21 rue de Paradis, above the Maison de la Porcelaine. Chambre de bonne means maid's room, but Greta thought it meant Room of Good, which made sense, because it was good.

An email pings: *TRAD SCRIPTE URGENTE.* Oh well. COMMERCE. It's actually a relief. Easier to be a good girl, a working girl. Bring home the bacon. Feed the young. Dating app web copy, deadline Monday.

Ping. A new agency wanting to 'test' me. Do I still have to say yes to tests? Yes, says the businesswoman in my mind. Too risky to say no yet. We need every speck we can get. And who knows what anything may lead to?

Clients, clients, clients. The more clients, the more security if one falls away. The faster the work, the more in each hour, the more billings. Yes yes yes, always say yes, soon you'll have a buffer, the security deposit saved, and then you'll be able to create space to breathe and do other things.

Ping ping ping.

Translation adaptation accroche tagline headline subhead body copy hashtag call-to-action.

M says I could start charging more for last-minute turnarounds. The businesswoman in me says no, too risky, we still have no fallback, no sturdy ground.

Funny. Being grounded was always something I avoided. Now I want to feel the firm ground beneath my feet. Hard, faithful dirt.

Nature

Cool Agency
Big Agency
Dating App Agency
Agency Out in the Boondocks that I need to quit but can't afford to
Corporate Pharmaceutical Agency
Corporate Agency Boulogne
Beauty Brand over périph

Today is Cool Agency, on the rue du Château d'Eau. There is *clim*. I'm working with a guy called Thibault on a video about a breakfast biscuit. I'm doing the writing and he's doing the art and it's turned out that I'm doing the voiceover too, which is great as I'll get them to pay me for that too. They don't know this yet. Perhaps I can get back into voiceover work – Nadine did a lot of that when she was here, French ads with the leetle English accent. This biscuit ad can be part of my demo. It's not bad, and the writing is good. Ha. Thibault is passionate about this biscuit. I guess it's about bonuses, which I have no access to. I am scared of Thibault's ardour for brands, but he is young, and he skateboards. We spend all day in a small boardroom editing and cutting, rewriting and splicing, eating the breakfast biscuits, which are actually delicious. We take a quick lunch at Le Petit

Cambodge in between, my usual bo bun spécial, which I try not to slurp. At five he skates off – summer hours, he'd usually work until 10 pm – and I head down rue de Lancry to Club in the dank heat.

She's not the last one there, thank god. I never want her to be the last. Like I'm winning some mother game – I'm not as bad as someone else. There was a birthday today, so her face is decorated like a butterfly: antennae on her forehead, wings on her cheeks, wings now all over my white T-shirt.

Maman!

Here, I'm Maman. At home, Mama, or Maman when she's feeling precocious. M is Papa outside, Dadda inside. I suspect she thinks everyone speaks English at home and French outside. Perhaps she doesn't know what she speaks.

There was a run-in today over a teddy bear. She's *sage*, says Maude, very calm and well-behaved, and happy playing on her own. But if you take her toy: ATTENTION. I like that she defends her toys, but I apologise about the bear. Maude wears a dry smirk, like she was rooting for her. The Chunk's nappy is dry, her singlet wet with sweat and drool. I hoist her into my arms, she wriggles back down. Baba walk.

She wants niflettes, and the thought of the boulangerie makes me want to melt. I try to foist some of the breakfast biscuits on her instead, but she does that thing she's started doing where her knees and fists go tight and her face turns red. NonNonNoooon! I can't be fucked with a tantrum, hoist her to Du Pain et Des Idées, where the lady, heat-swollen like a baked ham, hands me a bag of tiny fresh-from-the-oven pastries and one of the last baguettes. A cool Orangina for me. Courage!

Clean Park
Dirty Park
Sandpit Park
Pig Park

Swing Park
Hospital Park
Récollets Park

We go to Clean Park for a bit, then cross the bridge of Atmosphère to play in Dirty Park. Every time we hit the top of the bridge I say, This is where I proposed to your dadda! She still doesn't care, standing with her face pressed against the metal bars, watching the ducks. Canard! Canard! We're still looking for the otters we saw on the nature documentary on the plane from Australia, which showed the hidden wildlife in Paris: foxes prowling at dawn, otters in the canal, giant whalefish in the Seine, a silk moth imported from Japan in the nineteenth century that only bears its young in a small park in Montmartre. All the wild we see each day is ducks and pigeons and métro rats and the occasional fly.

Canard!

She slides down the pigeon-shit slide in Dirty Park, and we dodge the dogshit to play chasey around the broken ping-pong table. Then we run back over the bridge again to Clean Park, climb the shiny new steps to the new plastic playground and she goes down the slide, over and over again. Then we hide in the stinky little cabin to eat the niflettes. No kids her age. No other parents playing with their kids on the playground. One day I won't be the Australian park-kid-player. I'll sit like the other parents, reading my phone, my book. I wonder what it's like to have a nanny, an au pair.

Other people can't give the love you can. When Mum was sick, she started a list of parenting advice for us. She didn't get it finished, but I made the few dot points she'd written into a little book for me and my siblings.

Always give unconditional love. Be there for your children. Other people can't give the love you can, especially when they are zero to five years of age.

Always encourage them – give positive support – give praise because they are trying.

Never put them down or tell them they are hopeless.

Read books to them from the time they can focus (six weeks).

Always trust them and assume they are trying to do the right thing, even if things go wrong.

If punishment is needed, always be consistent and don't threaten if you don't intend to follow through or are likely to cave under pressure.

As parents, be one with discipline and don't discuss differences of opinion in front of the kids. Go into another room.

Allow them to have an opinion and respect it as you expect them to respect yours.

She did it as a gift for us, but now the words fit around me like an iron maiden, reminding me how perfect she was, though I know she wasn't – she just can't tell me now how she struggled to achieve these things. In death she gets to be the accomplisher of all. All I remember is her grace. We lived in a house with doors, I didn't see her mess, her struggles. I know she didn't imagine the words to be so fixed. How could she know how they would resound in her absence? They would have been aims, goals, but now she's gone they're pillars, rigid, cold. Reminders of all I'm doing wrong.

Home time. I strap on the carrier, put the hot Chunk in it, and trudge up past the Récollets, the old building hovering over the park like a parent. Wave to old Mama! Coucou, old Maman! The Chunk wants to go in the gates and play on the slide. I say no. The knees go stiff but she flops back into my chest, exhausted.

Possum, out.

Stop at the Monop' for milk, pasta, jarred pasta sauce (M won't know), toilet paper. Julhès for parmesan, nod to Rasta Man, wave to the guy in the wheelchair outside El Papi Chulo who never waves back. The Chunk bends back to wave too. Up, up the stairs, and we're home, and she's free and I'm cooking while she watches *Pocoyo* nude. Doing it. Look, it's a breeze, getting in a rhythm. I like myself like this. I'm less half of everything, less bad. Just parenting and work. And he's coming back.

Next day there's no Club, so I work from home for as long as possible, then grab the Hello Kitty scooter we found dumped on the street and push/pull/carry her up the hill to the Buttes Chaumont. Swing Park she calls it, because of the old iron swings. I swing her, then take her to our special spot near the stream and within seconds her clothes are off, her feet in the little waterway. It's the only place I know in Paris where her feet can connect with 'fresh' water, ignoring the occasional bits of stuck rubbish in it and, one time, a condom.

The tall trees create total shade over the expanse of grass. I will never tell anyone about this spot. I can't remember who first brought me here – Marie-France perhaps, or Nadine, during our student days. *Splash splash splash*, it's a mountain stream, in the middle of the countryside, we're freeeeeee! The Chunk paddles and splashes with her little hands, my black jeans are rolled up as high as they'll go, which is not high, the ankles too tight.

Last week here, the three of us, M fell asleep on the rug. It was only a short nap of ten minutes or so, but it intrigued me that he could do that in her presence. Let go. It drives me crazy. Even if he's with her when I'm there I can never disconnect like that. In my head I call it *New Yorker* syndrome: somehow, M can read *The New Yorker* at the kitchen table while she is there beside him. I am glad for him, but I want to be able to do it too. It's like certain parts of my brain's capabilities have been switched off and others switched on. Even the

French women's magazines that Sido forgot to cancel, intriguing and untaxing, feel impossible. I can't seem to take anything in. I'm too aware, too open, all my senses on guard for her and what she'll do next. And the place is a mess. I pick up toys wildly, on stage, always alert, the theatre state, never able to turn it off unless everything in the whole place, and our life, is perfect. M turning his page, sipping his coffee, the Chunk playing with blocks at his feet, the Rockwell painting of parental happiness. Me wanting to set that *New Yorker*, and him, then myself, on fire.

It's not his fault that he can find peace in the family setting, that he has an outline around himself, neatly drawn. My outline leaks. I have no barrier. I am a smear in the blurred singular realm of motherhood, my existence now one with all the mothers who are and ever were.

It's exhausting, omnipresence. I wonder at what age the Chunk will look up on the hill and see me asleep under my *New Yorker*. Closed off to her, in my own world. I try to picture a woman asleep on a hill with a *New Yorker* as her (perfectly safe) child, next to the awake parent, plays. In the dead of night in my parents' bedroom, my mother always knew I was in the doorway before I even walked in. She was always present, awake for us, even in the depths of sleep.

As the Chunk knocks her ball around the grass, I open my laptop, but it's hard to see the screen, and there's nothing that can't wait an hour. I pull her onto me and raise her in the air. She squeals as I bury my face in her sweet, sticky skin, blow a raspberry. Mamaaan. Mama. I'm your mama. C'est toi ma maman! She jumps on my belly, slobbers on my face, I hold her up, blocking the sun with her milky back. She squeals as I draw her down and up again: Op op op! Encore! Giggles and drool and she's off again, this time to the woman on a rug beside us, sunbaking and reading Houellebecq. The woman looks towards me with a scowl.

We stay until she's overtired. The walk home seems impossible. We need food. Thank god I strapped on the carrier, it means I can carry her with my arms free for the scooter. She can't walk at more than a trot and, besides, walking with her is uncomfortable – I'm so worried she'll dart into traffic I have to bend over constantly to hold her hand. It's easier to carry her, though it's bad for my neck and back, and the sweat makes me insane. Her nose runs and I'm unprepared as usual, no tissues, wipes, etc. that mothers bring. And I need to pee so bad there's no way I can make it home.

The café toilet is as squalid as expected, but I'm grateful. I hook the scooter on the sink and hover with her on me, thighs mother-fit. Paris-mother-fit. Paris-no-pram-mother-fit. Shit-mother-fit. The piss comes out wherever, damn, hover lower, pull out the tampon, which she marvels at. At least life for her will come as no surprise.

No fucking upstairs tonight.

Une Femme Est Une Femme. Such a condescending title. What does Godard know about being a femme. In French, a woman and a wife. A woman is a woman. A wife is a wife.

A wife is a woman.

A woman is a wife.

I return to the start of the movie. Angela swans down the rue du Faubourg-Saint-Denis, lost in her thoughts. She walks in the fading sunlight towards the boulevard and turns at the arch to enter the Zodiac strip club, where she works. She breezes through and does her show, her beauty, youth and insouciance breaking the screen. Blue. Purple. Red. Back out in the street, she plays romantic games with Alfred, Jean-Paul Belmondo's character, a friend of her boyfriend Émile's, who has no idea of the depths inside her, her earthy desires.

He asks what she's thinking about.

I'm thinking that I exist.

Her friend in the strip club has given her a fertility tool that shows when she's at her peak. She wears bright red stockings. I need these stockings. Her eyeshadow is blue. She lives next door to a radiant prostitute. To make the bed in her simple apartment she pulls her sheets up high while standing then falls on the bed.

She seems so happy there, alone. Free. Then Émile comes home. He has brought her the *Marie Claire*. She puts on her apron. He sits and reads the paper.

It's dirty in here! she says.

We eating soon?

Why is it always women who suffer? she asks at the dinner table. She has announced that she wants a baby and he has agreed, once they're married. We'll get married right away then, she says, excited. No hurry he says. Once we've got the baby we'll get married.

She is deflated.

Women are, or woman is, the cause of suffering, he says.

Shut your face, she says. Or I'll shut it until you have no face left!

He rides his bike around the apartment.

I hate you, she says.

He calls her a filthy communist.

She drops the eggs.

He says he finds a crying woman ugly.

I think modern women are stupid, she says, crying. Women who don't cry. Women who want to imitate men.

Alfred comes over to their place and they ask him to give her a baby.

Is this a tragedy or a comedy? he asks the camera.

With women you never know, says Émile.

Alfred and Angela go into the bathroom. Sexy lighting.

Do you want me to stay? asks JPB.

Oui.

Do you want me to go?

Oui.

Émile rides around on his bike.

What am I? she asks nobody.

Je t'aime.

Je t'aime.

Je t'aime.

What did you say, Angela?

JE NE T'AIME PAS!

She stuffs a pillow in her jumper and pretends to be pregnant, admires herself in the mirror.

I remember that feeling, being pregnant, so whole, so satisfying. Such an adventure, a mystery. There's a photo of me in the same position as Angela, in the mirror in Montmartre, my striped T-shirt stretched over the pillow that is not a pillow, my face as fresh and delighted as Angela's, no idea what's coming next.

You always want the impossible, Émile tells her.

They are children. Playing grown-ups. Playing with infidelity. She bangs a pair of scissors into the table, hair in pigtails. He plays with his face in the mirror, making noises like a car. They live in the tiny flat together, above the Napoléon, on top of each other. They have no personal space.

She's Danish – an outsider, but not on the outside.

Her French is fluent with a light foreign accent.

Time

Saint-Malo is old. Middle Ages old. The kind of old that gets my dad all het up. There are old walls and castles and forts in the ocean that at low tide you can walk to and accidentally get stuck on when the water rises. Chateaubriand buried in a tomb with a flag on it. Ramparts. Lots of people walking the ramparts and the tombs, poking their nubby heads into things. Teenagers chewing gum, leaning against the ramparts, wishing there was a disco.

How do we comprehend the age of walls? From the year 500 or 874? That they really did have people living behind them and climbing on them and getting ready to fight in the carved-out bits of them? People having sex behind them and making babies that eventually become our French boyfriend? To see it and imagine all those lives, all that time – what those walls have seen. It's incredible. But then I think, Let's jump in the ocean. Let's go eat moules frites. If we can or can't connect with time in this way, does it matter? I don't know if I even want to.

Time. Shakespeare sometimes gave it two syllables. *Ti-me*. I think that's what they said at drama school. So much in my brain these days is from dreams, French miscomprehensions, and memories that didn't happen that way or didn't happen at all. I've had some trauma now. One, two, three. Three meetings with death: Mum's, mine, the Chunk's. Mum's death came suddenly. She was fine one day, we were on a family beach holiday, she had a rash and a cough. She didn't smoke, it wasn't the flu. She looked fine, other than the itchy rash behind her knees. She got antibiotics because the rash and the cough were annoying her and she wanted to enjoy the holiday. The water there on the coast was ice-cold, like here, even in high summer, but she plunged straight in every day. A year later she was dead.

I couldn't wake up from it. We were unmoored. I got into the theatre school in Paris, somehow received a scholarship that gave me a residency for two years at the Récollets, my school fees paid. Those two years were a blur of creativity and sex, I didn't want to stop, and I did not, more than anything, ever want to look back, or return to Australia, its lack of Mum.

One dark night, after school was over, I was in a stairwell when a young girl called my name. I looked over the rail and was almost killed by the elevator descending at the same moment. In a mysterious coincidence the lift stopped just above me, allowing me to dislodge my head before it was taken. My neck broke but I was alive and, by some miracle, walking and moving. I had almost no residual damage other than scars and neck pain. My career in physical theatre was over, marionette shows and acrobatics, but other than that, minor fragility.

I'm sure it does something, to touch death. Life becomes something else, a bonus. The cord is cut. But it means that nothing is fixed, images float, when I catch them they fall right through – perhaps one of the reasons writing the novel is proving so hard. Nothing stays still on the page.

Francine is proud of Saint-Malo, and their humble apartment in the vieille ville, or intra-muros as she calls it, where you can see the sea over the rooftops, a deformed triangle of twinkling blue. She would never move here, she tells me as we wander the ramparts. It's for visiting, not living.

But if you love it so much, why not live here all the time? I ask.

You love it because you *don't* live here, she says. And you love Paris more, because you have here.

This somewhat dilutes my image of Francine as a die-hard Parisian, but I accept it.

The sea is tame from up here, obedient, greyish. European beaches can be disappointing when you come from a place with extraordinary beaches, natural beaches without kiosks or floating garbage, beaches with nobody on them where you can throw off your clothes and jump into the water in your underpants, deadly beaches that swallow you whole, clear, savage, constantly changing beaches. Is it because I have them that I don't need them? Because they're there?

The Chunk isn't bored, though I have to carry her a lot. We reach a statue of a corsair pointing out to England with his cutlass, and Francine tells me there used to be an inscription on it that read *SUCE LES ANGLAIS* but it got rubbed out in recent times as it wasn't very 'politically correct'. Oh, I say, because it means 'suck it Englishmen'? She is confused. No, not *suce*, she says. *SUS*, as in the old language, meaning towards or defeat.

It's an inscription from the eighteenth century. I don't think they had expressions like 'suck it' back then. But I like 'suck it Englishmen' a lot better and try to explain to Francine why it's funny, the men in their costumes calling out to sea, Suck it! Francine loves Monty Python – she pronounces it MontiPitton, and it took me weeks to figure out what she was saying – but she never laughs at me, mostly smiles, confused.

There is a pirate in town who sits outside the supermarket on his computer, in full costume even in the heat: pointed hat, beard, heavy coat ... smoking a cigar. He winked at me last night as I walked out with my cornflakes. He would get it. He appreciates the absurdity of it all.

Francine has made a traditional French soupe de poisson, which you eat with grated gruyère and toast and the stuff called rouille. She's been slaving over it all day, and I hate it so much I gag. I've had it once before and the same thing happened. It is repulsive, soupe de poisson. It smells like sweaty vaginas in a hot bus. I just can't do it. Watery fish. I think it's the only thing in life I can't eat. I apologise: I'm deeply sorry, Francine, I just don't like soupe de poisson. You could have told me before I started making it, she says. I should have, I say, like a child. But I forgot I don't like it.

Francine is direct, and I like it. I always know where she stands. The night we met she brought champagne, no hugs, a kiss on each cheek. She introduced herself – Jacques's mother – though I knew who she was. Sido had told me she was going to come over to collect some pregnancy clothes for her from storage, but I hadn't imagined she'd come so soon, and unannounced. She was wearing a thick red coat and a scarf tied in a knot, and the champagne was glistening. It was not a good night – the place was a mess, I hadn't been sleeping, M and I were stressed about money, we didn't have the office yet and were tripping over each other to work. I was hating Paris, frustrated by days lost at the commissariat trying to get my international driver's license and in Paradise City, being dragged over the coals for a simple address change. I was bedraggled, greasy, in pyjamas at 6 pm.

She didn't care. She plonked herself at the kitchen bench, the naked Chunk grabbing her thigh. I liked her instantly – her big glasses, her togetherness, her professorial air. Indeed she was a professor, specialising in linguistics. She told me about her work, the book she was translating from English to French about a gay man's life in 1960s America, had we settled in OK? No of course she wouldn't eat, it was l'heure de l'apéro! She had dinner waiting at home.

She asked how I was going, really. Caught off guard, I told her I was finding parenting tough and wondering if we were mad for doing it in Paris.

Nonsense, she said. This is a wonderful place to be a mother and to raise a child, the home of art, literature, ideas, imagination … As if I didn't know that, as if that wasn't the exact problem. I could see the city, feel it right there, but never quite get to it. She moved to the sofa and started writing a list of her favourite places for me, like I was a tourist. Le jardin d'Albert Kahn, le Château de Vaux-le-Vicomte, le Marais …

The Marais? I interjected. She told me she lived on the rue des Francs-Bourgeois, she adored the Marais. I know the *Marais*, I scoffed. You don't know the Marais, she stated. Come to my house on the weekend and I'll show you. Bring la petite.

We arrived at 10 am on Saturday. She made us tea and a petit chocolat chaud in her dim, rambling apartment cluttered with books and art and cats and her husband, Jean-Philippe, in a reading chair. Then she led us out the porte cochère and down the street to a building that looked private and pressed a buzzer and led us past the modern block and into a shady courtyard with grass and people reading. It wasn't a private garden, people just didn't know it was there. The Chunk played merrily on the grass because it wasn't forbidden and we talked. She asked about theatre and what I was writing and taught me how to use tu m'étonnes in conversation, which had been plaguing me. A small, shaded path led further behind the buildings and hôtels particuliers, with nooks to sit in and flowers growing, and the Chunk was calm because she was free and we were calm too. My shoulders dropped.

Francine led us to the Institut Suédois, which I had passed many times but never gone inside, and in the back there was a garden and an ice-cream seller and an outdoor library that would lend you a deck chair to sit on if you borrowed a book. The Chunk took *Que du Bonheur* and read it upside down and I thought to myself, Yes, what joy, and we read and licked and talked and listened to the sound of a fountain. Then I put the Chunk in the pram and she fell asleep in a hidden rose garden, then we wandered in the gardens behind the Musée des Archives, which I'd never bothered to explore. The Chunk woke in the Musée de la Chasse et de la Nature, among the taxidermy leopards and elks, and took it all in with her glazed eyes. The guards asked her to find the petit souris and she ran around until we found it finally, painted low in a corner.

Francine led us back, pushing open all kinds of gates that looked closed to outsiders but revealed worlds of green, of music, of artists' ateliers down breezeways, and old ladies playing cards, drinking wine from small glasses. By late afternoon we were exhausted and Francine was satisfied. She asked us to return any time. We would, I said, and she said bon and à bientôt.

My heart felt better. We saw each other every week, mostly in her neighbourhood. She took the Chunk on little adventures, coddled her in ways that made my heart light, and the Chunk swelled with the love, like she needed it. I started to wonder about asking Francine if she'd be interested in a weekly babysitting date, but never found the right moment to ask, or the guts, and still haven't.

She looks tired but animated now, sipping her soup, her prominent eyes seeming larger behind their frames, shadowed with fatigue. The Chunk doesn't like the soup either, dammit, so I get up and make her a bowl of pasta. Francine is annoyed, and she makes it clear, then moves on. There is no trace of annoyance in her warm voice as we talk about writing, and I show my ignorance once again of classic French texts, making notes in my mind to read Voltaire and Verlaine and Rousseau as soon as my brain starts functioning again. I have read Colette, and ask Francine what she thinks of her writing, given Colette was such a provincial and said the reason she loved Paris was because it was *province après province après province.* It was her countryside. From her window in the Palais Royale she'd look out and see farmers in their fields, gardeners trimming hedges. Could this be why Francine loves Paris?

Nononon, pas du tout, says Francine, bristling at the word province. But she, of course, adores the writing of Colette. How couldn't one? Jean-Philippe concurs, sipping from his spoon. Colette *is* French writing, I suppose. Is that true? Neither Francine nor Jean-Philippe will commit to such a sweeping generalisation. Still, it is an interesting thought – that of Paris and nature, and Colette seeing the city as her abundant natural landscape. Living in the Palais Royale was one thing (and back then it was a lot less polished, of course), but where we live is pure concrete. There are more small parks and squares than in, say, the 9th or the 18th, but still. I've never thought of Paris as my countryside.

Francine has bought mousse au chocolat from the traiteur for dessert. The Chunk looks up with dark muck around her lips like a beard and we all laugh. Look at us, a little family around this table. The Chunk gets her comedian face on and goes berserk with sugar and attention, running around the room before I grab her and wash her down in the shower. She keeps saying bah oui – or is it Bowie? Francine reads her a story in the living room, one of Jacques's books from when he was little. It's about Oui-Oui, the French version of Noddy. I try to explain to Francine how the Chunk calls her pee oui-oui but she doesn't quite get it. And she is also sure the Chunk is saying bah oui, not Bowie. I'm a little disappointed.

We say goodnight and I go into the bedroom and sit cross-legged on the floor, the Chunk climbing onto my lap to suck at my tired flapjack tit. I didn't intend to breastfeed until she was two and a half. In Australia I went to a breastfeeding clinic in Dad's seaside village and the instructor had hair down to her navel and breasts about the same and three children crawling on her like maggots. The oldest was six. I asked the woman how she knew when to stop breastfeeding and she looked at me with a drunk expression. *Stop?* She was so, so tired. And I thought, I respect that, but I don't want a bar of it. Now here I am, still breastfeeding, my own hair trailing down, falling out in clumps.

French women aren't big breastfeeders. Not Parisians, anyway. Sido was back at work after three months, and I think she stopped feeding at six weeks. Marie-France too. On the bottle, off to crèche. Sido's a doctor, but even when Marie-France wasn't working she had Emma in full-time daycare. Women go straight back to work here. They're not at home watching *Trotro*, getting sucked on, writing taglines. Recently in one of Sido's French magazines there was a detailed story on why you should never feel you have to breastfeed. It was almost an advertorial on why breastfeeding is bad. Probably sponsored by one of the evil companies I work for.

In Australia, you're at risk of being strung up if you *don't* breastfeed. *Breast is best!* Also if you don't stay at home for at least several months, aren't the perfect 'natural' mama, and don't simultaneously have a successful career and keep the house clean and tend to the grown male and his needs (if you have one – many don't and are no worse off). In order to make their lives work, many of my friends with kids in Australia have had to move to the country or their old suburbs to be near their parents.

Here in France, daycare is a state-given right and breastfeeding not a high priority. It feels like female liberation ... is it? Breastfeeding is my female liberation because it's something regular I've been able to give the Chunk as we've transported her from country to country, home to home, bedroom with another kid's name on it to bedroom with another kid's name on it. Boobs are portable. They helped me feel I was doing something right, at least. They liberated me from appliances, formula ratios, sterilising bottles, and they are comforting. For me as much as her. To feel her warm body against my skin, her fingers in my hair, her tiny heart beating. From eight weeks her face would take on an arrogant look of achievement as she drank, like she had mastered something already, she was champion of the world. It gave her confidence rather than made her needy, and me too, my body producing what she needed like magic. I was never able to pump the milk out, so I never actually saw what was going into her mouth. It was symbiosis, something between us the world would never see.

I try to nudge her head to see if milk is actually coming out, but she has fallen asleep and comes away. I'm sure there's nothing left in there. The sight of my exhausted flesh, the feeling of being drained in my every cell, at that moment, breaks something in me. It's over. We're done. It's official. *FI-NI*, I whisper to her like an incantation.

I lift her into the narrow bed, close to my body. There is a cot, but I want her near me. It's me who wants to eat *her* now. She is a dumpling, in her little singlet and nappy, skin all warm from the bath and the nudie runs and being pressed to my skin. She smells like ice cream. How not to lick her? It is the dead of night, and the first time since she was a baby that I've had her in bed with me, I have never managed to sleep beside her, too excited at her existence. She molests me now, under my pyjama top, like a tired old drunk before falling back to sleep, face wet with rejection. I can see her face in the moonlight. So still, like a doll. Her flesh smells like the Strawberry Shortcake doll I used to bite, though it never tasted as good as it smelled. Bet the Chunk would taste as good as she smells, if not better. Just looking at her I think my heart might burst inside my chest, just as her cheeks might explode inside my mouth like a juicy peach. Oh, to ingest her, to have her part of me again. I remember wanting so bad to crawl back inside my mother. If I could only have this child in my body again, and me in Mum's, all would be perfect.

She rolls into me. I nestle her face, careful not to wake her. Send a message to M: *Boobs are done.*

He sends back love hearts, and I know they are for me. It's good to stop the feeding. I need to get myself back, separate from this dual being, get strong, use my body for other things. Be with him. Be a man.

Still, a tear runs down my cheek. I will miss it.

Francine and Jean-Philippe take the Chunk to the merry-go-round so I can work. I tie up the edits on the coffee job and send it off, then have a long shower. The sun is shining in the mirror when I get out. Mirror of truth: more wrinkles, two more grey hairs sparkling on top of my head, two sunken lumps on my chest. I am losing control over the direction of my being. Perhaps deep down I thought I could overpower age, but the little grey assholes keep coming and stomping on my head screaming, Death! Death! Death grows closer every day! I am trying to look less in the mirror, what I can't see can't hurt me, or at least dimmer ones. Thanks, girl from high school who said, on discovering I carefully constructed my hair at the back each day using a pocket mirror, Why?

I hate my clothes. I go into the village and buy a '60s-style yellow skirt off a sale rack, put it straight on and walk down the hill towards the water. Another half-hour won't hurt. The skirt makes me feel slightly new and not so myself, and I can't remember the last time I felt like anyone else.

There is a café on the rock wall and I sit and put my feet up on the chair and feel slightly Bardot-on-the-Riviera, basking in the sunlight with my book and beer. And I take off my top because it feels right and sit in my bikini with just the skirt on and am reading my book when I realise I need a cigarette. Now I'm not hinged to someone else's body, I can. The sadness I felt last night is replaced by a powerful joy. Perhaps I'll reverse-age now, rediscover my youth, the years I've fed away will return to me twofold. To my right, a young man sits smoking, looking out to sea. Keeping the Bardot feeling inside of me, I purr like chocolate, Excusez-moi d'interrompre votre moment sublime, mais … He is fine with me interrupting his sublime moment and lights my cigarette with flair. God it feels good to sit back and smoke and for a second be just, whoever this is.

I sit as long as I can, which is not very long, then walk back up to the lovely old square, where Francine and Jean-Philippe are waiting. He is JP for short – Jiy-Pay. The Chunk calls him Jippy. Francine is Foncy. She loves Jippy like a grandfather, snuggling in his arms like she would my or M's father's, back in Australia. It always provokes a small, sad feeling in me, which I block, knowing this is the closest thing to real family love over here. It is real.

The Chunk spots me, and runs into my arms and we hold each other tight, her tiny sandals digging into my back. Then we all go and eat moules frites undercover as the rain rolls in. The Chunk sucks on her dummy in the high chair. She has always spat it out, but Francine tells me how as they waited for the manège a child passed in a pram drawing coolly on one, and the Chunk then sought hers out in the nappy bag and began sucking it with attitude. It was fashion, says Francine, laughing.

The rain clears and we decide to go for a long walk. I bring the baby carrier, and stick the Chunk in it at intervals. The wind whips our faces. Jippy tells jokes and stories of coming here as a child. He was born and raised in Bretagne, which is perhaps why he's so jocular and fun. Francine looks youthful as she walks, her deep grey hair dancing on her ruddy cheeks. She and Jippy seem fulfilled and happy, not as weighed down as most people I know their age. They're still active, protesting and learning and engaging with the world, coming home late at night like the couple in *Amour*, hanging their coats in the entranceway. I want to be like them when I grow up. I want to be like them right now.

The sea air fills our lungs. It looks like rain again but it passes over. En Bretagne, il ne pleut que sur les cons! says Jippy. In Brittany, it only rains on idiots! I tell him one I know: En Bretagne, il fait beau plusieurs fois par jour! In Brittany, the weather's fine several times a day! It's not warm enough to swim but we kick off our shoes and paddle.

So this isn't *province*? I ask Francine as we make our way back to the old town. Does *province* only mean the countryside?

Yes of course, she says. This is a village. There is life, vivacity, culture. When I think of *province*, it is the dullness of everyday life. The houses, the televisions, the cars. We need stimulation as humans, she says. Connection. Ideas. Discussion. We need to live amongst people who are not only like us. We need to share, to walk, to use our bodies every day. People are happier in the city, she says, even if they don't look like they are. In Paris, people are on top of each other, but they are happy.

Are they happy? I wonder to myself as we arrive back in the town. I am. I'm like Francine, I love the movement and life, like here now in the square, festive with music and movement and colour.

You like the action, I say to her.

Yes, in the winter here it's another experience. I don't like that, she says.

I think I would like the winter quiet. I picture myself alone here, writing by Francine's fire, eating bare essentials, chatting with the pirate.

My shoulders are soft in the living room that night. We eat a relaxed dinner of pasta, which I make, and once the Chunk is asleep I creep out of the bedroom and play cards with Francine and Jippy, drinking something strong called Lambig and eating the leftover chocolate mousse with vanilla ice cream. Yves Montand is on the record player. Do they ever listen to anything that's not French? Bien sûr, they say, but they do love this old stuff, especially in old Saint-Malo. Do they know any Australian music? Rock? They don't. INXS? Un excess? Midnight Oil? Minanoy? We laugh and laugh. They feel young, the two of them, Francine on the carpet, Jippy leaning from his chair, the lines in his face prominent in the lamplight.

I wish M were here. Francine lights a cigarette, then one for me, and I feel a surge of happiness here, in this old place, with these old people. I feel young and old. Older than them.

Francine and I are tidying the kitchen before bed when she brings up the year to come. Soon it will be the rentrée, and she'll be giving some new lectures at the university. The book will take another year or so, she says, there's no hurry, it will be done when it is done. She asks about my work, and M's, and I tell her the situation has improved for me but M still hasn't found any paid work. Hopefully the EP will mean more shows, I say, which will mean more connection with the industry. She asks about the Chunk and Club, and I seize the moment. Might she consider taking her for an afternoon each week?

She dries the fork and lays it in the drawer.

Non.

Everything goes white.

Only a second must pass between the non and my laugh – Of course! Pas de souci! – but in that moment the floor falls away and I'm floating, unattached, in the abyss. My heart thumps, my ears burn, I smile and fold the tea towel, hang it over the rack, wipe down the benches, tell Francine I'm off to brush my teeth. When I come back through the living room, she has gone to bed.

The moon is bright, the Chunk's body damp in the sheet. I lie beside her, feeling shocked and stupid and spoiled. How naive to think I could have my cake and eat it too. My family – our families – feel very far away. I've always thought we make our own family. That's how it felt before in Paris, with Kiki, Nadine, Marie-France. It was different then, I guess. I didn't have a child.

Something moves on the wall next to us. I shine my phone on it: a spider. It gives me a fright, but I remember I'm in France and breathe out. Here, a spider isn't an omen of imminent death, and if I see one, especially in Paris, I usually count it as good luck. The spider on the wall is large for a spider in France. It's also holding on to a big white egg sac, which makes it look even bigger.

I'm not sure what to do. I know it can't kill us, but I don't want it crawling up my pyjama sleeve or hers. My mother instinct prickles. I want to kill it but I can't – it's a mother too. And I've been teaching the Chunk to be gentle rather than squash bugs. I peel my arm away from her and grab a book – a tattered copy of *Les Fleurs du Mal*. It's too thick but it's closest, and to die by Baudelaire wouldn't be so bad. *Ange, plein de gaieté, connaissez-vous l'angoisse?*

I nudge the book towards the spider, inviting her to climb on, but that just encourages her to move up the wall. She seems slow and dumb. Exhausted, no doubt, from filling that sac with eggs. *Sac.* Such an ugly word. Bag in French. The spider's handbag, full of child. I keep nudging her, but she still doesn't take the hint. She has found where she wants to be.

I try to sleep, but the sick feeling from the exchange with Francine and the thought of the spider landing her sac on my face is too much. I turn the light back on and get the Baudelaire and more aggressively nudge her, threatening squashing. She takes the hint this time, but instead of compliantly climbing on she moves into a hole carved into the stone wall for books, ambling right down between a row of paperbacks, eyes glowing out at me.

I climb back into bed. She is technically gone, but still there. I'm not worried about her crawling on me anymore, but then I start to worry about her babies in that dusty hole and barely sleep anyway. I lie watching the child sleeping, her face still a marvel to me, so blank in sleep, so unmarked by life.

Angel, full of gaiety, she knows not anguish.

The next morning, Francine pours tea like all is well. In conversation she drops in how busy she will be this coming year, with her work and looking after her ageing mother. Of course, I say, of course. She lists childcare options like she did for places to visit in Paris – local holderies and crèches and nounous, all of which I know. The way it is done, quoi, you don't ask other people. Even if she were my family, she should never have been asked. I feel so, so stupid.

On the train back to Paris I can think of nothing else but her non. That maternal feeling I'd allowed to develop between me and her and the Chunk sucked up like a hairpin in a vacuum cleaner. A cultural moment, perhaps – an Australian asked the same question would likely have fumbled, made excuses, apologised profusely. Or said yes though they didn't want to do it. That's what I would have done. Her non ricochets through my heart, my being, reminding me where I am: far from a familiar, placatory yes.

I hope I haven't lost Francine. I need her, love her, love the friendship between her and the Chunk, our talks about books and translation and writers and art and Paris and history. Also I admire her and want to be like her, want to age like her, stay in my power like her, stay intoxicated by the world like her, say non like her when I want to.

It shocked me that a woman, a mother, could say non. The limits of myself have become so porous I don't know where I end and yes begins. A firm non right now to the Chunk, as she grabs at my chest. It does not come naturally, not one little bit.

Nausea

It's sweltering back in Paris. The city is cloaked in a thick, soupy haze. Pollution spike. Kids are advised to stay indoors, which is fine by me – I'm crippled by a debilitating nausea that keeps me hovering near the bowl. My heart races, head spins. The floor is best, on the cool tiles, where I can still watch the Chunk dive her little hands into the bucket of cool water I've put down in the living room, splashing it all around.

Mama! Piscine!

Another wave hits. It comes and comes until I don't know whence it is coming. My soul, my depths, my ancient history. I want to puke up my past, my now, everything, that soupe de poisson I didn't eat, Francine's non, the spider, myself. The Chunk thinks it's funny and laughs at me, pointing, then when I tell her Mama feels sick, she bends over and puts her small hand around my neck. Pauvre Maman. Now she is the doctor, her crayons on my back, fixy Mama with da médicament, poupidou didou, le lapinou! Like her paediatrician, doing the little rabbit at her check-up, and now I have the little lapin on me, all over my skin, killlll meeeee.

One great thing about her is that once she's found a game she's happy. She creates a relay between me and the swimming pool, diving her little arms into the bucket, then toddling back to give me check-ups. This lasts what must be hours. I drag myself to the kitchen and find what food I can for her, keep her water bottle full, then slither back to the tiles. M texts to see how I'm going and I tell the truth without thinking. Why did I do that? Now he's worried, but I tell him I'm fine, I'm fine, it will pass, we're safe and fine and please don't worry.

In the late afternoon, a knock.

Dadda!!!!

The Chunk goes sliding to the door with her wet feet and fists, banging into it. I imagine for a moment it's Francine, come with a picnic hamper of dry biscuits and flat lemonade. *There there, I'll take the child, you run yourself a shower and hop into bed, don't worry about a thing.* The Chunk claws at the wood, soaked nappy around her ankles, as I crawl towards the door to reach up and open it.

Claire.

I slump at her feet.

Jaysus.

Claire is an angel from heaven. Her black hair is in a rough topknot and she's wearing beach clothes that look like they've still got sand on them. She looks like summer, like peace, like she's been reading books beneath an umbrella that hasn't quite covered her face, a strip of diagonal pink from her hairline across her forehead. She scoops up the Chunk then says, Oh shit, it's not contagious, is it?

It's just me, I say. It's not a bug, I don't think.

Too late now anyway, she says, letting the Chunk play with her necklaces as she carries her into the kitchen, leaving me to sprawl in peace. Just having her here makes me feel slightly better, and I manage to crawl into the living room and up onto the couch. In the kitchen, she unpacks groceries and starts tidying up, as the Chunk plays with the bucket.

Wimmy poo!

What a good swimmer y'are!

How did you know I needed you so bad? I groan.

Never you mind.

Her voice is a warm Irish blanket. All the rounded vowel sounds and funny ways of saying things. M and I are constantly finding new ways to provoke her into saying: Are you not? Amn't I?

I never puke, I say, flannel on my forehead.

Do you not? (Pause.) ASSHOLE!

Well, in fact I don't. I almost never have.

I don't believe you. I don't believe a single word you say.

She brings me a glass of iced water and hands the Chunk a small ice cream.

You're a godsend, I say, moaning as I sip the cool water. I'm still going on this fucking coffee job …

Forget it, she says. They can wait five seconds.

Claire works in advertising too, but full time, a Suit. She is also a poet. She likes to keep work and art separate, and they couldn't be more polar opposites, a fact that suits her fine. One pays, one should never expect payment. This is what's hard for M, he is having to pressure his art to pay, something he – and most of us – have never imagined possible.

We met Claire at a gig he was playing at the English bookshop. Songs from his first instrumental album, with a hot cellist whose hair fell over her instrument without getting caught in the strings as she played. It was a beautiful night, the first time I'd left the apartment since the birth, and I felt like a set of organs with no skin and also like a superwoman. The bookshop was full all the way up the stairs and into the reading room, the music played all through the shop and outside through speakers. With the blossom trees in full bloom outside, the music's hypnotic gentleness, and a new baby in the room, the feeling was almost biblical.

Afterwards, M's director friend from LA invited us to dinner at Bofinger with a group of film people. I said M should go, that I should go home, but they convinced me to get in the taxi. I remember a feeling of liberty seizing me, my life was not over, the baby was out of my body now, we could be free again. M beamed with pride as we flew through the streets, the Chunk nestled in my coat.

Upstairs, in the grand old restaurant, the four males bantered and jostled for superiority in that way successful men do. To my left was a beautiful woman with black hair and wide green eyes. I excused myself and went to a curtained-off part of the restaurant to breastfeed, unsure how to be both a mother and a public person. The baby drank and drank. I wasn't sure how much I was supposed to feed her. I let her drink until she fell asleep. It still hurt so much I had to stamp my feet on the carpet.

Back at the table, the men were still talking and I felt a confusion in my body at how to sit, what to say, who I was. No longer an actor with any chance of being cast by any of them, post-birth bloated, unslept and overweight, wearing a giant pad with womb blood still seeping into it. None of them asked me a single question – not about who I was, or what I did, or what it was like to have grown a human being inside my body and then bring her out through myself and into this room we were sitting in. They were talking about the movie *Magnolia*, which I'd loved in my twenties, but M and I had rewatched it recently, and found it melodramatic and flat.

It doesn't hold up, I announced to the table. Usually, in such a circle of males, I never would have offered my opinion so forcefully. I went on. Have you watched it lately? It's actually quite schmaltzy and sentimental.

There was a feeling of shock, or was it irritation. I had dared contradict the renowned filmmaker on his all-time favourite film. It was rude. It felt good. The baby nestled into me. M agreed it was nowhere near as good on rewatch, and the men turned to him and they all continued discussing.

For the first time in my life, I didn't give a fuck who liked me besides the creature in my arms, and M, and perhaps the woman to my left. The feeling astounded me. As the men murmured, the woman leaned across to me and said in a thick Irish accent:

I agree. It's a fookin load. She held out her hand. I'm Claire.

She was from Dublin and worked at the Big Agency on the Champs-Élysées and we realised we had worked together several times without meeting in person. She had assumed from my name and my use of exclamation marks that I was a jolly round American. I had thought she was a cold bitch Englishwoman. This made her shudder – not the bitch, the English. She told me she had thought I sounded nice. A good, nice girl, but she could see now that I didn't match my name.

You don't match yourself either, I said to her.

Do I not? she said.

She then asked me a hundred questions about what it was like to grow a human inside of me then bring her out through myself and into this very room we were sitting in.

A few nights later, we invited her to dinner. M cooked vegetarian lasagne. Claire came with wine, which she and M shared, and a big box of macarons. We discovered we had much more in common than work. Her dad's name was the Irish version of my dad's name. Her mother died the same year as mine. Her dad had a 'lady friend' with the same name as my dad's 'lady friend'. Our full names had the same number of syllables. She once lived in Australia for a year, in the suburb where I was living, working temp jobs and dating an Australian who broke her heart. Her face was ancient, pale, with freckles, her raven hair and green eyes like Irish ponds or the green grass of the Galtees, which I climbed once with my classmate from Lecoq. This impressed her. She was tall and strong, buxom, and wore clothes in earthy tones, with lots of jewellery around her strong, pale neck and wrists, which created refractions and clinking sounds as she moved. On the couch that night, she laid the baby between her knees, just like my mother or my sister would have done. I sensed the baby's calm. Seeing her at peace, so far from my body, made my own body soften in a way it hadn't since the birth.

We told each other our stories of Paris. She moved to the city the year after I came to theatre school. It was just for one project, but they offered her a contract and she thought, Why the fuck not. Now Paris is home. I told her about the accident and the story of the Chunk's birth, and we sat for hours, talking about the craic, the thing Irish people value most highly. It is pronounced 'crack' and is the Irish way of saying something very specific that has no real equivalent in English, like the French *juste* or the Spanish *duende*. It sort of means fun, as far as I can tell, or storytelling, or being good at storytelling, or comedy, or being able to make people laugh, but the craic is not only laughter. Perhaps it just means a very good time, with a lot of laughter and possibly tears. Realness. You can either *be* the craic, or *bring* the craic, or *have* the craic in, say, a bar, or be *craic audience*, or a good *craic listener*, which are the people who don't necessarily *bring the craic*, but facilitate it. M suggests he is *craic audience*, but Claire suggests that just because he's quieter doesn't mean he's not the craic. When I suggested I am the craic she announces I officially am not and never shall be, as nobody, especially a non-Irish person, may ever declare themselves the craic, the highest honour there is. After we establish that though it is many things, Paris is not the craic, M lightly suggested that perhaps the craic is not everything. Claire said she was going to pretend she hadn't heard that. Then when I asked, Is the craic everything? She said, Yes.

We asked Claire to sing a song to the Chunk. Since I was pregnant, we'd been singing a medley of Twinkle, Twinkle, Little

Star, Goodnight, Sweetheart and Paul Kelly's From Little Things Big Things Grow, a favourite of my mum's. Claire sang a quiet song about summertime and leaves gently bloomin' and wild mountain thyme.

Will ye go, lassie, go?

And we'll all go together ...

It was like an ancient Irish breeze. The baby seemed asleep and then she screamed and I put her on my boob, where she had basically lived since birth. Claire felt a special kinship with the baby, and was particularly pleased she had been born on St Patrick's Day. Claire made me sane in those first few weeks with the Chunk, especially when M went to play a show in Greifswald and I was left wandering the streets, feeling like a criminal who had stolen a baby. We would meet at the same brasserie near Saint-Paul in the mornings. She took a photo one day of me waiting at a table outside for her. You have to zoom in to see that I'm breastfeeding a little stowaway. This photo pleased me, because it showed I was out in the world, living normally, you couldn't even tell I was a mother. It also amazed me I was visible from the outside.

Claire isn't sure she wants kids. She likes her freedom too much. Right now she isn't seeing anyone – the last few left her anxious and bereft. She wants a dog, and to renovate her tiny deux-pièces, but the landlord won't allow it. Her dream is to buy her own place in Paris, somewhere in her neighbourhood, the 11th, make it hers, have whatever animal she pleases.

She told me upfront to stop trying to mimic her Irish accent, I sounded like Nicole Kidman in *Far and Away*. It hasn't stopped me, but I'd better stop writing her here with an Irish accent. She, on the contrary, does a brilliant Australian accent, ripping the *I* sound in fish 'n' chips, bloody bewdy, she makes me ashamed, not only of the awful sounds but of her ability to master them. I'm the trained actor. Her Dublin accent is as thick as ever, despite surely needing to 'universalise' her speech as I did. *Can you please just speak normal*

English? my students used to say. Her French is pretty good, but if I try to speak it to her she says, Shot op, ye fookin eejit.

Claire sits on the opposite end of the couch to me now, and we watch the Chunk splash water all over the floor, roll in it, paint with it. Are you pregnant? Claire asks, and I assure her, No, I've just bled like a demon. Think I'm just seasick, trainsick, motion sick, emotion sick. It's nearly gone now, I think.

If Claire hadn't just returned from Lanzarote, who would M have asked to rescue me? Nadine's back in Australia now. Marie-France is away and, anyway, has her own kids to deal with. Francine? I doubt he has her number. Valentin, our old waiter/actor friend from across the canal? I try to imagine a hungover Val coming on a Sunday to rub my back and bring me iced drinks. He would, I'm sure, and he would bring three chicks. No. I would have been OK. The Chunk would have been OK. There is food in the freezer, I would have figured it out. Claire turns and smiles at me, her lovely ironic smile. Would I have called her and asked her to come myself? I'd have asked my sister or dad. You don't hesitate to ask family.

Would you contact me in a case of spew? I ask. Like, if you needed help. Like you had the flu …

I would.

That makes me happy.

Then she says, I know you needed me to say I would so that in the future you can ask for help. And I'm glad you asked, because I *do* need help sometimes and it sucks to be alone. And I'm too proud to ask, or worried about disturbing people. So now I'll ask. So thank you. And you always must ask, not wait for M to do it.

A dull wave of vertigo passes. Claire and the Chunk go into the kitchen on a silent mission, leaving me to lie back and stare at the ceiling. A few minutes later they come out and present me with a glass of Badoit with some grenadine in it and a few other unidentifiable floating bits. The floating bits make the nausea rise again, but I sip the liquid through tight lips as the Chunk watches on and the touch of sweetness on my tongue is so kind I almost cry. Claire takes the Chunk and gives her a proper bath and organises *Frozen* for us to watch on my laptop on the couch.

It's the French version. Instead of Let it go! Elsa sings Liberate! Deliver! This troubled artist, needing to run into the neverlands to figure out how to use her talents, her sadness, her magnificent solitude. In English she says the cold never bothered her anyway, but in French she says the cold, for her, is the price of liberty. What a cultural leap. To be fine with the cold is one thing, but to actively flee and seek your liberty in the cold place is another. It's the difference between running from warm Australia to actively seek your liberty in cold France and just ending up in France, where you are fine with the cold.

I like the French version better, though it has way too many words for the rhythm of the song.

I wake in the early hours of the morning in a sweat and can't get back to sleep. *Une Femme Est Une Femme* is still whirring in my computer. I watch it from the beginning.

Angela wants a child right from the start of the film. It's not explained why. She is free, she is young, everyone is in love with her. Her body is light and tight, childlike but womanlike too, in its white lingerie with ribbons sewn into the bra. She is alive on the rue du Faubourg-Saint-Denis. Why does she so desperately want to break what she has? Émile knows, intrinsically, the impingement on his freedom a baby would create. Perhaps he is jealous that she wants something else. Perhaps he doesn't see why. Does she understand what it means? Is it just that she wants to look cute, like she does with the pillow up there?

In that picture of me, in the mirror, I am pulling a stupid smile. I have no idea what's ahead. How can I? Ours will be different, we think. And they are different. And having them is not different. Having them is the same, but we feel unique inside of it because it is ours, and only we can know, and that is why it is terrible and wonderful at the same time. And we can't express our feelings out loud because the children are gods. We have birthed a god and who are we to complain? We are mere vessels. I don't want to tell Angela not to do it, and I can see that she is searching for something more meaningful in her life, something more than the showing of her beautiful body and hanging out with Émile and Alfred. I get that. But what will happen once she gets what she wants?

They sit on the stairs, she and Émile. She says again that she wants a child. He tells her to shut up. She frowns. She smiles. They kiss. He says her tartan skirt is ugly. She says, I'm off to the Zodiac. Go, he says, take your clothes off in front of men. We can't live on your lousy income, she says. They kiss. She wants a baby, she repeats. He says, Shut up or I'm leaving. She says, Where to? He says, Mexico.

Is this a comedy or a tragedy? Émile asks the camera.

She has slept with Alfred. Now she could be pregnant. Émile comes around to the idea of them having a baby, but it's too late now. Unless … they realise if they fuck right now the problem will be solved. Eh bah voilà, the deed is done! She is not *infâme* – abominable. She is *une femme* – a woman. Goodnight!

It is a comedy, the film, not a tragedy. All ends well, nobody dies. Or *is* it a tragedy because Angela is unable to find the simple beauty of her carefree life enough? She wants the impossible. She thinks she can have it all. How can I reach into the film and tell her that her entire life will change, her entire self, her entire way of seeing the world, everything that gave her joy before will no longer be the same, and she will have new joys, but she will have to leave the others behind, let go, let go of all she ever thought she knew of herself, who she was? She might even have to leave the Faubourg-Saint-Denis, the little flat, her colourful life, and if she comes back it will never be the same.

If I could step into the film – burst in when she's wearing the pillow, tell her everything – I know that nothing I could say would ever stop her. She will never know until she does it herself. Would I change what I have done? Do I regret having a baby? No. With everything I am, no. Would I have done it if I knew how hard it would be? Yes. I think so. Would I have kept the life I had, like Angela's, on the rue du Faubourg-Saint-Denis, messing around with boys, rolling about on stage, flinging my clothes everywhere, dreaming, for eternity? That would never have been possible, even if I hadn't had a child, and I think that's why I'm writing the novel. If I can write my time here on the street, as things were, then perhaps I can keep it forever.

Most of my friends left the city after school finished. A few from Paris are still around, or have moved to the suburbs, but I'm the only one still in the Faubourg-Saint-Denis. I have changed. And yet I am still here. I am living and reliving that time, as I do my grocery shopping and as I write, and as I pass the theatre school and all the old versions of me in the street. Would Angela have stayed here in this street with her baby? She's Danish, not French, in real life and in the movie, would she have returned to Denmark? Hard to imagine her here, pushing the stroller down the street, with Émile the attentive father.

Anna Karina never had children, she was married four times including with Godard the first time, and they fought so hard she tried to kill herself and was institutionalised. Godard didn't make films about mothers. I wish I could see the film that might have come after this one. *Une Mère Est Une Mère*. In it, Angela and Émile will be living in the same apartment above the Napoléon, she will be inside with the baby, losing her mind from lack of sleep. She will breastfeed for a bit, her sweet lace bra replaced with a heaving udder-holder, then she'll move to formula, their tiny kitchen filled with bottles and powders and dirty appliances. She will be all torn up from the birth, or afterbirth, and unable to shit, so she'll be stressed as well as exhausted, and scared. Perhaps she'll have encountered a monster like I did, and be shell-shocked, traumatised, unable to speak of it. No one will care, because the child is healthy, she should be grateful, this is what it is to have a child.

She will sit crying as she feeds the baby, loving it so much it is beyond herself, and mourning the fact that the baby is no longer a dream of all she could be, but is real and needs her in the most real ways possible. She will mourn that the baby is no longer part of her, that it is lost now, will go out and live its own life and not need her, just as she once set off into the world no longer needing her own mother.

She does still need her mother, though, especially now, more than ever. Perhaps her mother will come from Denmark and stay at the Ibis near the Gare de l'Est, downing a crème at the Napoléon before heaving her matronly Danish body up the stairs to the apartment, taking the baby from Angela's arms and ordering her to shower, passing her a tab of stool softener through the curtain, Angela no longer caring if her mother sees her naked body, scarred and bloated, the thighs that have thickened, the breasts that, confused, are still full but starting to sag. Her mother will send her out for lunch, to get some fresh air, and though Angela is grateful, she will feel every moment separated from her child like cold steel, longing to get back and press her flesh on the baby's flesh. Her mother will be passive-aggressive, always hinting that she is a better mother than Angela, she knows what she is doing.

I don't know why I'm imagining the mother like that – supportive but nasty. My mother would have been perfect, I bet. She always said she couldn't wait to be a grandmother. I want Angela's mother to be an asshole because I want to see Angela ruined, diminished to the natural peasant-state of motherhood, cankles and farts, overhanging post-birth belly, mother-thick, stooped. Destroyed by her dream of mother, of baby, of a love so big it could end you. I want having a mother to be worse than not having one there, if that were possible, and I know it's not. Mother is a presence greater than the woman herself.

A mother is a mother is a mother. Godard couldn't make it. If I made the film, and it were M and I instead of Angela and Émile, I'd call it *La Menace*. A tragicomedy about a musician and an actress trying so hard to have it all they almost push it off the edge.

La Menace

Sydney

I'm in a perspex box when I feel the flutter. An avant-garde retelling of Lorca's *House of Bernarda Alba*. Two male and three female performers, including myself, all playing women, in the box as the audience watches from three sides. The program reads: *Being born a woman is the worst punishment.*

Being born a woman is not the worst punishment, M and I agree. There are far worse ways to be punished. Being burnt, for example, or waterboarded, or stoned in an open square. Guillotined?

My character, Amelia, stiff in her black bodice, sits on chairs or moves ghostlike around the set, occasionally doing ballet, until a climactic moment when she dances violently with a whip. My neck is fine, the movement is choreographed, though I do one night almost crack one of my sisters with the whip. That would have been the worst punishment.

M made the music for the production in Melbourne, but didn't come up for the Sydney run. All these weird songs full of light and shade. Duende. *The mysterious power which everybody senses but no philosopher can explain.* I think Lorca would approve of the play's mix of darkness and weird humour. There's a moment when the guy playing the mother does a headstand and crosses his legs Buddha-style to display his upside-down dick and balls. Like a stack of mushrooms, reports my dad. I'm not sure if this is duende, but it does provoke choked laughter, groans and quite a few walkouts.

As I sit fanning myself at the back of the set, I try to imagine that I too have a dick beneath my dress, what that would feel like. I would rather have been born a boy. Correction: I would have liked to be a girl without all the *stuff*. Girls get to have babies, Mum would say. Great, I'd say, more pain. A different kind of pain, she'd say, a pain with the greatest gift of your life at the end. I liked what she said, but still.

There it is again, the flutter, in my abdomen, beneath my gown. A butterfly trapped in there. It's not nerves, I don't think, though this play is terrifying. I feel out of place somehow, more than usual, more aware of my presence on stage, in this theatre, an old train factory. My mouth is very dry.

You're pregnant! says Kiki the next morning, making eggs. For the play's Sydney run, I'm sleeping on her floor. She could be right.

M and I agree to wait until I fly home to Melbourne to do the test. Seven awkward days. He greets me at the airport gate and we return to the house, excited as children. Two lines. We lie staring at the ceiling for a long time, clutching hands.

He tells me to dress up and takes me to dinner, a French joint. We order champagne and toast to our good fortune. After eighteen months of 'leaving it to the gods', we had assumed the gods had decided for us. Now we start the new chapter of our lives. Move back to Paris. Have our baby.

We've been planning our return pretty much since we arrived back in Australia a year ago. We had our reasons for leaving Paris:

M's track job had folded, and we'd been kicked out of our apartment in Belleville. His old Melbourne band wanted to make a new record, and I'd been offered two theatre jobs – one playing a sickly boy who vomits blood, and this one in the perspex box. After the accident and the so-called end to my acting career, it felt defiant and right to take those jobs. It seemed I still had some options as an actor, albeit playing physically restricted or ailing characters.

It was good to be back in our place of origin. Like me, M grew up in suburban Melbourne, and his siblings lived around the city, his parents not far away in the country. M's track boss from Paris asked him to create a Melbourne outpost relaying details on the races, and M put together an office in his friend Kev's bungalow down the road, employing him and three music friends who liked the weird hours. We were grown-ups now, ready to move forward, work in our own language, and I was ready to embrace the city I grew up in but had fled. Ready to be an aunt, a sister, breathe in the big air, swim in the deep ocean. We got married in an old church near my dad's place, Mum's ashes watching from the hill overlooking the sea. We said the old vows, it was dreamlike, placeless, our feet didn't seem to touch the ground.

Every day we talked about Paris as if we were still there, and as time greatened the distance we became nostalgic. We couldn't help it. It was what we knew, where we'd gotten to know each other, fallen in love. Though we were Australian, our relationship wasn't. It had grown from the Belleville streets, the halls of the Récollets, the sticky carpets of the Studio Bleu. I kept wondering, If you're always looking back, does it mean you're on the wrong path?

We were in the moment there. Here, I could feel myself softening into the world of my childhood, my culture, the life one was supposed to live. It felt confronting, exposing, I missed the detachment of Paris. There, I didn't notice myself so much, there were fewer human mirrors.

But we would need a very solid reason to pack up and leave again. A *bon plan*, as they say. Something solid as a brick that nobody would expect us to refuse.

A bon plan could be:

A real/proper/good job.

A cheap/free apartment.

A scholarship.

An auspicious visa.

Something unarguable. We'd announce it at a barbecue: Guess what, M got a new job in Paris, too good to refuse! It would be uncomfortable to move back without concrete justification. We were ageing, growing up, supposed to be solid people. Was this *Revolutionary Road*? We should never have rewatched that film, it impregnated us like the devil. *Is this our chance, Frank? Our one chance?*

To our little baby! says M, raising his glass again across the table from me.

To our little family! I say.

We clink, and add up dates on a napkin. Merde. The baby is due the same day as my sister's wedding. Impossible to miss that.

Oh well. We'll have the baby, go to the wedding, *then* move back to Paris.

Won't we? Won't we, Frank?

We enrol at a hospital for the birth, the one where Mum worked. There is a portrait of her in the hallway, with her birth and death dates on a plaque below. They have a scholarship in her name, for midwives who want to pursue further study, a pathway she pioneered. She is smiling in the photo, proud, hair thick and glossy, no sign of sickness, no clue this smile to camera would look out at us so soon through death.

When I was little, I would ask her:

When I have a baby, will you deliver it?

No, she'd say. But I'll be right there with you.

It bothered me when she said that. I thought it was because she didn't want to. Then, after she died, I thought she must have said that because she knew she would be dead. Now I realise she probably said it because back then midwives weren't allowed to deliver their own children's babies.

The nurse confirms this. She also says there's little chance I'll be attending my sister's wedding, whether the baby's late, early or on time. Then she hands us a show bag with lots of weird samples in it.

I'm going to be one of those fit pregnant women. The ones with the sports leggings and the bump you can only see from the side.

Ha! says Kiki. That's what I said!

I sign up at the gym. But the next day I can barely walk. The pain of shifting the weight from one foot to the other is too much. I barely have a bump and am shuffling with my hands on my back like one of the women I saw on the gym tour, on all fours bending upwards like cows. God, they looked like cows.

It's a condition apparently: pelvic displacement … something. The doctor shrugs it off like it's a cold. It may be like this your entire pregnancy, he says. But it could ease up at some point.

Could?

I'm going to write. Be productive. Finish the book before the baby comes. Send it to the agent who is waiting for it, has been now for over six months. She liked the sample chapters I sent, and asked to read the whole manuscript, and I said, Sure, I'll send it in two weeks. Then I realised there was no manuscript. Just the four relatively well-built chapters, the giant stack of notes I gathered over the theatre-school years in the Récollets, a few loose bits stuck together, a lot of questions, and pages and pages of embarrassingly bad writing. Well, now I have time to focus on it, I can't walk, and the only copywriting job I've got is the print campaign for sterilised cats.

Special care for your sterilised cat.
Tailored nutrition for sterilised cats.
New food. New cat.
Oh god. I've done nothing with my life.

I'm going to get published, yes, before thirty-five, before becoming a mother, before I'm old.

Yes.

Yes.

I have three days of writing before the nausea comes. Three days of flipping between present and past tense, first and third person, trying to unstick the story from myself, but even if Greta's a redhead she's still flamingly me. The nausea won't let me think, won't let me do anything but moan. Not morning sickness. All-day sickness. The pain of the neck injury was easier than this nausea – the inability to decide what to eat and yet the need to constantly eat, the disgustingness of toast and, even worse, crumbs. The mere idea of crumbs. The fact that in some place, somewhere on the planet right now, there are crumbs, makes me want to hack myself to bits.

My mind is subsumed by vertiginous gloom, a numbing incapacitation dizzying me into a thick state of darkness. What is the *point*, I'm nothing but a bug, bacteria, a cow on all fours, arching. I dream of Paris, of whizzing through the streets on a bike, on a motorcycle. I dream of the métro, the boat ride in *Willy Wonka & the Chocolate Factory*, there's no knowing … where we're going … I dream of drowning, waking up on the beach near my dad's house, stranded on his rock.

The nausea slowly subsides. We learn it's a girl. M spots her penis on the screen, which it turns out is a labia. A good, throbbing member. He practises saying 'my girls', which makes him beam.

The sun pokes through. And then, M's phone rings.

It's an old friend of his, a circus guy who now runs a dance-theatre company in Berlin. They've been rehearsing a new show about age and gravity, using music from M's instrumental albums. Would we consider coming to Berlin to perform the songs live on stage with them? A paid gig, six weeks in Berlin, in September and October, then a month in Paris in November, and possibly other shows in South America and other parts of Europe in the new year. The Paris and travelling shows would be a pared-back version requiring just M on guitar. I would play keys in Berlin.

Bon. Plan.

We announce it at a barbeque. It's not a permanent solution, but we'll see Berlin and get our fix of Paris, make some inroads before the baby comes. We could stay in the Récollets, I could drum up new copywriting work and finish the book.

The dates are perfect. We'll be back in Melbourne mid-December, before it's too late for me to fly. Kev can step up to manage the horses job. We won't have to pack up, or even say goodbye.

Berlin

The producer has put us in a fifth-floor walk-up. He chose it because of its location near most of the dancers and crew, and the easy access to the bus and train for getting to rehearsals on the outskirts of Berlin. The damp, dark studio has been sublet from a guy who has Tibetan murals and pictures of the Dalai Lama tacked to the walls along with postcards of Ol' Dirty Bastard and Masta Killa from the Wu-Tang Clan. There's a grimy shower, a filthy toilet and a low glass table with worn art books all over it and knitted cushion things to sit on. Scent of old hash and incense. Sticky kitchen, suspicion of crumbs, which, though I'm through the nausea, still make my toes scrunch in my sneakers. Jackhammers blare from a construction site opposite.

We smile at each other as the producer closes the door. What the fuck have we done. We're used to living in shitty flats, but this is worse than Belleville. We name it the Wu-Dojo. The bedroom is a ledge high on a platform with a dodgy ladder, and there is nothing up there but a thin futon mattress with no base. Tears choke my throat. My pelvis has gotten worse, making it not only hard to walk but to lie down. M takes me in his arms and rubs my back, then climbs up the steps to drag the futon mattress down onto the studio floor. My queen ...

It's way too hard, so he drags the cushions off the couch and I lie on them like I'm on a high raft on the sea, him in the water below, like in *Titanic. Jack!*

I'm in pain, and also horny. A confusing combination. These *tits*. The tits are someone else's, a Page Three Girl's body has been transplanted onto mine, and I get to feel what it's like to have serious tits for the first time in my life and to rub the tits and curves, and so does M and he is very happy. I realise how much making love is making love to yourself. I could gladly stay on this shitty mattress and masturbate all day long. I wonder how I will feel about losing these tits. I remember Mum telling me that after breastfeeding she understood for the first time why people sought implants. I never remembered that before now. It seems I've entered a new doorway of knowing her.

It's a terrible place, the Wu-Dojo, but it's in a cool area, Prenzlauer Berg. There's a rock'n'roll burger place down the road that makes hand-cut chips, and we meet there with the theatre gang, a funny, rough-and-tumble group of dancers, circus people and actors from Germany, France, Austria, Liechtenstein, and the director from Australia. They drink hard, shots at the bar, and the bartender gives me shots of Sprite so I can sit with them and feel part of it all.

Drunk on Sprite on bikes through Mauerpark, we ride past the mirrored sports centre, my reflection in it, a kid with a basketball up her top. Men salute, pregnant women are hot in Berlin it seems, at the ping-pong nightclub in a wartime bunker as the troupe drinks cocktails that look like embryos in lab fluid, a guy asks if I'm pregnant, then if I'll go home with him, unperturbed by M next to me, holding my hand. In a café in Kollwitzplatz, as I wait for the bathroom a large German man says, You nice lady I will like sponsor your eat, and follows me back to the table where M is sitting, still awaiting my reply. I'm everyone's now. Perhaps it's that they can't impregnate me. Though nature rarely wants what it can actually have.

Sounds of kids. This neighbourhood, we're told, has the highest birth rate in Europe. Kids everywhere. Playgrounds in cafés, strollers and bikes, children part of the city, not like in Paris. I still don't think I've connected with the fact there will be an actual child. M has. He says he will be the Michael Jordan of parenting, which makes me laugh so hard I almost leak.

I don't think we've ever been so happy. Close as close, holding hands everywhere like children. Working on a play together, making music, getting paid. Not *Revolutionary Road*, far from it, the future is open and bright and there's potential in everything.

At first we catch the bus, then cycle each day to the outskirts of Berlin, where we rehearse the show in an old warehouse. Our rehearsal room is high above the main space, up a ladder, a small office with windows through which we can see the actors and dancers fly and twirl through the air, suspended from the roof with pulleys and ropes. Dieter, a sombre redhead guitarist, joins our small band and teaches me to say weiss so I don't have to have my coffee schwarz anymore, like M.

In the show, we will stand on stage with the performers and play our instruments and the whole cast will be wearing the same costume of a plain khaki worker's uniform, and the same old man's head, made of silicone. The heads are very realistic and give us all the creeps when not being worn, sitting in sunken piles around the theatre space, lifeless yet full of expression.

We grow accustomed to the Wu-Dojo, though I never make friends with the bathroom or kitchen. My desire for food, of expansive variety, is insatiable: all-day brunch at the Frida Kahlo, tacos and Ms. Pac-Man on Danziger Strasse, Chinese, Thai, no more schnitzel, things get boring fast. We avoid the Wu-Dojo as much as possible, but M figures out a way for us to eat cereal from there in the mornings at least – we are overspending our stipend. The hardest part is getting up all the stairs after a long day. I tiptoe up the first few levels, then crawl the last.

Being born a woman is the worst punishment, I joke to M.

He doesn't laugh.

My pelvis hurts. This constant feeling of being split in two. There's a dermoid cyst in there, and a fibroid, they told me at the pregnancy scan. Just part of the décor. They'll remove the cyst after the birth, they say – it should cause no trouble, though there's a remote chance it could twist on itself, causing excruciating pain, in which case we must call an ambulance immediately.

I wish I hadn't asked my doctor what a dermoid cyst was: a ball of biological material that can actually be made up of teeth and hair and flesh. I can't help but picture it in there – an angry flesh-ball poking its mutant teeth out at the baby – but M assures me it's not possible for the cyst to frighten the baby. I don't see how he knows. The pain is getting annoying and I wonder if it could be the cyst, though it's not excruciating. Just in case, M confirms we are definitely covered for an ambulance – for the first time ever, we took out basic travel insurance. I learn the word for ambulance. Krankenwagen.

I wish I was pure in there. Is it lumpy, full of knots, caverns of old blood, the ghost of the first tampon I shoved so high inside myself as a teenager in order to stop the blood forever, make the womanhood go away? The cyst, a feral gob with teeth in the back of its head, all those random, misused bits of me rolled into a ball. I would like to reach in and pull that cyst out, like the creepy doctor who extracted that tampon. *Tight in there!* I'd keep it in a jar like I did my wisdom teeth, confirmation the fuckers were out of me.

Sleep gets worse. I hear jackhammers, even in the dead of the night. It's me, the construction site. I can feel the baby in there, making space for herself. I used to tell people at parties I was in construction when they asked what I did. I thought it was clever. It was supposed to stop me feeling like a failure because I had nothing solid to show for my life: unemployed actor, experimenting writer, sort-of copywriter … I dreamed one day someone would ask me and I would shake their hand firmly and say:

Writer.

Awake, asleep, plagued with dreams of stinking masks and sagging wombs and wrong costumes. Mum, appearing silently, backstage. I don't think I've slept a full night since we arrived. M snores, as he can't roll onto his side on the thin, hard mattress.

Jack!

Jack!

Jackhammers. Every morning, same hour, real this time.

Perhaps I can't do this. Perhaps my body isn't meant for it. Perhaps I'm too weak. Why does it hurt so much? I'm barely halfway!

We call my doctor in Paris. As always, he picks straight up. It's OK, he says. The pelvic issue happens to lots of women, the pain should pass. He gives us the name of a doctor in Berlin in case we need it, and tells us to call a krankenwagen if it becomes unbearable. He will check me when I come to Paris, but he's sure I will be fine.

Knotty hair, sunshine and bicycles, rain and buses, fare evasion. My bearings feel awry. At rehearsals I lean on what I think is a rail but is actually a very tall ladder and almost fall way down into a stack of steel offcuts. M is shaken. Me too, but I put it out of my mind.

My sister asks for photos and I ask M to take one of me standing behind a pole with just the belly sticking out. He never takes photos. It bothers me. If I'm not recorded, I don't feel real. I have to ask him and then he does it but the moment has gone and it becomes a thing – the feeling of the photo becomes stilted and he always leaves the sound on so you can hear the camera noise. He lives in the moment, he says. It just doesn't occur to him to take himself out of it, ruin it by freezing it in a photo. I appreciate this. But my instinct is to preserve everything I can, for that moment one day when I get to sit down and look at it all. When I'm dead, probably.

He thinks I'm ugly. Yes, I decide, that's it, and cry myself to morning jackhammer non-sleep. I need a woman, suddenly, to hold me in her arms. A larger, older one who can make me small when I'm now so big.

He hears me sniffling, holds me tight, tells me I'm not ugly, silly, it's OK, it's alright, you're beautiful, I'll try to be better with photos.

He instructs me to take the day off. The jackhammers stop, I sleep until early afternoon, think about masturbating but don't have the energy. Open an art book in English with a list of creative assignments:

11. Photograph a scar and write about it.
14. Write your life story in less than a day.
21. Sculpt a bust of Steve.
52. Write the phone call you wish you could have.

Hello, Mum?

By evening I feel a lot better.

On the way to the dress rehearsal on Kastanienallee, I realise I've left my wallet upstairs and go back to climb the stairs but my body won't let me. M runs up to get it as I sit on the step with my head in my hands.

Why do you insist on pushing ahead when it's too much? he says, coming to sit next to me.

I don't know! I don't want to rely on you.

He tells me we have to rely on each other now, we're a family. It's not just about us as individuals anymore.

Got it.

Opening night. M walks on stage alone, sits down in his mask and uniform. Another old man comes on and hands him a guitar. M begins to play the guitar and five more old men enter the scene, including one with a quite pronounced beer belly.

The men begin to dance and to play instruments. They spin, fall, struggle, fly, leap, die, fight, try. They play. They are all kinds of men, and they are one man. As I play my keyboard on the right of the stage, breath amplified in the mask, I wonder if it is the man the audience sees or the feelings. Strange to have a tiny female ballerina twirling in the air, in the shape of an old man. We are all this man, I suppose. Each of us is old, our femaleness removed, yet not. One day I'll be an old man too, I won't bleed or reproduce. But I couldn't feel more female right now, or young, I suppose. Young in the sense that I am not dying like it seems the old man is. I am creating life.

Someone takes a photo of M and I sitting on the set in costume, my belly in the overalls the only thing betraying our difference. Or is it? My head is inclined in such a way as to betray me as female, I think. M's body is upright, protective.

Acrobatic, clownesque ...
Foggy memories, ungraspable pasts ... bodies soar
and fall, twist and contort to evoke the impotence
and ubiquity of age.
A fascinating, soulful piece ...

The show is a hit. Word spreads and offers come in to tour to other parts of Germany, Panama, Liechtenstein. M is excited, thrilled.

I am thrilled to leave the Wu-Dojo.

Paris

On the train to Paris, I feel strange. Stranger than usual. I can feel the baby moving, which comforts me, but something is strained in my lower centre. Such an odd feeling, to be growing a human. Nobody in this train can see what is happening inside me. Sometimes I can see it, her tiny body swimming around in me, making a home, putting up pictures. M sleeps as the signs outside change from ichs and iebens to illes and ères. His face is total peace. His body must feel the same, same as it always has. I can't imagine that. What that would be like.

The pain subsides as we step off the train at the Gare de l'Est. Because I'm home? I suddenly feel light. M buys two pains au chocolat. The sky is clear, the paving stones outside the Gare de l'Est have been cleaned. The tall white walls of the Récollets across the street look grimy in comparison, a reversal of the way things were before. We walk in through the gates, ghosts at every step: Adrien beneath the arcades, M reading his book on the step, me and my classmates rehearsing on the lawn.

Chantal, the directrice, beams in the entranceway and comes to hug us. She places her hands on my belly.

Un bébé des Récollets!

BAM.

Her first kick!

She's knows she's home, says Chantal, showing us our room. As she pulls the door shut, the kicking stops. M and I stand together in the window, third floor this time, a lower roof, but the same view of the park, same rickety cupboards, same plastic chairs. I drink in the familiar smell of age and Ajax.

M unpacks, fusses over sleeping arrangements, massages my neck. I stay looking out the window. Kids are playing in the park. Now they're real as real, the little imps down there, soon to be ours.

It's unseasonably warm out in the street the next day: people on terraces, wearing dresses and colours, before the inevitable greys and blacks take over. M looks more alive than ever as we walk towards the canal, eyes bright, this place he loves just like me. He seems more masculine suddenly, his beard thicker, his stride more forthright. As the baby grows, so, it seems, does his manliness. Or is that just my vision, programmed to see him that way.

Our first visit is to Nadine and Didier's new place on the rue d'Hauteville. Nadine beams in the doorway, puts her hands on my tits first, then my belly. *KICK*. The baby's gone nuts, kicking and banging. M has nicknamed her Hit-Girl after the violent little superhero in the movie *Kick-Ass*, which we watched on the plane.

She wants to get out! says Nadine.

She looks radiant. What is it about Paris that makes women radiant? Men too, perhaps, but you don't notice them as much. Is it that she's épanouie? I don't know what that word means, only the feel of it, expansive and airy. Didier tells me it means fulfilled, as he shows us around the small, corporate-type apartment, with Nadine's bohemian character dotted throughout – the painting Kiki gave her of the house floating in the sky, the second-hand coats on the rack, my worn red velvet chair, her tattered paperbacks in neat shelves next to Didier's finance textbooks.

Yes. Women are fulfilled in Paris. A huge and incorrect generalisation. But they seem alive, engaged, whether they're liberated or not. Are they liberated? They have universal childcare, that's one thing. They are outside, doing things, out to dinner, having lovers, throwing utensils at them, never seemingly trapped in homes cleaning enormous living rooms in the death camps of suburbia.

The men are there, they seem involved, the young ones anyway, one this morning zipping past our window at Chez Prune with one kid on the back and one in the front basket, no helmets.

This apartment feels grown-up. I guess Nadine is one now. Not long ago we were students here together, riding around on bikes. She's still acting, mostly doing voiceovers and corporate stuff, and teaching English here and there, luckily Didier makes some coin. She rolls a cigarette and opens the double-glazed windows, allowing the silence to be broken by the loud street outside. L'heure d'été hasn't ended yet and by the time we leave it's still light, so we wander down the rue des Petites Écuries to the rue du Faubourg-Saint-Denis, feeling like tourists. Tourists of our old selves. The selves that, seemingly minutes ago, were dancing around these streets like children. Now we are outsiders. I don't like the feeling much, though the perspective is interesting. I can see the city better, the new and old shopfronts around the canal, the graffiti on the bridges, the movement of people, thickening through Belleville as we walk without intention through the Buttes Chaumont to our old street. For some reason we kiss outside our old apartment in rue des Annelets, as if to seal in a memory, and a dizzy feeling sweeps through me, a feeling of placelessness and fatigue.

M knows what I mean. He says he's never quite left here either, his body now picked up where it left off, his mind in neither place.

We've arrived earlier than the dance show crew, so we have a few days to wander around and do nothing. We are both aware there may not be many more days like this, if ever again, especially in Paris, so we plan to suck them up, drink in the city and our freedom as much as we can. I feel everything in a heightened way, being pregnant seems to have softened my edges. The pulse of the city seeps right through me, the life force, the flurry, and I gather it up, passing it to Hit-Girl, who kicks and punches her way through the streets, gathering the aliveness to build herself with. People smile at me now as I pass. They give me their seat in the métro, and I even get a shoulder-touch and smile from a ticket inspector, which makes me feel warm and also like I now have a free pass to commit petty crime.

Kiki wants photos, so I send selfies in métro mirrors, shop windows, café-wall reflections. On the side, mostly. The seams strain in the underarms of my coat, the basketball so low on my frame I think sometimes I might drop it. I visit Bérénice Bayeaux, the kinesithérapeute I was assigned after the elevator accident, and she says my neck is very stiff and agrees I am carrying low and gives me a special belt to take the pressure off my pelvis. It does make it slightly easier to walk. Sometimes the pain goes away for a bit, but then it comes back from nowhere. I have no control over it. Even lying down hurts.

We ride shonky Vélibs around town, visit friends: Valentin, Marie-France, her little Emma and baby Assia ... Our old friend the Dodger comes from London for a game of boules and a foie dinner at the Bariolé. Most things feel like we left them: Ahcene at the Carillon for apéro and music and overmoussed coffees, Bruno and Omar at Prune greeting us like we've never left. Grég at Chez Jeannette is playing one of M's songs on the stereo when we walk in, a surprise that makes M blush. Val now works at Chez Hugo in the Place des Vosges, and gives us free omelettes. He looks terrible, drawn, exhausted. From fucking, he says. Who? M asks. All the corners of the globe, dude, says Val, they all want the French waiter. I tell him to be careful or he'll end up with one of these, pointing to my belly, and he says, Good, he wants one anyway.

We walk too far, all the way over the river. Michel Gondry's *The Science of Sleep* is playing and the seats in the cinema are so soft and supportive I almost weep with gratitude. The film is called *La Science des Rêves* in French and it drives me crazy they've changed it from dreams to sleep in the English translation. Why? It's not a sleep study. In the movie, Gael García Bernal plays a young man called Stéphane who has a condition where he can't tell when he's dreaming or awake. He can't get things right, in life. His mind blurs across the boundary of consciousness. He is so cute and full of joy and sadness, unable to temper his insecurities, his inappropriate thoughts. He tells Charlotte Gainsbourg's character he likes her boobs, they're unpretentious. She finds him strange and charming, and she is an odd person too, obsessed with crafting things with scissors and glue. I identify heavily with Stéphane's inside–outside state, the fogged edge of reality. Right now my dreams are so strong they stay with me all day, and I'm never sure what's real, which country I'm in, which body.

We stay until the lights come on and a man with an eye-patch kicks us out.

The pain has changed to something new. Sharper, lower down. I picture the cyst with its bung eye and piranha teeth eating at my body, threatening Hit-Girl, Hit-Girl staving it off with her kicks and blocks.

M's French music publisher, Franck, invites us to lunch at his place, and his lift is broken, so we walk up. Marie-France invites us to her new apartment in the 11th, on the sixth floor, no lift. I'm living in an Escher painting. Crawling, crawling, crawling up staircases, a baby full of baby, pick me up!

The Récollets. Blessed, functioning lift.

M rafts me on the bed with pillows.

Six months now, twenty-four weeks.

Val invites M to a gig and I insist he go and I try to read *I Love Dick*. Kiki has insisted I read this book, or specifically, that I insert it into my vagina or she'll never speak to me again. It's an impossible read right now, though I want to put smart things, art things, inside me. The narrator is agony, I want to tell her to shut up just like she is saying in the book that the world wants to shut women up and this is making me realise I am part of the problem too and I don't want to know that right now. I keep throwing the book down then picking it back up again.

Invitations in my inbox to barbecues and Christmas parties back in Melbourne. Reply yes, yes, yes. Sister's hen's day with her girlfriends, yes, M's old band's new band's Sunday gig at Pure Pop, yes. Sun, soon, starting to rain here, sky greying to winter. I do love the winter here. The days when the streets outside the Gare de l'Est are wet and all the lights from the buildings reflect on the ground. Though I guess it's easy to romanticise it all when you're not living here.

My sister keeps asking what date we're coming back, and I keep avoiding answering. I have a feeling we'll be leaving sooner than we thought, after M's finished the dance shows, even though we've sublet our place in Melbourne. I'm just too uncomfortable. I can't sleep.

I close the computer and go to the window. An old woman sits alone near the playground. She is nestled in her jacket, looking content. She doesn't seem to be waiting for anyone, or there to watch children. She has no book or food. She is simply sitting, just being alone, I think. It is hard being alone, but I learned to here, twice. First as an au pair in the lonely chambre de bonne, second as a theatre student, before I met Adrien. I would stand here in the mornings and evenings, smoking, wondering, thinking about sex and plays, remembering my mother. At some point I started making decent food for myself, tired of living off biscuits and cheese. To feed myself was a certain sensation, weird at first. A particular kind of honouring.

That was when I started writing. There was nothing else to do at night, only shonky internet, no television. I dumped stuff on a page, and that's what I'm trying to make the novel from now, though I have no clue what I'm doing.

The wind blows through the trees. I climb up onto the hard bed, take a paracetamol, fall asleep.

Backstage. Someone taps on my shoulder. It's Valentin. He asks me to please stop worrying about myself and take a crate out to the stage for the lighting check. I pick up the plastic crate full of old diaries and junk from under my childhood bed. It's heavy. I carry it onto the stage, feeling a hot, sticky sensation down the insides of my legs. I look down, and milk is leaking out of the bottom of the crate. It's tech rehearsal and I mustn't move. As the lights flicker and change around me, the milk trickles down my bare legs, filling my shoes until it spills over and forms a puddle of white around me.

I wake. My legs are dry, but the pain is incredible.

I shake M awake.

Something is wrong. I think it's the cyst.

It's 7 am. I call Dr Medioni, he tells me to take more paracetamol and to come see him at 8. The métro ride is an eternity.

Dr Medioni smiles. He says I look a lot different from the last time he saw me, and asks how my neck is. Then he sees I'm not up to talking and comes to my belly. He says things seem OK, but sends us straight to a radiographer further up the Boul'Mich. I squeeze M's hand in the waiting room. Finally it's our turn, the baby is fine, it's actually the fibroid in there creating the pain. But it should be fine. Take paracetamol and go home and rest.

I clench my teeth, breathe. I knew birth was supposed to be agony but didn't realise pregnancy was too.

Back at the Récollets we get more pillows from Chantal, and M props them all around me in the right places. We watch a short, infuriating documentary about James Baldwin in Paris, the stupid white filmmaker asking him stupid questions. It's painful to watch, in all senses of the word, but watching things seems to be the answer, they take my mind off it, keep my focus tight and small. But the pain only mounts, rising, tightening, and even the pillows don't help and I wish we were in the cinema and then it gets really, really bad, so bad I have to moan out loud, weep, What is wrong with me? Women do this all the time, why am I not coping? It gets worse, and worse, and by evening it's too much, and M calls Dr Medioni, who tells him to take me to the Hôpital Franco-Britannique. Métro will be fastest.

A small sense of relief. The pain is believed, it's real, no longer on the verge of sleep or dreams. Something is definitely wrong, I know it because all I want is to be in hospital now and I really, really hate hospitals.

On the métro every jiggle, every swerve is a knife in my belly.

At the hospital, I wait, then they look at the scans, take my temperature.

Take paracetamol and go home, they say.

I hunch over myself. The tears are deep. The nurse turns kind. She pulls up a wheelchair and helps me lower myself in. Was she waiting for the display of emotion? I am never leaving this wheelchair. My hands grip tight. The nurse wheels me into a room behind a sheet and helps me into a bed. The pain is hot, burning. A female doctor comes in.

Is it OK if I examine you?

I don't care. I am gone. I close my eyes, feel M squeeze my hand. Afterwards there is silence and the doctor leaves, then comes back. I open my eyes, then close them again, my mind drifting in a strange place. The doctor speaks to M.

Alors, she's in labour. That's why the pain.

I open my eyes to speak, but don't. The doctor's face is blurred. There is a pause as M looks down at me.

But she's only twenty-five weeks.

It's OK. We think we can stop it.

Drugs have happened. The words in the room swim through me in colours: regular contractions, dilated, 1.7 centimetres, cannula, Loxen, morphine –

Morphine? says M.

It doesn't cross the membrane.

She could have had that sooner?

What is it? What is happening?

Menace d'accouchement prématuré.

What does that mean?

Menace of premature delivery, the French doctor tells M in English. *Threat.* Threat of premature birth. Or late miscarriage. Fausse couche. False carriage.

Menace.

The fibroid had begun to necrotise, causing the pain. This led to the contractions. She needs to rest now. It is very late. You should too.

They won't let M stay.

At the Récollets, he proceeds to gain an education in gynaecology.

Sunrise.

I am nowhere.

M is beside me.

Am I still in labour?

No, the medication stopped the contractions.

Was it my fault?

Of course not.

What if I go into labour again?

If you stay still they say you should not go into labour again.

What happens when I stop taking the medication?

It's slowly reduced until it is certain there are no more contractions.

What happens to my dilated part?

The doctors are talking about cerclage. A cervical stitch. They are giving you antibiotics in case they have to do this. Also in case of infection.

52. Write the phone call you wish you could have.

Mum?

Sit tight, honey. I'm on my way.

I look him deep in the eyes. Whatever a cervical stitch is, I won't have it, I tell him. Even the sound of the word makes me shudder. My body is tightening around my centre, closing.

In the early morning I am helped to the bathroom. Every movement is measured. In the mirror my eyes are different – the eyes of my baby, my mother, the eyes of women, God. Why am I thinking so much of God? I never did before. I don't believe in God. I am praying, I notice. I've never wanted anything so much before. Please, please, let this baby live, please let her be OK. Back to bed, on tiptoes. Must not awaken God. Let her live. The world feels gentle around me. This space, all of my own. Bed, walls, window, bathroom. Incubate myself incubating the baby. Every hour she stays in there counts, they say. Every minute.

M looks at me with his soft, concerned face.

How am I in a Paris hospital again? Can we pay for this?

Don't worry about that, we've got the insurance. Your only job is to stay calm. Forget everything else.

What happened? I ask.

A menace, he says. But it's going to be OK.

I feel very menaced right now, I whisper, face hot.

I know, he says, kissing me.

A broad male doctor comes in with a female nurse and gives M a look to make him stand up. The doctor speaks in English with a deep French accent: We are controlling the contractions. We may have to do the cerclage, to close the cervix and keep the baby inside.

It is a sensitive procedure. There is a risk of miscarriage. We will talk to you about this more once you are stabilised. But, he continues, pronouncing his words slowly, I'm afraid you will not be flying any time soon. You'll be giving birth here, in Paris.

Of course I'm giving birth in Paris.

I was always giving birth in Paris.

Sometimes Paris doesn't feel like a physical place. It feels like a plane in my mind, somewhere between waking and sleeping, life and death.

Child, I'm sorry.

She doesn't seem unhappy, flipping and punching.

We are a team, with one goal. My job is to be soft, and warm, to breathe, not tense up. M's role is to get through the shows and find us somewhere to live until she's due, let our families know what's going on, keep talking to the doctors back home and my doctor here, keep me and thus her incubated. He is deep in a document called 'The Incompetent Cervix' that gives the pros and cons of cerclage. Talk of it continues, despite our repeated refusal. Eventually, it is decided the stitch is off. Too risky. As I have been saying all along. Would they have forced me to do it?

Every second is alive, breathing. Sensations like contractions come, and I panic and press the buzzer as I've been told, and they come running, and it happens more and again, and I buzz to be sure, until I start to understand the general feeling of having a moving life inside my body, what is the baby and what is myself and what is danger. I hold my tits in the night. My white hospital gown makes me feel small, a little girl, her little girl, my little girl. It is an intensely female place, this room, this bed.

M is beside himself, face drawn with concern, hands warm. He is lonely for us. He can't know what it feels like, he will never know. I feel an incredible sadness for him, just like Mum would say,

Boys don't get to have the babies. Who would want to, I used to say, all that pain, that heaviness. She would give me a knowing look. *Oh, you wait.*

Once I'm able to walk to the bathroom alone, I stop at the window and look out at the Levallois street, the buildings opposite, the moon. My reflection is a lunatic, a ghost attached to a pole with god knows what running through it into my arm. Funny to be in Levallois, this suburb near Adrien's place, where I'd ride my bike all the way from the 10th through these streets late at night to him. The suburb feels safe, familiar like a blanket. I look up at the sky, and I can feel the baby looking with me, and also at me, and all my history.

In the nights we commune. I speak to her. *Stay.* She moves inside me, and as I lie motionless I can feel her curiosity, her calm. Being so still I get to know her. She is feisty, brave, Hit-Girl saving cities in her sassy way. Trust her to try to be born here. Trust her to know where the adventure is. I can't be sure she won't pull another stunt, but I sense she feels safe, in the silence and the comfort of the miraculous hospital bed that can be manipulated with buttons to support all the right places.

Long, foggy days. I lie still, watch *Treme* on my laptop, try to read *Dick* but switch to the Franzen brought in by Nadine. M comes and goes, I lie in my cocoon, transforming.

That visit to the local strip mall in Melbourne to buy the cheap travel insurance has paid off. The hospital fees are taken care of, as well as our accommodation in Paris until it's safe to fly. M has chosen an apartment in the village on the other side of the Butte Montmartre.

Wait till you see it, he says. There's an actual bed.

I am anxious about leaving the hospital. Scared, in fact. On a razor's edge. The only thing preventing her descent is my will, my concentration, my calm. I have to try to suck her up, keep her in, but also relax, as too much tension is also dangerous. In the hospital the lack of free will is ideal, the being waited on, the remote-controlled bed, the convent-like nothingness. I am reliant on M, and I know he will be perfect, but my autonomy is dangerous and I'm not sure I'll be able to keep it in check.

On departure, the doctor gives strict orders not to move until the baby is at least thirty weeks old, when her lungs will be fully developed.

No going outside, no walking, no even leaving your door.

No exercise.

No cleaning.

No socialising.

No activities.

No lifting.

No laughing too hard.

He didn't say that last one but when I asked if I could laugh he just gave me a stern look.

Outside, the sky is a brilliant, freezing blue. Dormant Christmas lights are strung up in the trees ready for December. We pull up outside a red-brick block in rue Francoeur, a sloping street in the village behind the rue Caulaincourt market strip. Marie-France has left a package in the entranceway, with a note for us, in English.

> Hit-Girl will born in Paris, in the start of spring when the little bird squeaking for first time and the flowers show their new dress ... Everything gonna be OK now, perfect! M close to the guitars shop de Pigalle, perfect to bring some first sound to Hit-Girl so she sleep quietly here in Montmartre, where a lot of the artists like Van Gogh, Malraux, Gabin ... born and lived. And you two will play music and write the book and Hit-Girl be the little fight baby that did live.

It's a nice, small apartment with two whole bedrooms and a real kitchen that is clean. Windows that look out over the corner of rues des Saules and Francoeur, and into a kids' dance studio on the ground floor opposite, where lots of jumpy little beans in tutus are flinging themselves around. M has been fussing around like a bowerbird, hiding the landlord's ugly artworks away, buying a coffee machine, and filling the kitchen with lovely things from the markets and shops around Caulaincourt, Mont-Cenis, Marcadet, and Château Rouge. He helps me to lie straight down on the bed and, once satisfied I'm comfortable, goes to look out the window.

There's no tomorrow, he says. No Friday. No Saturday.

Um, what?

The forecast says snow, he says. Snow tomorrow. Snow all weekend.

I laugh and explain to him I thought he had just announced matter-of-factly that all time had ended. Which right now, in a way, it has. Time has become something else entirely.

I grow rather used to keeping still. Being brought beautiful food, fawned upon by an untiring M. I sleep a lot. Read Helen Garner. Jean Rhys. Bits of *Dick*. Learn Final Cut. Watch the entire series of *Mad Men* with M, enjoying Peggy Olson's story very much, her carving her way into the man's world. I remark on how little things have changed in advertising, still the same swinging dicks, just now in sneakers. Smatterings of freelance work come in and I deliver them as normal, not telling anyone what's happened because why. Sometimes I work on the novel, but the writing requires a physical part of myself I can't access, as though to dig in there would be to dig her out. The idea of finishing before her birth starts to fade. It's more important to try to keep my thoughts light, on the surface, protective, conscious. I make a video clip for one of M's songs from old footage of my sister and me at our dance concert. She is pregnant too, due three months after me. That was why she was so keen to know when I was coming home. I'm sad I won't be at her wedding. Or there for her pregnancy. She will be doing it without me, without Mum.

Sometimes I hear my watch ticking. Sometimes I don't.

Each week the wise woman comes. In French, midwives are called sages-femmes. Wise women. M gives it a porno narrative, making sounds as Patricia knocks at the door – *Ba-bow*, the *midwife* is here for your *examination* – which lightens the mood of my least favourite event, which I must step out of my own body to endure.

Out the window, snowflakes blow like a trillion baby-bird feathers.

We make it to thirty weeks. Ideally she'll live in me six more weeks, or better yet ten, but if she exited now she is very likely to survive. I can relax a tiny bit, walk around the flat, step out into the passageway, breathe. A fragile liberation.

Snow melts in the night, thumping the windowsill. M sleeps through it soundly, but each dump feels like it's trying to get my attention. Now that the preoccupation with Hit-Girl's survival has eased slightly, a new, uncomfortable awareness is dawning. The feeling is moorless, bottomless. I don't know how to articulate it to M, though I try. He says now that things feel more concrete, less abstract, we are probably realising what has happened, that we're far from the home we had started to build in Australia. We've been so focused on getting through these weeks, it's like we haven't prepared for life when she actually arrives. Now we're awake to the fact we're in a short-term rental in Paris with none of the usual infrastructure around us. We'd normally be making a place for her, preparing, connecting with the reality of it.

He hugs me and brings me toast. Then he sets about creating some tangible solidity for us. He goes to the Monoprix and buys some clothes, size 000, returning with stories of connection with mothers in the baby section, who found him adorable. He collects baby supplies, makes an impromptu cot out of couch cushions in the spare room, though we won't even use it – Marie-France has dropped off an old Moses basket. He buys a small lambskin rug because Marie-France has told him my sleeping with it will imbue it with my scent and then we can take it with us wherever we go and make her feel secure. He buys a plastic tub, and puts it on the bathroom sink, and a small, soft hooded towel, for when we lift her out.

I feel much better knowing that when she comes we can feed her and bathe her and put her somewhere to sleep. I should feel wonderful, but there's another feeling beneath all that. I am ashamed that the nesting hasn't put the feeling to rest. It's something deeper within me. For days I sit inside it, unable to talk about it with M, as the only thing I know is that it has something to do with him and the baby.

Then I realise what it is: I'm not a man.

M laughs when I speak the deeply stupid words. But they come from a real place.

Our connection has always had a gender-ambivalence to it. We've done everything together, best friends. The balance of our masculine/feminine has always been fluid, sliding and equal. We each have our days and moments where either side presides. Right now, he is the housewife, cooking and cleaning for us. I am the fat fuck lying around playing online poker. I like to be the male. I pride myself on my masculinity. M is very male, but also completely at ease with his feminine side, unthreatened by my desire to fuck the world with my giant dick.

Of course, I am also female, and since the beginning, M has had the most wonderful way of making me feel that. And he is also male, with his desire to protect and provide, to dominate a ping-pong table, to make money so we can eat and explore and be free.

But now, this divide. I am a woman and I am going to have a baby. And I will never go back to the way I was again. From now we will be forever different. He will never feel the way I do. He has humoured me through the nesting, but inside himself it's a problem solved with a few jumpsuits. The deeper urge I feel, to build a fortress of security around us, is not something I have ever felt, or wanted to feel. It is furious, ancient, murderous. It comes from a place I don't understand.

The lonely feeling around it is intense. I am going to be a mother. M can't come with me there. No, he will be a father, and I will be a mother and we will be a family, and as much as we try to be gender-neutral, there will be roles. He can't breastfeed, as much as his nipples are sweet. There are things I already can't do. I can barely walk, for goodness sake. I certainly can't climb a tree. I can't drink real shots in Berlin. I can't *not* wear a bra.

Our islands are, for the first time, completely isolated. I want him to feel what I am feeling – a creature in my body, dancing and twisting. I want him to know what it's like to swell up and become round, so we can share it, like we've shared everything else. But I can't, we can't. We are alone together.

It's a grieving. A letting-go of my boyhood. In French they call a bachelor party an enterrement de vie de garçon. A burial of the boy's life. That's what it feels like I'm doing. Putting to eternal rest this striving inside me from when I was young to deny the weight and responsibility that would come with womanhood and instead build my inner self with the traits I associated with maleness: liberty, detachment, power, control.

M listens to me and says that part of me will stay alive, there will just be a different balance from now on, especially in the beginning. Perhaps it's not just about losing the boy, but losing the independence to do everything you want all the time. He feels it too, he says, that trepidation. But he understands it must be an enormous shift from boyish female to mother.

Our roles will be defined, I tell him, by our gender.

Not necessarily, he says. Aside, of course, from the obvious things.

He holds my hand. The cloud has lifted slightly. I realise I'm always waiting for M to get angry at me, for my true thoughts, and he never has.

I turn thirty-five, blow out the candles, gently.

The book is not completed, as I'd hoped. I'm not completed, as I'd hoped. But the baby is baking well. Thirty-two weeks now. I'm taxied to the hospital for a check-up, a strange feeling of insecurity at seeing the big world outside after so long in my cushioned bower. The streets are grey slush. We're late, putting the doctor in a bad mood. Then I answer truthfully on the forms if I've done drugs, though I haven't in years, and the doctor reprimands me. You're a mother now, she says. Time to give up the hard drugs.

As if for punishment I have to splay myself, French-style, no modesty sheet, and undergo an examination so rough it causes contractions again and I have to stay all day for monitoring.

I am wild after that. I didn't even need to be checked – the wise woman did it only days earlier and everything was fine.

I don't want to be a woman anymore, I write to Kiki. *I changed my mind.*

I close over like a garden slater, determined not to let anyone else inside of me, or out.

Nadine and Didier break up. She and I cry together in my bed. She will return to Australia. To the water. She longs for it.

I would like to give birth in water. Not like my own birth, heaved with salad tongs onto a dry dock. None of the panting, being split in two with a knife, men with utensils, vacuums, blinding lights. An old high-school friend of mine, April, who has a morbid fear of pain – and spiders (so much so, you can't even say the word *spider*) – swore she had two pain-free births, all because she was so calm, surrounded by women, dim lighting, she was able to just breathe the babies out. This sounds good to me. I'm not affixed to natural ways, but it makes sense to me that to be tense is to not allow things to flow as they should, thus requiring intervention, and once that starts it seems there's no way back. Women have done it since the beginning of time, surely if I can be left alone unstressed, I – and Hit-Girl – should know what to do. If I can make it to thirty-six weeks, I can go to the natural place on Avenue Parmentier where they have baths, and where Nadine's friend Tess the magazine editor did a vaginal breech birth, no problem. Tess tells me the place is gentle and warm and underused because Parisian women generally find the idea of natural birth insane. After reading books and watching movies April recommends, including one that showed women having orgasms as they birthed, I'm committed to the natural way. I just hope I can get there.

After Christmas, the instability feeling rises again, this time with force. The friends subletting our place in Melbourne move out, and rather than pay for a place we won't be in for months, we give up the lease, and our families move our stuff out. Once the baby is here, we're officially homeless.

On New Year's Eve I am finally allowed out for a short walk. We tiptoe in the snow up the hill to the bistrot on the corner, eat burgers and share one glass of champagne.

This is all *telling us* something, I say to M, as I savour the bubbles. We knew we wanted to move back here. Maybe Hit-Girl made it known via the Menace she agrees with us.

What are you saying? M smiles.

We need to find a place here, now.

He reminds me we can't actually stay here long-term. We don't have a visa. And Hit-Girl may not know it, but being born here doesn't automatically get her a passport, or us. And M has a job back there ... sort of. So far it's worked fine for him managing it from over here, and it's not likely to be a long-term thing, and I don't have any commitments there other than emotional ones ...

I start looking online. Whether we find a place or not, the grounding action feels wholesome and good. We will stay here in Paris as long as we can after the birth. Then we'll go home, see our families, get the visa, and we'll have a place to return to.

M isn't sure at first, but the more we talk, the more it becomes clear. It feels right. We've got the time now to work out how to get the right visa, find a place, get set up. Nadine knows an excellent immigration lawyer and M goes to meet her. We're sure with my copywriting work we could apply for an auto-entrepreneur visa, but to his surprise she says our best chance is with the carte de séjour compétences et talents, for him, with his music. It would limit him to working in the field of music, but within that he can do whatever he likes: composing, playing, teaching ... I once applied for the same visa as a theatre practitioner but was rejected – not enough competence or talent. I was later told they barely ever give them out, only a handful have ever been issued. But the lawyer says M has the credentials, experience, evidence required and, if he is prepared to put in the time gathering all the paperwork and securing the job offers and supporting documents, he is certain to get it.

One thing M has is time. He sets about ticking every box.

We don't have the paperwork or the deposit to get our own long-term rental, but Nadine tells us about a site for furnished places for academics, a well-kept secret, which could tide us over while we get set up. There's a place in Belleville near the park. It's tiny, cluttered, but has a small second bedroom and is available long-term from June. It will be a start, an address, a base. M goes over to meet the owners, and puts down a deposit.

The feeling of solidity is tremendous. I sit, fat in bed, squatting on my egg like a good, stable hen.

Magic number thirty-six. We made it. If she is born now she will be small, but fine. The relief.

In the waiting room of the natural place for births, the young receptionist asks if we have a name for her yet. I tell her the list of five we've narrowed it down to – long, elegant old French names. With each name the young woman pulls a worse face, laughing. You can't call her that! She'll be bullied at school! I'm grateful for her candour. Marie-France tells me later that old grandma names are not at all cool in France as they are in countries like Australia. Naming here, it seems, is less about what's original or evocative or visual and more about what doesn't get you punched. Now I think of it, I've never met a single Bleu or Henriette or Mélisande.

Our wise woman appears. Fabienne, sixty-something, with a glowing face, round body and soft hands. She takes me into a room and asks a lot of questions then does some osteopathy or something, placing her hand under my pelvis, taking its weight, which feels incredible. She tells me they have baths here in which to birth, and takes me to see one, large and oval-shaped, in a room looking over the city. She asks if I'd like a bath right now and I swoon with desire. She runs it for me and puts in scented-oil drops, watching me get in naked, then telling me to fill it right up as she leaves. There is a drought back home, buckets in the showers again. The midwife returns and asks why I haven't filled it right up. I love her standing there, unfazed by my naked islands, like she's my mother, or I'm now part of the greater sisterhood, not a singular body.

Now I'm overdue. It's like I don't know how to let her out, after all these months of tucking her so deep inside myself. Fabienne says they'll have to induce me tomorrow, but she does have an old wise woman's remedy …

I drink the castor oil with the almond meal and apricot juice and a dash of champagne. M just drinks champagne. And we wait.

And nothing happens so we do another round. And it begins. The shit-torrent opens the gates of eternity. Once there is no shit left for the rest of my life, I hover over a chair and tell M to turn off the fucking Arvo Pärt, and the scented candle and the mood lighting I had specifically asked for. The wise woman tells us on the phone to wait, wait, wait, now come. She is not Fabienne – Fabienne had an emergency somewhere else. She is Nathalie, and she speaks very little English, which is sad, as that was part of the plan, so we'd both feel more at ease. The taxi driver, nervous, takes us the shortcut that is the long-cut over every speed hump in Paris.

Nathalie greets us at the elevator. How an elevator this small is supposed to transport women this pregnant I do not know but am too delirious to care. Nathalie tries to speak English, though we tell her not to worry – she says 'water of bath' and 'back of woman' – then M follows her into another room where she lies down on a couch and crosses her arms across her chest like a vampire and says your wife knows what she is doing and that he will know when to call her, before closing her eyes. I sit in the water and M sits over on the bed and I tell him not to approach me or to do or say anything and he obeys my every order, watching me but not too hard. The Eiffel Tower is in the distance, twinkling. The tower surely wasn't there. Was it? M assures me later it was. Six months from now this building on the Avenue Parmentier will be boarded up and remodelled as a finance school. The whole thing will feel like a dream.

It's scary, terrifying in moments, a strange sense of destiny, weird portals and moments when I am sure I am being born myself, remembering things I've never known, horrible thoughts, I'm a monster, hopeless, what am I doing in this bath, get me out of here, I want to go home, watch *Mad Men*, be somewhere else, someone else, something else, anything other than this. Here it comes again, the thing bigger than me, too big. I can't stand it, can't do it, I am watching myself from the outside, an amoeba, a slug, a whale, primordial, swaying, strange sounds coming from somewhere. Earbuds in my ears, the stupid American lady saying peace and calm, wanting so badly to believe it: *peace and calm, peace and calm*, I am *one with my baby*, I am safe, oh god, how – how – how – how. Ow. Fifteen hours of this one moment, fifteen hundred years.

There is a time when you go so far you don't know if you'll ever come back. There is no choice but to go there, it's like stepping off a cliff or hurling yourself on an electric fence over and over and over again, each time perhaps getting closer to the thing, but never quite knowing whether you are. The effort it takes to survive is extraordinary, but each time I do there's a small sense of relief, a glow, a glimmer of something else. I have no idea where I am. Somewhere very new. Watching myself, all of us. We do it together. I clear the fence this time, in one jump. I am over it. There is fire there in that water. And then, all eyes and hair and rope and silence, there she is.

On my chest.

Everything slows.

She is perfect, and my body is fine, but they are pulling me out of the bath, to dry land, I have been in the bath so long the air on my skin is like cold blades. Something is wrong.

The placenta hasn't come, explains the wise woman, I've forgotten her name.

It's too late for the injection now. I'm in a wheelchair, the natural light of early morning coming through, out and into the elevator. The baby is fine, in her dad's arms. Look, a baby! Down we go, far down, to a fluoro-lit bunker, sounds of metal clanking, voices, flurry of movement around me, emergency?

I would really like to ignore the next part. Forget it. Keep the fairytale. The bath, the night, the tower, the silent and respectful husband, the sleeping vampire wise woman entrusting it to me, to us. The dim light, the stagiaire I'd allowed to watch, the moment

I told M to look into my eyes during a contraction but I couldn't stand it. The wise woman guiding my hand between my legs. Head of baby, she said, feel, there, the head of baby, that is head of baby. The roundness of her skull, a child, here, but still part of me. The wise woman's fingers in my asshole, directing my energy there in order not to tear. The moment I had to choose between child and clit, and there was no choice.

I kept both. And somehow everything.

This is what I'll keep. My story, to laugh about later with other women over cups of tea. Not what happened next. That is to be bound up and removed from view. I will never, ever acknowledge it, or give it air, because I hate it, it cannot be part of this. I hate *him* for infiltrating it, he is not a part of it. The man in the spotlight, the bald doctor in a white coat, representative of the medical world I had managed to avoid. Fluoro lights, shiny implements, dungeon. The light burns the man's bald head. Women are around, milling, nurses. I am hoisted onto the bed, to sitting, gown pulled aside at the back, What is happening? Péridurale. But I've had the baby! Look she's right there! I don't need an epidural!

The nurse ignores me, flicks the syringe.

Why is no one is answering me?

This will hurt.

A pain in my back.

Soon you will go numb.

I do not go numb.

Pulled down, spread apart, French-style. Stirrups. Détendez-vous, madame. The bald devil stretches gloves up to his elbows. I try to catch his eye. Monsieur? Monsieur? He focuses between my legs. But I have my baby! This is all I hoped to avoid, this is my mother, me, extracted from her, detached from her, pulled out, salad tongs, what the fuck, women are here, they hold me down and I howl and struggle like a psychiatric patient WHAT ARE YOU DOING they test for numbness and it isn't numb but there is a flurry I AM NOT NUMB and I struggle more, a psychopath NOOOOOO one arm inside me like a cow

other monstrous hand pushes hard on my belly

that place that only moments earlier she had come from, that place where I had housed her, protected her, kept her from death

he pushes harder on the outside, pulling on the inside

and I am gone

blood, blood, a butcher's shop, pulling the liver from the carcass, the good healthy liver shining

VICTORY

he holds up the meat like a prize

in the spotlight

APPLAUSE TAKE A BOW

a nurse holds up a bucket

SLAP

SUCCESS!

the meat in the bucket

proud

the devil, up to his elbows in blood, gloves peeled off

FLICK

SNAP

into the bin with the flesh

the devil is gone, I have no end, I am gushing out, there is no stopping it, I'm a hose

an abattoir

Clean it down, women. Clean it up. Fix it up. Did he sew it up, the end of me? I don't even know, I don't even care, their faces guilty, the women, lost, bobbing around my end, padding me up. Close the gap, the hole, a country letterbox.

Baby on my bare chest, ha, funny, like play-acting, the baby is calm, she soothes me, M pats my forehead, it doesn't matter, she's here, look, ah, take a photo.

Wheeled into a room. Welcome, new mother. Time for a shower, up you come, *Maman*.

On my feet the world is light. Sparkles and now the dark. I'm in the sea, way down deep, I can breathe under here, such crisp clean air, it is dawn, a ray of light enters my underwater cave, the ray is bigger, now it's sharp.

My head in someone's soft lap.

You fainted, says M above me, holding the baby.

Oh.

I am on the floor. Strange to have left the world. Strange to have left the world for which I am now responsible.

Bed pan from now on, reprimands a nurse.

I am naughty. The baby is perfect. The baby cries. There's no milk. Naughtier still. The nurses bring in a pump to help it come. Bizarre kind of agony. Dizzy, bleeding, car wreck, nipple pulling. No shit, thank god, I shall never shit again. M sleeps on a cot at the end of my bed. The baby in her crib starts to scream and doesn't stop.

She's starving, I'm reprimanded.

But I don't want her to have formula!

The stuff hits her lips, silence. Calm.

Snot comes out of the baby's nose. I suck it out like an animal.

M walks down to the mairie to register the birth. It must be done within three days. None of those long feminine names would have suited her anyway, it is clear she is no flower or fruit. We give her a little boy's name that sounds twinkly and charming in English, and like a beefy German man in French. The woman in the registry office says the name is not allowed, but M tells her we're Australian, and soon to leave. Which is sort of true. We do give her a French middle name, a female one, so she doesn't sound entirely like a male in France.

We take her home to rue Francoeur, like thieves, with saucer eyes. The world is new, everything is peach fuzz.

I lie and stare at her, lying next to me. Close up she looks like a foetus or a very attractive alien. I miss her when she is sleeping. And the days are nights, and the weeks disappear. I can't speak in sentences. I forget what I look like. In the mirror, my face is all Picasso and my body too. It feels like I've been taken apart and put back together again. And the mornings (which are evenings) bring on delirious joys, and the nights (which are days) bring on terrors beyond my wildest nightmares. Every world sadness seems to pass through me, every badness in me, and the outside world, like a sort of cleansing, detox, I'm scared to tell M in case he thinks I'm mad. Anyway I wouldn't know how to describe it. We communicate in gestures, smiles and looks. Honeymoon period. Nightmare period.

I take showers at dinnertime (which is lunchtime) and miss the baby as the water falls. The little black knob in her belly button falls out and we marvel at it then throw it in the bin. We change her nappy like amateurs, though I did it all the time with my brothers. Her vagina smells like vagina. I realise I have never smelled another vagina.

Will she play tennis? What will her laugh sound like? Will she marry? Will she be vegetarian? She is alive and one day she will die, and so will I and I will leave her alone. I grieve and grieve.

Slowly the soft edges turn to more solid outlines. When the baby is six weeks old the insurance company tells us we have to move out, but Nathalie writes us a letter to say we need six more weeks, so they move us to a place on the Île Saint-Louis. It's the only place available.

We play down our excitement. Who in their lifetime gets to live on the Île Saint-Louis?

The apartment is on the third floor – no elevator – with sleigh-style beds and more bad art, plus some old, dead cheese in the kitchen, the smell of which M spends hours scrubbing out to no avail. There's a view down the street to the water and the sounds during the day are of glasses clinking and tourists shouting and the nights are calm, ghosts of the Middle Ages blowing through the narrow streets, ghosts of the cows that once grazed here.

I am a cow, being milked on tap. I have barely put her down since she was born. I'm not sure I'm doing things right, but holding her feels good, and she prefers it too.

Nadine comes, and Tess, and Sido, and Claire, with food and toys. Marie-France shows me how to superimpose two cheap tank tops and cut a hole out of the under one to feed out of. The women pick the baby up and play with her, serving rosé and cakes to me in the window that looks out over the river. She cries to come back to me and I feel flattered.

Marie-France calls her T'choupi, after the little penguin character, for her hairline that comes down at the front, bald at the back. M and I call her the Chunk. The little love chunk. She is warm, sticky, the back of her neck is unbaked dough, her arms steamed dim sims. Her fingernails are sharp as claws. If she is upset and is shown a mirror she feels immediately better, consoled by the fact she exists. What does she feel? See? Think? I ache to know, and look for signs but I can't be her, even though I made her. Well, half. Well, nothing. She is silent in slings and loud in mornings and delighted by the sight of me – never have I felt so important, so popular. She sucks her pointer and middle fingers with such earnestness she makes me wonder about doing the same to my own. She likes Biggie Smalls. She is absolute in her rejection of sleeves. She murmurs in trains. If you blow in her face she pokes out her tongue and her eyes go wide.

It's hard not to do that a lot. She's a wind-up toy, a Kewpie doll with no clothes on. She likes the feel of her skin in air, in water, against things, my skin. She is not afraid.

I miss her already, though she is right here, on my skin. We spend hours trying to take her passport photo, but she's so new her face is barely capturable. I take pictures and pictures and hope I don't drop her in the desperation to capture every instant of her before it's gone.

I make a little world in the living room, with the lambskin rug and the mobile Dad sent her of ships in the sky, and all the little fluffy and floaty things she's been given. We call it Chunktown. There's a wind-up box that plays La Vie En Rose. There is a satisfaction to creating a small home for her. One that, wherever we go, can stay with her.

We have a small party. Claire comes with champagne, Valentin comes with an older woman. Sido and Jacques come with their toddler, Jojo. Marie-France and Hakim arrive with Emma and baby Assia, who Marie-France places in the bedroom then comes out to socialise. I find this intriguing. Marie-France seems to be back in her life again, striding ahead, while I'm still in the sea. I'm not sure if it's because it's her second time or because she's French or because I'm not doing it right. There's no one to ask, other than M, who insists I'm doing a great job.

When I'm alone I try not to look out the windows with her in my arms. The height terrifies me. How easily she could die, in so many ways. Flashes haunt me, of suddenly dropping her out the courtyard window. Because it could happen. It won't, I tell myself. But it could, and that is enough to keep me in a state of terror.

And I can't stop thinking that, if I left her on the side of the road, she would die. The thought plays over and over. If it was an outback street, no passing traffic, she would simply die.

I try not to think of this, but when M is out and I walk the length of the flat to soothe her my mind seems no longer mine.

Her passport arrives.

We're deemed fit to fly back to Australia.

She cries the whole way.

It takes us a year to get back to Paris. In Australia we seem to disappear, moving from holiday rental to holiday rental near my dad's, time warping, everything taking longer or shorter than expected. She crawls, then stands, then walks. My sister and I push prams together. M and I get fat on cookbook chocolate cake. We lose the deposit on the Belleville place, but then M's visa is secured, and I find a place we can rent for a year up the canal from the Récollets in the rue Eugène Varlin. An art historian and his family are moving to the Villa Medici in Rome for the next academic year. It's a small, nondescript place with two bedrooms and shelves full of books, and looks easy to keep clean.

We had considered looking for a place in a greener, more kid-friendly part of Paris, but we know the 10th so well it feels more comforting than starting from scratch. In Paris, it seems once a neighbourhood has chosen you it's almost impossible to leave. Especially with a child.

It's painful to rip ourselves away from our families. A visceral tearing. On the plane I can't stop replaying the image in my mind of the Chunk waving to my dad at the gates as she ate an apple, the handbag with the ponies on it he gave her strapped across her chest. Dad, smiling, happy, proud. They all understand, and wish us well, encourage us. Which only makes it worse.

It's a grim autumn morning when we arrive. Rain taps the windows of the cab. The Chunk sits in my lap, in the baby carrier with the straps loosened, dazed but awake, resting her head on my chest and looking out at the tall grey buildings, the narrow sky. M and I squeeze each other's hand. *What have we done.* At that moment the Chunk stands up on my lap and starts pumping her legs up and down, charging her fists in the air, like a victory dance.

When we enter the new apartment and stand listless, taking in yet another family's space, she sets off around the flat, mounting each piece of furniture to stomp and bounce, arms in the air, a mini-Napoléon claiming her land.

It's hard not to feel this was all her plan. To be born here. To born herself here. In French they say elle naît. She *borns*, rather than she *was born*. Like the classic Simone de Beauvoir quote: *On ne naît pas femme, on le devient*. One borns not woman, one becomes it.

It certainly seems, watching the Chunk in that room, face bright with determination, that she had some part in it. Either way, that she is happy brightens our countenance. We must be on the right track.

Le Bonheur

M is back. Strange to see him from this distance. We've been fused since returning to Paris, welded together. Come to think of it, since the pregnancy we've barely been apart. He looks amazing. Refreshed from a period of being a nonstop adult, a musician, a free being. His hair is unwashed and messy, like gusts of life have blown through it, the world outside, Tundra man, returned to the family with the kill: two guitars, a suitcase and a big bag of percussion.

She's Elsa now, I say as he picks up the bundle of tulle.

Toi, you Olaf, she says.

I'm *Arna*, I tell M, as she starts running from wall to wall. I think it's Anna, but it's pronounced, more dramatically, *Arna*.

He grabs for me and I like it, thank god he feels the same, better, he's back, he doesn't hate me, all is fine, we're a family again.

We kiss and I've made the salmon thing and the Chunk watches *Pocoyo* as he tells his stories, of the recording, the guys, the bars, the loose producer. The work is good, he says, but he won't let me listen to it yet. I can't wait to play it on the record player, I tell him. He is positively fizzing. This is the key. We just need to go out there and keep ourselves alive as individuals. Yes. He unpacks an array of toys and new vinyl from Amsterdam. Youth Lagoon, the new National, a Marvin Gaye. The Chunk runs around with a ribbon he bought her, tied to a stick. Then he bathes her while I work.

The next night I've booked Bastien to babysit. It's balmy and I'm dreaming of a terrasse. Though I know there's no chance whatsoever, I call the Bistrot Paul Bert and to my surprise not only do they have a table but they are fine to seat us en terrasse. The guy seems surprised at my surprise and I hang up and think, Perhaps this city isn't as difficult as I thought, perhaps I should try more to call last minute, perhaps I sound important, perhaps I'm famous now and people know my name, perhaps I should believe more in possibilities, perhaps I should loosen up. I'm smiling as I get dressed, giving M a hug from behind as he does up his shirt, his body responding to the unusual feeling of my gentle, caring touch. The Chunk is excited when Bastien enters, lifting her high above his head.

Bistrot Paul Bert has never heard of our booking. I tense up. What the fuck, no way, check again. The guy sighs. Look, is it possible you called a different Bistrot Paul Bert? There's another Bistrot Paul Bert? The guy hustles back inside. I call the number on my phone. Yes. I have called Le Paul Bert in Fontenay-sous-Bois. Pu-tain! The terrace tables are lit with a dying sun. They have opened the windows so those on the inside of the restaurant are facing out and enjoying the heavy city air. Everyone is having the greatest time in the whole wide world. I smile at the waiter, who is back outside with a tray of wine, and try the charm that used to work. There's no chance at all of a table?

He doesn't hate us, and gives us the chef's table, right up next to the grill. Sweat glistens our faces, but the food is delicious, and we are smiling at each other and we're back.

Walking home up the canal afterwards, I ask M if he's happy. It's a scary question to ask and once it's out of my mouth I wonder if

I should have asked something so naive and yet so loaded. What even is happiness? My dad would say:

Something to keep the rain off.
Something in your belly.
Someone who likes you a bit.

M does that thing where he sees the question as not relevant. He makes sure he's happy, he says. This prickles me as though he's implying I'm difficult, hard to please. He's not. He is just answering my question. Yes, he's happy, he says, sensing my annoyance. It's a particular time. We're in the trenches, he says, quoting someone who said anyone with kids under five should expect nothing much of themselves, just surviving is enough. I ask if he thinks we're surviving. We're thriving, he says.

Are we?

Look what we're doing. We've got a roof over our heads – a nice one – in Paris. Our kid is great, healthy, having a ball. You're getting work, and working on your book – not enough, I know, but there are little windows – and I'm going to work as hard as I can to give you more. I'm making music, following the thing I've always wanted to do, which might just be the ticket to actually earning money. What else could we want?

He's so optimistic sometimes I want to smash his face in. But he has this way of pulling everything off you for a second, giving distance to things, so you can see the picture from afar. And the picture of us, in Paris, is very nice.

You're right, I say to him, and squeeze his hand. He doesn't ask if I'm happy and I'm glad. What was I thinking, asking that question? I would have no clue what to say, where to start.

Why have I heard of Fontenay-sous-Bois? I ask, to change the subject. The place I booked the restaurant? He starts laughing and so do I, until we are both holding our stomachs. The guy was so pleased I was calling!

He reminds me Fontenay was the place he used to go on about when he worked at the track. Once, there was a métro strike, so he rode his bike to Vincennes and got lost, and ended up in this little town that, though just on the other side of the bois, felt like a village. It was full of trees and grass and little houses, and after that he would deliberately take the métro the extra stop so he could walk to the hippodrome from there. He would come back to the Récollets or our place in Belleville and say, Let's move to Fontenay-sous-Bois! It always made me laugh.

I didn't come to Paris to live in the 'burbs, I'd say.

He would tell me how leafy it was, and quaint, right on the edge of Paris, and close to the whole Vincennes park area. If we ever have a kid, he would say, that is the place to live.

I just realised, I tell him, Fontenay is the place the woman and the man live in *Le Bonheur*.

At nights I've been slowly watching Jacques and Sido's Agnès Varda box set: *Vagabond, Daguerréotypes, Documenteur* … In *Le Bonheur* the family live in Fontenay-sous-Bois, or I think it's called Fontenay-les-Roses. The perfect couple, François and Thérèse, and their two perfect children – one girl, one boy – live simply and happily in this town of flowers. They are actually played by an actor and his real family. Theirs is a real, sweet, wholesome love. The dream.

Then he meets a woman who works in the post office. She has just moved to Fontenay from Paris. She prefers the excitement of the city. She looks strikingly like Thérèse, but more sophisticated, worldly, and they start an affair. François is so happy he tells his wife about the affair one day as they picnic in the park. He describes his and Thérèse's love as a perfect field, and that he has seen a beautiful apple tree outside of their field and brought it in to join their happiness. Le bonheur, ça s'additionne, he says. Happiness is cumulative.

Thérèse is happy for François, they make love, then while he's napping she goes and drowns herself in the lake. He replaces her with the post-office woman and all is well for François. As the credits roll, the new family walk together in the sun, as if Thérèse never existed.

There is a moment early in the film, where in the background a TV is playing the old Jean Renoir film *Le Déjeuner sur l'Herbe*. The movie plays as the live scene unfolds, François, Thérèse and the kids fussing around with their relatives. On the TV, the man says, *Le bonheur, c'est peut-être la soumission à l'ordre naturel.* Happiness is perhaps submission to the natural order. The natural order proving not to be the simple, sweet family life, but the impossibility of being satisfied with it.

I remember going out to Fontenay once when I was dating Adrien, to visit the father of one of his friends, a writer. We sat in the garden of the spacious two-storey house beneath a lovely gnarled, weeping tree. I remember feeling distinctly uncomfortable, as though the comfort itself was disturbing. Part of the reason I loved Paris, I realised then, was its discomfort. It made me feel real, awake, alive. Here was a place to become content, and complacent, like in the suburbs I grew up in. A place to submit, become soft, to surrender. A place to die.

This is going to be a great year for us, says M. We'll have more time, more freedom. We've come a long way in eighteen months. It's only going to get better.

I believe him, I do. I do I do I do.

Every day I get up for work, kiss them goodbye. She has Club five hours a day now, except Thursdays, either at Old Club – the Gavroches – or New Club, the municipal one across the road from us in Petites Écuries. From the outside, New Club is heartbreakingly bleak but, like so much in Paris, there's a whole world behind the unassuming facade: down the back there's an entire courtyard area with a tree.

When she's not tired after Club, M takes her out, to parks, cafés, museums:

The Chocolate Museum

The Bonbon Museum
The Cereal Museum
The Yoyo Museum

The first one exists. It was a bust. All she wanted was to eat chocolate. At the end they gave her a tiny piece.

The Fish Museum (the aquarium)
The Dinosaur Museum (the natural history museum)
The Pomp-di-dou (the Centre Pompidou and its kids' room with all the interactive game and toys)
The Petites Museum (the Maison des Petits at le Centquatre)
The Mouse Museum (the Musée de la Chasse et de la Nature)
The Zouzou Museum (Café Zoïde, where they do singing and games)
The Kids Museum (the Cité des Enfants at the Science Museum)

He has his routes planned, knows each park, each nearby café where they can use the bathroom, where they can go for a snack, and where he can shelter with her if it rains. He has enough places sussed now that any new place he goes, he knows he's not far from one of the safe zones. This enables him to feel free to explore, while knowing that nobody is going to sit in a wet – or worse – nappy.

Trampoline Park (Les Tuileries)
Horsey Park (Jardin du Luxembourg)
Flower Park (Parc Floral)
Boat Park (Bois de Boulogne)
Picnic Park (Bois de Vincennes)

And he takes her to kick soccer balls or throw basketballs or to the Piscine Pailleron or Château Landon, with his *maillot*, that he resents, after a pool guard made him change out of his shorts and buy a too-small lycra pair from a vending machine.

On Thursdays, when she has no Club, he likes to take her somewhere new: on a bateau-mouche or to see a play or to tour Versailles or the Palais Garnier, which she lasts ten seconds at. Or different wings of the grand galleries, if they can be bothered in queues.

The Big Museum (Le Louvre)
The Clock Museum (Le Musée d'Orsay)

He often ends up around Madeleine, where they'll look in shops and eat by fountains, watching the tourist women in their dreamy bliss and the husbands checking their watches. M dreams, wanders with his girl, goes where things lead him, like he used to with me. It's all filling her up, he says. And him. He seems to love his role as domestic custodian. He never complains about the drudgery of wandering around, thinking of food and toilets, missing adult conversation. He loves to watch her interact, he says, and he's learning a lot about the city. This week, he took her to the Cité des Enfants to play her favourite water-splashing game and put her hands in the different-textured holes, and there was a new installation called the Cabine de Tristesse – the cabin of sadness – a dark enclosure with only the sound of different voices weeping all around her. She loved it, M said. Sat there for ages.

Only in France would they have a cabin of sadness, he said with admiration.

I get sad that I'm not doing more things with her. But also I'm relieved. There's a sense of achievement that comes with working, delivering, being part of the adult world. It's more clear-cut to go to work, even if my job is messy.

He usually sends me a picture in the afternoon. Her in the pram, asleep, squashed up next to his knees at a table, usually outside, with a beer or a coffee on it. He gets about an hour each day, dependent on the weather and where they are, to stop and think and breathe, for himself.

I take her on Wednesday afternoons. M rehearses with the band, and it's a quieter time for work, as all the kids are off school after lunch and people are shipping them around to grandparents, sports, et cetera. At first I'd take her to the menagerie to see the flamingos, the red pandas, the chimpan-zeens, and the crocos and iguanas in the vivarium. Or the Pomp-di-dou or the Musée de la Chasse et de la Nature to look at the bears and search for the mouse, or the fish at Porte Dorée or the jungle gym at the Parc Floral. Now I take her to ballet.

When I was twenty-two and first lived in Paris as an au pair, I never discovered the inner parts of the Right Bank, sticking to the grander places in guidebooks: gardens, monuments, boulevards. One night, I found myself in the Marais for the first time, walking down what I now know was rue du Temple. I think I was on the way to meet some boys who had invited me to go dancing in a nightclub. As I walked down the narrower, darker street, a paved driveway caught my eye. Most doorways were shut, but the two heavy blue doors were propped open. At the end of the driveway was a building with tall windows and warm lights, and in the windows were the silhouettes of people dancing. Couples doing the tango on one level, gliding ballerinas on another, and right at the top a darkened studio with a solo dancer bent over a barre. I stood in the cold and watched for a long time. I didn't dare cross the doorway into the courtyard – it felt like a private place, secret, and I felt it might simply disappear. The scene stayed with me, and though I tried many times to retrace my steps I was never able to find the place again. I began to think I'd dreamed it.

Now I am here, and the Chunk is one of the bodies in the window. Or she would be, if she was tall enough to be seen. Coming here is like stepping inside a memory. Her sweaty little palm in mine reminds me it's real.

Her classroom is high in the rafters, up three flights of stairs, an attic of sorts with poutres jutting down so low the teacher has to mind where she walks. The little blobs of flesh in their regulation pink jump and squeal and jiggle, hurtling from wall to wall, twirling and waving their arms like wings.

Parents are not supposed to stay, but I haven't been kicked out yet.

THE SEA IN THE METRO

In the little changing room, damp with tiny ballerina sweat, I change her out of her costume and we walk back to the bus stop to take the 38. Before becoming a parent I had never taken a Paris bus before. Now we take them everywhere, especially the 38. The 38 is the best: it runs north to south, and you can fit the pram on it. You don't have to worry about the métro steps, and she can look out the window, point to things – la trottinette, la dame aux cheveux bleus, le toutou.

Once we're home I try my best not to look at my phone until she's asleep. Then, when she wakes, I focus on her as best I can, playing, watching, painting, drawing, cooking, shopping, whatever. I like it when we have a project. My least favourite thing is the imaginary games, improvisations. My body turns to steel and I have to grit my teeth and set a timer in my mind to endure it. Perhaps it's a reminder of the theatre in my body, the theatre I'm not doing, may not ever do again. It's like I've shut that part of myself off.

If I can control the game it's better. I like tea parties, for example. They have clear rules. Or strict theatre exercises I know from Lecoq. Sometimes we do melodrama or pantomime or tragedy. She loves it when I direct, when I have ideas, when I propose. Pierrot and Columbine is a favourite: a pantomime piece we learned at school. We draw out the scenes using our bodies, exaggerating the characters as wildly as we can:

PIERROT

Me, I love you. Come with me and I take you to the seaside!

COLUMBINE

The seaside? No. Me, I love Gilles, with his big shiny car.
You, no.

PIERROT

But me, I love you! Look! I will take down the stars and give them to you. I will take down the moon.

COLUMBINE
Stars and moon? No. Me, I love money! With Gilles's money,
I can buy myself a beautiful necklace.
You, no.

Pierrot suicides

Her favourite part is the suicide. Life and death are the same game to her. We find lots of ways to kill ourselves, squishing our cheeks together too hard, pushing up our eyebrows till we die, tying her skipping rope around and around my shin until, Aghhh! I'm dead! She loves my seriousness and engagement in the game, different from the random dolly games.

I love you! And I cry! I cry bigger! And BIGGER!
You see the moon?

COME A DA SEA COMBILLY!

Sometimes she talks about Tinyland. Before she came to live with us, she lived in Tinyland, with her tiny mum and dad. In Tinyland, bonbons are good for you, and vegetables give you a bobo tumtum. In Tinyland, being naughty is good and being good is naughty. In Tinyland, she had three sisters: Strongy, Aren't I, and Teeny. They all had separate bedrooms, but sometimes they would swap, and occasionally they would all sleep together in one of the rooms.

Did three of you ever gang up on the other one? I ask.

No, she says.

Stuff like that – adversity, jealousy – never seemed to happen in Tinyland. In Tinyland they lived in the one house forever and never ever moved. The Chunk misses her tiny mum and dad, and talks about them every day. Their names are Matt and Coraline. She can still visit them, but I can't. I'm too big. If I came I would squash them and all of Tinyland. The Chunk can visit them because, though she's big, she was born in Tinyland, and when she wants to visit they just magic her tiny. She was borned twice, she tells me. First in Tinyland, then in this land. In Tinyland they currently have a sign up in the street that says *No Big People*. I would go to prison if I came.

That's a shame, I say. I would love to visit Tinyland.

No, Maman. No Maman inna Tinyland.

One day, she tells me, she was in Tinyland with her tiny mum and dad, and the clouds suddenly went away and all these holes opened up in the sky. She climbed up a very tall tree to the holes and had to choose one of them to go inside.

How did you choose? I ask.

She makes a sniffing motion and explains to me that she went up to each of the holes and sniffed and this one didn't smell good and this one didn't smell good … and then this one smelled like Mama! She liked the smell. So she climbed up into that hole. And that's how she came to live in my belly.

I like the idea that I smell good and that she just climbed into me. It makes sense to me that she would have that kind of volition, even prior to being.

When she's tired, we watch *Frozen*. We must have seen it twenty times now, alternating between the English and French versions. I love the over-intellectualised garble of the French, but she doesn't seem to have a preference. I'm not sure she even notices the difference.

Liberaaaate! Deliver! I will not lie anymore! I left my childhood in summer … lost in winter … the cold is for me the price of liberty.

She loves to lie stretched out on my body, the computer propped on a pillow on my lap. Sometimes she sits on the couch, me on the floor, and plays with my hair while we watch, pulling it with her sticky fists, which annoys and hurts me but I bite my lip and bear it so she can show me the affection. She wants to play Elsa and *Arna* constantly, and my heart hurts with the desire not to, but I put the towels around my body and we chase each other and build snowmen and sing and she hides in her room. I'm always *Arna*, banging on the door, begging to build a snowman. The Chunk inhabits her role, demanding I GO WAY. I didn't know she would be Elsa this long. She walks the streets in the too-big blue dress I found her in the rue de Paradis dépôt-vente, singing a mashup of both languages, letting her voice really goooo. People bend down and ask if she's going to a party. Kids don't wear costumes in the street here, it's rare to see a Spider-Man or a random princess just going about their business. I don't think my sister's son has worn actual clothes since he could walk.

It seems clear to me that *Frozen* is all about depression and its relationship with creativity. Elsa, the snow queen, has a gift, but it's tied up in her sadness and nobody can understand. She has to hide herself away to dig into it and see what it really is in there. It is not because I'm depressed that I'm saying that, or creative. Depression – what even is that? The word was said to me a few times back in Australia: postnatal depression. How could anyone NOT be depressed, I wanted to ask, when their entire life has been turned upside down? Who wouldn't be depressed after being in a car crash, only to turn around and nurse those who survived the wreckage? Who wouldn't be depressed after months of sleeplessness, isolation, bleeding, leaking, having their tits pulled, nipple-crippled so bad they have to bang their feet and howl? Who wouldn't be depressed at the loneliness, the strange hours, the separation from the world and what you thought you knew of yourself, the desire to see nobody? All this is *normal*, part of life, and if you talked about it you would only sound ungrateful, and offend others, who may not have been so lucky as to have a baby, or may be completely fine, or may not be fine and your sharing your experience will trigger a misery they weren't sure they had, while casting a negative light on yours and their baby's very existence.

I love my girl. I love her more than I've ever felt love. I also need to flee to an ice castle. It's possible to have two things living inside you simultaneously, isn't it. Many things, simultaneously. That's the problem. How we're expected to have just one thing in there. Be purely one thing.

Elsa is two things: a kind and loving sister *and* a young woman dealing with this other side of herself, this other her she can't control. She needs to run away to learn what to do with it. Then she makes everything better.

It's fine for the Chunk to play Elsa. I'd much rather be *Arna. Arna* is my opposite. She is one thing, balanced, in harmony with herself. Stable. All she wants to do is play, but Elsa keeps the door shut.

I dun *wunna* buildy 'nowman.

It doesn't have to be a snowman!

The good thing about Elsa is she shuts you out so you can lean against the door staring at the wall for quite a few moments, or even sneak into the kitchen and grab your phone. I came up with the perfect tagline for the sportswear print campaign that way. But she is in there, being Elsa the whole time. I know it, it breaks my heart, I am evil. I make sure I'm back in my role by the time she bangs on the door and says, OK, *Arna*, play the babies, but the feeling is cheap.

Then it's back on, the door slammed and *Arna* can sit back and slam one strong, merciless coffee.

Francine and Jippy's new apartment on the Boulevard de Strasbourg is a ghastly space, the high walls swamping their modest Marais furniture, which they've arranged in awkward clumps as if they're camping there. A huge salon, tiny old closed-off kitchen, cavernous cold bathroom with rusting pipes, two tiny bedrooms. They are happy as pie, windows always open despite the pollution and noise. Francine's mother, Louise, is often there, in her mid-eighties but as fit and spritely as ever, though Francine claims she needs a lot of looking after. She wears sneakers and jeans, and plays with the Chunk, always with Crocos or Fraises Tagada in her pocket. Francine arranges the snacks for apéro on a large tray: usually olives, charcuterie, chips paysannes in beautiful mismatched bowls, and small champagne glasses shaped after Marie Antoinette's breasts, into which she pours the fizz I always bring from Nicolas, the cheapest one but always *de Champagne*.

It's the craic but tonight I got so relaxed I accidentally tu'd Louise. We'd been talking politics and books and Mai '68, when the Chunk started picking her nose like fury on Francine's lap. Don't do that, I said in English, It's yucky. Non Maman, said the Chunk, C'est yummy! And we laughed as Louise handed her a tissue and I asked Louise what she thinks of the new place and, in a lapse of concentration, accidentally tutoyer-ed. Francine has used the informal tu when speaking to me from the start, and I've tutoyer-ed her back – after first asking her if I should, like I've learned to in the office when I'm not sure. Generally in advertising, there's no vous, but you can get it wrong. Calling Louise tu hit me like a bomb – she clearly noticed but didn't say anything, and I quickly switched back to vous, and I could tell it was wrong, from Francine's face.

Tu/vous is a craic-killer. Each time I start to relax I get bitten. Even though Paris is getting more casual – less formal dress, more chefs throwing away their Michelin stars – I still, ten years later, have trouble with it. It's especially hard as an Australian person because our MO is to never act greater than anyone else in any given circumstance. Maaate. Being casual in general in French is difficult. For example, An offhand *nice to meet you* doesn't exist – you can only say you're ravished to have met someone, or greatly pleased. At parties you generally use tu, but not always. The public world, people you don't know, are mostly vous. Though yesterday a guy came up to me on the métro platform and when I apologised for not having change, said, Nique ta mère, ta mère la pute. Fuck your mother, your mother the whore. The tu-ing adding that extra taste of absolute disrespect.

There's a woman about my age who looks like Charlotte Gainsbourg and brings her one-year-old to the Mère Denis café on the rue du Faubourg-Saint-Denis where I take the Chunk sometimes after Club. Her little boy, Isaac, and the Chunk play together – it's a tu situation, surely. But the other day, out of the blue, she vous'd me. I'd asked what she (tu) was doing on the weekend and in response she said, Et vous? It spun me out. For a week I was afraid of seeing her, but then she tutoyer-ed me again. Then it dawned on me – she had been talking about us, *plural.* What are *you all* doing on the weekend? I felt stupid. But then I also found it interesting that she had assumed that my activities would involve the family, whereas I'd assumed she'd be doing things solo. Because she seems like that. An active, sexy, young woman who happens to be a mother, but would certainly not be at home watching *Pocoyo* on a Saturday night.

It's a fine art, socially guided. The rules are blurry. Grandmas: always vous. Children: tu, though that feels so blanket disrespectful that I sometimes say vous, and then sound patronising. Creative directors: tu. Managing directors: vous, but shoes can affect this. Sneakers: tu. Suit and shined shoes: vous. Bank manager: vous. Parents at Club: tu. Childcare workers at Club: vous. Omar at Chez Prune: tu. Pharmacist: vous. Acupuncturist: vous.

Louise forgives me, and never shall we tu. She says tu to the Chunk, and the Chunk uses tu back, but she's allowed to because she's a kid and they have that special rapport.

M uses tu for everyone. Even the fonctionnaires in Paradise City. They don't mind. They find him charming.

On nights when M is home and the Chunk is asleep and my work finished, if I have the energy I'll ride to Claire's and we'll lie on her floor or go to the pizza joint Val now manages opposite Square du

Temple or sit at the bar at Grazie on the boulevard with the funny bartender Cyril who didn't know what a wedgie was. And she will moan about work and her writing and rejections from publishers and the dates she's been on and I'll moan about my ugly, abhorrent female rage at the pressure I feel to earn and its accompanying festering resentment towards the male in the room, who is trying his best. It's disgusting, heinous, a bog inside me I don't quite understand, and it took a long time for me to finally let it out to Claire. What is he *thinking*, I puzzle into my drink, how could he think this will work, even a job in a record shop would be better, why am I so alone in this, where are his friends telling him, Wise up, dude, where is his family saying, What the fuck, where is my mother telling me, Jayne, be careful, do you want to lose him? And Claire will sit and listen, in the way she does, the greatest craic listener I've ever met, as well as the craic herself. Rather than give me advice she'll lay out questions:

Is it possible this is about other things, for you?

Do you think M is a good man?

Do you think M feels all this you are telling me, even without you saying it to him?

What is it like to be a parent?

It feels big, this small thing, this glitch, because M and I have always talked about *everything*. Every single thing, honestly too, about our work, our impressions, feelings about art, writing, music, our deepest most inappropriate thoughts and desires. To hold back even one tiny thing feels epic and shakes me to the core. But I can't talk to him about it, what I feel is too big and confusing and likely damaging, and anyway, who am I to tell him what to do or ask him to alter his path, he's a grown man, he knows what he's doing. We've always supported each other, trusted each other. Have I stopped trusting him? Yes, I suppose, in some way. I suppose part of me is afraid he's blinded by his own ambition, that he's not seeing clearly, and that scares me. We need pragmatism now, solidity, we need to pay the bills. I guess, in a nutshell, what I don't trust is that his decision to start a band has been made in the spirit of supporting a family instead of to pursue his dream.

A loss of trust, yes, though when he justifies it to me it all makes sense. The visa, the cultural shut-out, the autonomous potential of his own band. But justifications, I've noticed, don't work on my female side. My female side is her own monster. She has grown from god-knows-where, since that day in Montmartre I buried my manhood. Despite my loathing of traditional gender roles, the monster wants the man to bring home the bacon; despite my lust for freedom she wants *foundations*; despite my horror of the domestic life she wants me to spend sweet time with the child, nurture and coddle her, obeying Mum's pillars of attention and care.

This conversation never kills the craic between Claire and me, it's just part of it, the evil interlude. It feels amazing to let go of some of the foulness building up in me, so much suddenly feels taboo, my challenges with parenting, my egotistical desires, my frustration at having to bin my ambitions, that I'll be forty in a few years, I'd hoped to *be there* by now, whatever *there* is, have accomplished something, not still be selling my soul to the axis of evil each day, and only more and more. The idea of the whoring to advertising was always to take its rewards and give them to good, to art, to living, to making the world a better place, but now all I feel like is the whore. What was that Artaud line, the whore, the slut wanting eternal happiness, eternal bonheur, unwilling to compromise for any price. Mademoiselle Lucifer.

I want it all. Money, love, art, the craic, the child, the city, the entire garden of earthly delights. I am Mademoiselle Lucifer – or *Madame* should I say – and now Claire's laughing and so is Cyril and he's pouring us shots. And I will ride home full of craic and a toxic sadness to have betrayed my love who I know is only trying to be everything I want, and because of one lousy decision, has to stick to it or die.

Dreams

This is the picture in my mind of our life in Paris.

We live in an impasse, behind a tall gate, in one of those hidden laneways, shut off from the noise, though it's very noisy and wild in the street outside. It's a dead end with cobblestones and plants and a few little tables outside for warm evenings. The buildings are old ateliers, workhouses, with high glass windows, the ones on the ground floor mottled so you can't see in. There are balconies and flowers and ivy growing up the walls, children playing, cats, dogs with names everyone knows.

Our place is one of the ground-floor ateliers. It's humble, messy but not too messy, open plan and full of books and art and nooks. Not that big, but spacious and full of light, and in it is a writing space for me and a music studio for M – both of which are private but somehow also open plan – and in the middle is a makeshift kitchen where people are always hanging around, the Chunk and her friends, friends of all ages, sitting on benches kicking their feet out, relatives and neighbours, hanging out, and we're making some money doing jobs here and there but mostly we're making art, it's a big art warehouse and people sit around until night and food somehow gets cooked and dishes done and clothes washed and put away and nobody seems to lift a finger.

People are always there. The place is open, doors never locked, and there's a feeling of unending joy and freedom. Unattachment. It's unpretentious, though of course the picture costs a zillion bucks. I guess that's not the point. There is balance. Music. Always music.

I think we're still in shock at the way things worked out with M's talent and competency visa. Friends in film and television, his agent, his music publisher, the cultural attaché at the embassy, all wrote glowing letters of support and promises of work … but when we arrived in Paris none of it eventuated. M spent months sending demos, emailing showreels, calling contacts, sending copies of albums, eventually posting notices to work for free at the Fémis and the other film, music and television schools, but there was barely a response.

Then he met Domenico. Domenico was an Australian composer who had lived in Paris for thirty years. He told M point blank he'd never work in the film industry here. It was a closed shop, limited exclusively to the French. Domenico, himself a French citizen with a catalogue spanning some of the greatest films of the past three decades, still worked here only as an assistant or uncredited in major films. The only chance M had was playing as a session musician, but he had never trained to read music, he'd only ever written and played what he made himself. That was when he started thinking about starting a new band, and singing too. He could play shows then, every night. Bars always need music.

He told me this at Nanashi, on a rare night out after we'd been back in Paris six months and were losing money fast. Was he serious? This was not the picture I'd had of us coming over here. Same for him, he said, he'd imagined going off to work each day in a suit, a working artist, with a special niche in this enormous, enticing French industry he loved.

The band idea was crazy. But I couldn't help but smile at him as he ate his green tea cheesecake. I love crazy. And, as he explained, having a band would mean he was free to work in the gaps, be independent, take charge of the kid, cook, shop, collect her, all that stuff, to take the pressure off me and my work. It was his dream, he said, to lead the band. I told him not to say that, things had to be firmly rooted in reality right now. He promised me they were.

He built the band with Dan and Jean-Yves from his last band and a new guy, Guillaume, on drums, and started writing straight away, practising his singing, rehearsing regularly. Each night he'd deliver the report.

Terrible.

Woeful.

OK.

Not as bad as last night.

He played me some of the recordings. I became afraid to give him feedback as I could only ever speak the truth, and creating a whole new band and leading-man persona was never going to take five minutes. So one night when he brought me a demo, I stole away into the bedroom with the headphones, already rehearsing ways not to break his heart – but it was beautiful. His voice was grainy, true, fragile as a leaf, but this time there was a confidence to it, a strength inside the leafness. Before this, his guitar-playing, mastered over two decades, had been dominating his voice, but now the voice was meeting it, guiding it, the guitar playing with it, not against it, allowing it to find its space. Tears ran down my face. I still didn't feel hopeful it would support a family, but M had always come through with all his crazy work, I remember him paying our overdue rent once at the Récollets with winnings from the track. To question his choice would only be to doubt him, and I didn't. I wouldn't.

The EP comes back from Amsterdam, hot in its vibrant sleeve. I cook the meatball thing and we put the vinyl on the record player, with wine that cost over eight euros and we sit on the couch and listen to the five songs, the Chunk whirling around with four costumes on top of each other, one on her head.

The sound is loud and bright and M's voice placed boldly inside of it. There's a feeling of risk to it that has come from all the pain of the last months. It feels alive, unsafe, on the edge … a success! We jump up and grab the Chunk's hands and dance around in circles. M's face is flushed with joy, relief, apprehension. It's so good, I tell him. It's really, really good.

Perhaps I'm wrong about it all. Perhaps this will all work out. If only my brain would shut up. I remember a conversation we had about how it all plays out. The money is in gigs these days, M's favourite part of playing music, so, best case scenario: the band gets noticed, the EP gets airplay and the songs sell, they tour, play Paris, tour, record, tour. Not only will he be out every night, he'll be away for weeks, months at a time. Which I guess, if it works, takes the financial pressure off me, but leaves me here full time with the kid. Not a bad option, but not the dream. Discussing the subject is so sensitive and fraught we always back off. This is his only option, music. He has to find a way.

The band quickly gets two gigs: one playing first at the OPA on a Friday night, and another opening a big arts festival at the Australian Embassy. The latter is paid, and though once the money is split with the other band members and mixer the sum will be small, it feels like a victory. We celebrate with dinner at the Napoléon, the Chunk has steak-haché. Having the shows lined up lifts something in him, he is in a good mood, things are coming together. In the morning in bed he rolls over and kisses my face. I hold him tight, burying the monster in me. He smells good. I have to get to work but let him draw me beneath the covers.

At the OPA there are five paying audience members, including me and the Chunk, which M was pretty much expecting, and is ultimately relieved about. The sound is terrible, the band clunky and the live singing not working with the sound. But M has a saying: one gig equals ten rehearsals. Which I remind him on our way out, to cheer him up, but his mood is flat. After the high of the recording, he says he feels he's fallen backwards. But it will be fine. They just need to rehearse hard for the Embassy gig.

I can feel he's nervous but he doesn't let on. Over the next week he shuts off from me slightly, in order to present a brave front. I focus on my own work, leave him alone. He works in the office until very late at night. In the morning he doesn't share much about his progress, which feels strange. Perhaps he realises that if he shows any sign of difficulty, I'll suggest the band wasn't a good idea, that he should consider changing tack. And if he disagrees, he will be going against me. Better to keep his struggle to himself and continue moving forward.

On the night of the Embassy gig, we jiggle our way through the underground, M with his amp on the trolley, guitar on his lap. His natural state. The train stops at Kléber for its usual unexplained pause. The Chunk wriggles in the pram. I'm hoping she will fall asleep and I can drink some beer. M looks nervous. I'm not sure if it's about the show or about who will be there, how it will work, will this lead to more gigs, why is there so much pressure on a party show.

What are you thinking? I ask.

I'm thinking this is stressful, but I'm glad you guys came.

Of course we did! I say, tickling the Chunk.

He smiles again, looking more confident.

We're gonna hear Daddy play!

The train starts up again and he plays the game with the Chunk where he gets the bunny to climb the edge of the pram, straining to get to the top, then falling down again. We all laugh, and the people around us focus on not noticing.

She is restless at the gig and the floors are slippery and Claire gets held up so we mingle for a bit then I have to leave before the band has even started. Later, he recounts the humiliation: at first nobody listened, just kept talking loudly amongst themselves, then the band got louder and the crowd were forced to listen, despite a group at the back, including the guy who booked them, talking loudly. Then the requests started coming in for AC/DC, Midnight Oil, Kylie Minogue, people drunk and annoyed and impatient that the band couldn't play their favourite songs. Finally the band packed up and the events people played loud hits over the speakers, and people started dancing.

Not the craic, reports Claire. Poor M. Your people don't know how to listen.

Flâneuse

I never come to the Napoléon alone. If I had a moment to stop for a glass of wine I would go to Jeannette, or Vivant Cave or Chez Madame Gen or the Petit Château d'Eau or the Cadran. I am in the Napoléon because it's on my direct route home from the Cool Agency and my entire being is a rock, and I think I should heed M's advice and take a breath before walking through our doorway, rather than entering with the tension that sets the place on edge.

The Chunk loves the Napoléon. Whenever we ask her, Where shall we go? she says, The Napoléon! You'd think she'd like Chez Madame Gen for the chocolate squares they give her, or the Carillon for the dolly behind the bar, but she always chooses the Napoléon. When I went to school in this street, I never came here. I can't remember why. Perhaps it wasn't a student hangout back then, or it was more expensive than Jeannette or the Mauri 7, or just because it's one of those corner places that's always there and you never notice it. We come here a lot with the Chunk because it's relaxed and basic, and they have decent hamburgers served quick. They're not nice here, don't fuss over her like at Madame Gen, but they're not rude or annoyed either like in some of the nicer places. The disgusting-but-not-too-bad bathroom has a toilet with a thick red seat that we can lie her down on to change, and a urinal next to the basin with a large pair of red lips around it that I find funny and M finds disturbing.

At the bar I order a glass of chablis and sit, trying to breathe. If I could smoke indoors I would. Just breathe. *Breathe.* Today was my second day on a job with an intense directeur artistique trying to work his way up and getting shit from the senior creative team that he then poured on to me. My ideas were good, but he presented them badly, then when they cut him down he'd blame me. My articulation wasn't great, I didn't want to be in-house, jobs for the make-up brand and others mounting up as I wasted time in meeting after dick-swinging meeting. I drank too much coffee.

The wine helps. I would read, but I don't. I just sit and watch the people go by, like I always dream of doing. No one to have an affair with. I have been having two affairs. One is with Steve Saint-John. He owns a small, chic restaurant on rue Richer, just opposite rue Ambroise-Thomas, and another small, chic one on the rue du Faubourg-Saint-Denis. They're too fancy for me, but I sometimes go to the one on rue Richer and sit at the bar for a coffee, hoping he will be there. He rarely is, and if he is, he is usually out in the kitchen, planning the menu, talking with the chef, or doing housekeeping stuff like replacing the outdoor window ledge or painting the eaves above the entrance. Twice he was serving coffee at the bar. We said hello and I read my book. He didn't notice me.

Because he walks the same route as me – up and down the rue des Petites Écuries between the rues du Faubourg-Saint-Denis and Ambroise-Thomas – we are constantly passing one another. We say bonjour and I smile and he has a slightly confused look, like he can tell I'm having an affair with him. I would like to say our affair is torrid, him bending me over the chef's counter in his Richer place, or in the chequered bathroom of his Faubourg-Saint-Denis joint, but the feeling I tap into is the love I had for Steve Saint-John in primary school.

Steve Saint-John had deep blue eyes and wavy brown hair. In preschool the teacher asked us to name sounds starting with M. He said marching. I couldn't believe it: he heard the same sounds in his head as I did. I had always heard a *thoomp, thoomp, thoomp* when I lay down, and I later realised it was likely my heartbeat, but the fact that Steve Saint-John had marching in his head too, I knew he was for me. We played tennis at the same club, sometimes in the same team, love hearts came out of my chest and went swirling around him. In Year 6 I sent another child to ask if he would be my boyfriend. The messenger came back and said that he said no. In Year 7 another messenger came to me and asked if I would be Steve Saint-John's girlfriend. I sent them back to say yes.

At the school dance we held hands. I spent a week making a paper cut-out with glue and glitter that said *JT 4 SSJ*. He never returned the message, and when I asked him on the way to tennis if he got it, he said, Oh yeah, that dumb thing. I died on his mum's back seat. Not long after, the messenger came again and told me I was dumped. That was the end of Steve Saint-John.

But I held the flame for years. Much later, I realised the gift of the unconsummated nature of our love. If he had kissed me or even been kind to me, the passion in my heart would have been diluted somehow. My perfect love was untouched, untainted by reply, by his needs, by mine. That is how I feel when I pass French Steve Saint-John each day. I don't want him, not really. I've seen him at the Récollets park on Saturdays, bored, with his kids. I compartmentalise that, keep our story to the street.

I bet M has affairs too. I wouldn't want to know him if he didn't. I like to think I'd be fine if he had real ones, but I'm not sure. I tell him I would be. He says the same. I wonder where he would find his affairs. Near the snack machine at the Studio Bleu? Chez Jeannette after rehearsals? Gigs? In the park when the Chunk is napping? At the Monoprix buying nappies with the ladies? In the Capri Bazar buying capricci for me, the deli lady slicing his ham, thinly? Women here have always liked him.

My affair capacity is restricted to the street between the office and home, and the agencies. Nobody notices me sexually at the Cool Agency. Everyone is too young or jaded. I'm one of the boys there, in my black jeans and Converse. The Big Agency is different, more dressed-up and repressed. Corporate, tall glass windows and carpeted floors with desks in lines, people wearing glasses and smart outfits, holding unlit cigarettes that they take out to the balcony to blow over the facing Arc de Triomphe. When my eyes dart around the warren of desks and cubicles, they always land on a guy over near the window. Tall, neat, relaxed-chic, French. Cool in that advertising way. Effortless blazer, sneakers. But you can see he's of the upper ranks – people bring him things. He has the stillness of an upper-status Suit. Older, mid-forties, perhaps early fifties.

I go home with him, to his apartment with its sleek kitchen. Dinner out tonight with friends, I can afford the great shoes and sexy dress, we'll probably have a kid or two, he'll ride them to school on his handlebars, down past Prune, stop in for a coffee, propping the kids on the bar as Omar feeds them grenadine. It'll be easy, we'll spend summers at his family house on Belle-Île, not ostentatious, simple but taken care of. His family is French, so there are loads of babysitters for the kids. He has no interest in art, no desire to break himself apart to make something, just wants to take me to the country house on the weekends and watch me read. He admires my artistic tendencies, wishing he also had them, but being content to work in a 'creative' industry, using his skills to make big bucks. Perhaps he lives in the suburbs – Fontenay – but I like to think he has a loft in the 11th with a good coffee machine. It is laid-back but every detail is thought out and when something goes wrong he has the money to just get it fixed. His dishwasher doesn't leak. His sheets are excellent – soft, in darker colours that I would never choose. He eats fine food and has a cellar with good wine. His financial life is secure, I don't have to work in this office writing print ads, I have a small studio down a laneway, an old-fashioned atelier full of light and privacy, where I'm writing my seventh book.

I despise Suit man but, as I brainstorm new ways to say the same thing about cat food over and over again, I go silently in the lift with him down to his big shiny car.

An old man at the next table smiles at me. Can he sense my waywardness? Can't relax. Home is pulling me back. Jittery, I abandon the last of my wine and, as I step out onto the street, realise I'm mimicking Angela in the movie. She didn't finish her drink either. If I retrace her steps, will I become her? Would I want to? No. Yes. I cross the rue des Petites Écuries as she did, walk into Terra Corsa, the same shop where she looked at the newspapers and magazines Émile was selling in the papeterie. I look at the charcuterie in the cabinet and the wines set out along the walls, pick a saucisson and a bottle of Corsican white – the cheapest, they're expensive – and walk back out onto the street.

In the film, the street is filled with vendor carts, *les quatre saisons,* Francine told me they were called. Tonight it is bustling like a marketplace, as if the ghosts of the old produce sellers are still here, in the chained-up bikes, the people walking the thoroughfare, ignoring motorbikes and vans. It's almost dark and the lights are on. I keep walking Angela's path towards the boulevard, past the Middle Eastern delis and cafés down near the arch. She turned left down here, towards the club where she stripped. I turn back up the street, but instead of turning down Petites Écuries I continue up towards the Gare de l'Est, still abuzz with male energy from the agency that I need to turn female.

The rue du Faubourg-Saint-Denis hasn't changed much in the years I've known it, nor since the days of Angela and Émile. Not in its soul, anyway. This street is not imaginary Paris, it's a real place, for workers, drinkers, regulars. Francine told me that most of the people here each day don't actually live on the street – it's just where they spend their days, either working or socialising. Until the 1980s when the law of copropriété was passed, you couldn't actually buy a flat in Paris, only a whole building, so everyone was a renter, and they were mostly the people who worked at Les Halles, before it shut down in the mid '70s. Further back, as well as being a royal path into Paris, the rue du Faubourg-Saint-Denis was also once the route for workers from the suburbs to and from Les Halles. People with roots elsewhere. Regulars, not residents.

Though people do now own apartments, the feeling of this neighbourhood is still one of renters, loiterers and workers, socialisers, passers-through. No wonder I've always gravitated here. It's a limbo of sorts. People coming, going, from everywhere, music and life, travelling above ground as the métro rolls beneath, stopping to drink, eat, or continue north or south, to Marseille if you kept walking downwards, or Flanders if you went up. The other places I've lived were in areas that felt more still, settled, residential, but this is a quartier of action and activity, of transience. It makes it feel dreamlike, nothing quite fixed.

Je flâne. To Benjamin and Baudelaire the flâneur was male. The flâneuse didn't exist. Women, mothers, were best kept in the suburbs, in the home, away from city life. If they were to come to the city they might begin to dream, and for women to dream would be the death of the family.

Angela sings to the camera that she is no good girl, she is cruel. The subtitles say that she's no angel, she can be a real devil, but that doesn't quite capture what she's saying. I bet the subtitles were done by a man. To be cruel and to be a real devil are two different things. Cruelty is evil, deliberate. A real devil is cute, naughty. To be no angel is playful too, but to not be good – *sage* – is to be deliberately wanton.

Everything seems out to trap us, put us in a box. That is my feeling. I am overthinking things. I don't have time to think for myself and, when I do, I think of Angela or Thérèse or Betty Blue and take things around me to pieces. My eye is as sharp as a bird of prey's. I see death. Danger. I see sex. Old people, strange people, office people, teenagers, that couple there, now, choosing fruit, the possibility of it, that it's right there, that that guy and those two women are doing it, they just did it, are about to do it, how do they do it, what are their pleasures, are they unrestrained, do they have fetishes, do they use objects, talk dirty, watch stuff, do they visit clubs. The wine guy, the check-out girl, who do they do it with, how, what are their perversions, their fantasies, are they thinking about doing it right now, are they thinking about doing it with me. I don't want to *do* the sex, I just find it fascinating that other people do it, that we all do it, well not M and I so much right now, but we do, it's normal, it leads to the continuance of the species, but we feel like we're special, keep it secret, walking now, all clean and proper when in private we're real devils.

I don't want sex and it's all I see. Occasionally I do it, because I don't know where I am and I want to keep things alive until I can figure out what I do want, and where I want to go with my life. I can't make decisions now. To not have sex is a decision, and requires serious discussion about problems, and there's no problem, or if there is I can't identify what it specifically is right now. It's a lifeline, a confirmation, a high five to one another – hello, still here. I'm always glad to have done it and afterwards think, Why don't I instigate this more often? But it's the level of energy and spirit required to be summonsed that leads me mostly to pretend I'm asleep when M gets home from rehearsals.

I remember the exact moment my libido left me. It was in Australia. We had returned a few weeks earlier from Paris with the baby Chunk, and we needed a place to live for the months it would take to get our visas processed. We rented someone's empty beach house full of bunks in the village near my dad, and experimented with putting the Chunk to sleep in another room, which felt a world away from the bedroom where we slept, after our tiny quarters in Paris. One night, knowing she would wake soon, I went to lie down in the bedroom next to hers, unable to sleep. The thought of sex came to me and I considered going in to M, but he badly needed to sleep. Then I realised I didn't want to masturbate. For the first time in my life. I lay there and cried. It wasn't just the exhaustion, the feeding. It felt like that part of me, that fire just for myself, was gone.

I knew it wasn't the end of my sex life completely. But since teenagehood, that private spark, the excitement of my own flesh, had always been there. Now it seemed it had fulfilled its biological purpose and was gone.

The natural order of things.

I keep walking. A true flânerie is done solo, but M and I used to wander the streets of Paris together on Sundays, lovers' days, and the feeling of the solo flânerie, rather than being halved, was doubled. We were alone, but together, and they were my favourite days, walking from our place in Belleville all the way down through the Marais and across the river, letting our legs guide us where they would. I never thought you could enjoy that sensation of being lost in thought in the city with someone else, but together, somehow, we could. Now if we walk together, which is rare, it's specifically to get somewhere: a holdery, a quick lunch on the boulevard, a meeting with the bank manager, the accountant.

Every moment on the clock. Get to work. Get home. Which is why M tells me to do this – stop somewhere and take a moment for myself – but I'm always so desperate to see her I press send, throw on my coat and run down the rue des Petites Écuries into her little arms. Once there, and satisfied they're alive and well, the exhaustion, the rage hits. Dinner. Bath. Bed. Work. Work. Work. Bed. Office. Repeat.

Am I being a martyr? Registering my goodness on the ledger in the sky? To have moments-pour-soi would make my life seem balanced and it's not and I don't want him to think that it is, and I know his is not either and it's all on the ledger, every moment accounted for, and I hate that I hate it.

I do not deserve this flânerie.

I slow my pace. Benjamin wrote that, in the 1840s, it was fashionable for flâneurs to walk with turtles in order to slow their wandering. It feels wrong to slow myself down, but I try. Just to a normal walking pace. Noticing. Observing. Becoming myself again, slightly.

In the Capri Bazar, the young Italian woman with toned arms packs the gorgonzola I had a craving for, glowing with the affair she could be having with M. Imagining it brings us back to life somehow, like we're residents of the world, not just dutiful soldiers. The moon is close to full, a man and a woman hug passionately on the pavement, pleasure and vice, a fight outside El Papi Chulo, a band warming up at New Morning. A flock of pigeons attacks a kebab, a guy starts a motorbike and drives straight in front of a car, the driver honks and calls profanities, the motorcyclist is gone. Musicians outside the Studio Bleu, hauling instruments into a cab, my dreadlocked friend in his beanie outside La Ferme, smoking weed.

In the doorway, the Chunk runs at my legs. M is in a bad mood, she's refusing to go to bed. I remember he hates gorgonzola.

What do you want for dinner?
What do you want?
What do you want
What do you want
What do you want
What do you want
Do you

THE SEA IN THE METRO

>What
>Want
>I want Szechuan
>I want you

He dreams we have another baby. He says the feeling was great. When I ask if he wants one, he shivers and says no. I feel the same, but I do wonder if his shiver is more about me and the way I've been than anything else. I don't ask him.

My shiver is physical. I can still feel that place inside myself, what happened after the menace. I couldn't put something else there. The thought of it makes my toes curl. I can't even think about it. Can't even imagine it, for fun.

The wind is so loud in our room I can't sleep. I go and sleep in the single bed in the Chunk's room. It feels like desertion.

I dream of being hated. People fight in a bar. A man has a mutilated hand. Everyone is blaming me for the mutilated hand. I ride to the house of a couple I know, who I don't know, in Belleville, and ask them if they like me and they say, Frankly, no. I ask why, and they say, We just don't trust you anymore.

Mother

It's Sunday at the rue Alibert market and we're tasting strawberries when we notice she's not between us. I look around and see her – across the road. She is playing on the metal barrier fence, flinging around her Elsa tulle. We are stunned for what feels like minutes, then I'm over there without knowing how I got there and then she's with us back at the fruit stand. The narrow street is filled with trucks lined up for the market, confusing the line of sight.

One car is all it would have taken.

It's fine, says M, as the Chunk squats down to eat a slice of peach. She's fine.

Mustn't ever run away like that, OK? I say, buckling her in the pram. Mustn't ever cross the road.

OK Maman. She smiles.

I'm in shock. We walk across the canal. Neither of us speaks. My god. I don't want to make a big deal out of it, she's fine, and I don't want to admit it's my fault, I know it's my fault, in one second she could have been gone. After my accident I saw freak things happen in my mind all the time, all the random ways to die, right here, present everywhere in this city. M and I once saw two little boys almost crushed by a truck here on the canal. They were fine, but I couldn't stop replaying it in my head.

We wait in a long queue outside our favourite Sunday breakfast place. The Chunk sings Elsa. I think we need to eat, says M, like, now. We turn and go to the place above the markets on Château d'Eau that is not good but always has tables. We pick at runny eggs and drink our coffee, the Chunk eating spaghetti for breakfast in her love-heart sunglasses. I take a photo of her on the staircase, Elsa dress hanging over her pink sneakers. Oh, Elsa. I lift her down the stairs so she doesn't trip.

Back home I feel sick. I'm the mother. I should have felt her leave my side. M didn't notice either, but still, I feel the blame. He was paying for the fruit. Besides, she's my flesh, no matter what, a father will never be as responsible. I can't feel M absolving me enough, like he knows it was my fault, like he actually blames me. He says it was both of us, but I can see it in his eyes. *He was paying for the fruit.* I can't talk to him, retreat into a cave of anger and self-blame. He goes into the bedroom to read while she has her nap.

I blame him for everything, I realise. For my lapse in attention, which, the monster says is because I'm so exhausted and stressed from work, which is because it's all on my shoulders. For not taking the blame, though it clearly wasn't even his to take. For not wrapping me in constant cotton wool. For me being a mother at all. For me being bad at it.

I lie on the couch, the image replaying over and over in my mind. She's here, she's over there, she's next to me, she's over there. She's here, she's there, the truck …

I know this, the circular horror thing, like grieving. I just have to let the images play themselves out, until they lose their power.

The next morning I notice a pigeon nesting in our window box. Not an average street pigeon, a beautiful dove-grey one with a peacock-blue neck. She sits in the soil, doing an odd wiggly dance to root herself into the dirt. I wonder if she is dying, then realise she is laying. She looks distressed but controlled. It reminds me of that earthy feeling giving birth in the bath, the desire to root downwards.

The Chunk watches with me, then bangs on the glass and the pigeon flutters off to a windowsill on the other side of the street. A perfect white egg remains.

We both squeal. She wants to sit and watch a chick hatch, but we have to get to work and Club and by the time we get home that night it's dark and we think we should leave her alone, like my vampire midwife left me. The next morning we get up and race to the window. The mother pigeon is there again, in the window box, still and proud and grand. Her feathers are smooth. She could be porcelain.

What now? we wonder. She ruffles her feathers when the Chunk moves, but stays where she is.

After breakfast we return to see the pigeon making the strange movement again, heaving and puffing, her breast rippling and coiling. I back the Chunk away from the glass. Peace, peace.

We like that she has chosen our window, the one with my special curtain. She obviously feels safe. I feel proud, like a midwife. Like a wise woman. Like a very good mother.

In the evening when we return, the mother is gone and there are now two eggs in the ditch. Two babies! We wonder how many more there might be. A dozen? We wonder what they might look like. And how long their gestation period is. Will we see them breaking out of the eggs like in cartoons? What do baby pigeons look like? How long does it take for them to fly?

The next morning our lady is there again, still and silent. She trusts us. I think about giving her a little bowl of water, but I don't. My wise woman wouldn't have. The pigeon knows what she's doing.

We sit. We watch. We run to the window each morning. No more eggs, just the two. A still, careful mother who knows her limits.

M and I wonder over dinner what the sex was like, if she has other children from a former relationship, how many babies does the typical pigeon have in a lifetime?

Mama-pigeon-watching becomes part of our day. We watch and watch and watch. We set the red chair facing out, and the Chunk sits on my knee. The chair is off to the side, so as not to make the pigeon feel on stage.

Then one morning they are gone. The mother as well as the eggs. The Chunk is confused. I feel worried. Have they been killed, eaten? Did they fall? M peers over. No squashed birds. Are baby pigeons able to fly as soon as they hatch? M looks doubtful. But how could they just vanish? It's obvious, he says. Isn't it? I can't bear to think about the peregrine falcon from that nature documentary, perched on top of the Eiffel Tower, eyeing prey with its binocular vision over the whole of Paris.

I had envisaged watching the eggs crack, the heads poking out, the slimy babies emerging, the mother cleaning them off, sharing a glass of champagne with her and musing over our shared experiences, the mysterious joy of these weird new creatures entering our lives. Did her placenta come?

I feel sadder than I should about the pigeons.

M is out late, and, unable to sleep for thinking of the pigeons, I finally manage to watch Chantal Akerman's entire three-hour *Jeanne Dielman, 23 rue du Commerce, 1080 Bruxelles,* without interruption. I haven't managed to get through more than a few disparate grabs, and I realise it must be watched like this, in order to feel the sense of time. A domestic woman's life over three days. Each day condensed into one hour. A woman we all know. Not my mother so much, but my grandmothers, their mothers. Aprons and house shoes. Neat, proper, organised. But Jeanne has one difference: she makes breakfast, wakes her son, eats with him, clears it away, eats lunch, welcomes a man for sex, sees him out, puts the cash in a jar, goes shopping, prepares dinner ...

Tomorrow will be ten years since Mum died. I have been trying not to think about it. Jeanne isn't like Mum but the pride in her woman's work, her solidity, reliability reminds me of her. And she did lay the table, and things in our house were ordered. Clothes cleaned, kitchen clean, floors clean. No cleaners or nannies or au pairs, she did it all herself. How did she do it?

It's amazing how full Jeanne's day is, just looking after a household of two people, one who only comes home in the evening to eat and sleep.

One afternoon, Jeanne's order is thrown out. Something has happened in the bedroom with her client. Now the potatoes aren't cooked, now she has a spare moment to sit in the living room. Just sit. She is uncomfortable with this freedom. She is not free.

I'm free. But I still rush home to mother my child, to bathe her and do the things her father can't do like I can. I feel guilt over not cooking, though I hate it with a passion, I'd rather never eat again than have to cook. There's a violence to my feeling about it, all the Jeanne Dielmans lined up behind me, ancestress after ancestress after ancestress. A need to rebel. Like if I enjoyed any of these parts of myself the whole point of my being, and their struggle, would be lost.

We go with Claire to Notre-Dame. She leads us to the statue of Jeanne d'Arc, and each of the four of us lights a candle at 12.10 pm – 10.10 pm in Australia – and place it in front of her. That's what Claire does, every year, for her own mum. Claire always knows the things to do.

I like the idea that the light from my mum's candle might join Claire's. Notre-Dame is dim, the stained-glass windows sombre with winter light. The Chunk, done up tight in a red parka, doesn't want to let her candle go, so M holds her up to place the candle with the others herself, trying not to set her on fire. We stand awkwardly for a moment, then get caught in a wave of tourists and make our way out into the freezing mist.

At Les Philosophes we eat an entire formule: entrée, main and tarte tatin. No one cries. I feel nothing. I never do on the days I'm supposed to feel something. There is a homely feeling in Les Philosophes, with our four-top table, our family, the funny waiters and the sky outside so grey. M sweetly asks questions about Mum, what she was like, the things she did. The Chunk asks if she lives in Our Stralia and if she has a garden. She doesn't live on the planet anymore, I tell her, but she does have a garden, we'll visit it when we go to Our Stralia at Christmas. The Chunk is pleased.

In the bathroom I send a message to my family. Last night in a moment of desperation for connection I posted a picture of Mum on social media, announcing the tenth anniversary of her death at 10.10 pm on the tenth, and suggesting we all light a candle at the same time. Though she was a humble and unassuming person, I think she lined up the tens like that so she wouldn't be forgotten. *It* wouldn't be forgotten. She would have known the importance of marking such things, for our sake, but we don't do it much, we forget, and we certainly don't talk about it amongst our family. I do remember on the first anniversary of her death we all went to her plot, and it was my idea afterwards to sit around and tell stories about her. It was sweet, but awkward. There is nothing to be said, or done. We are alone, each of us have our own experience of it inside ourselves, which is almost impossible to describe.

I lie in bed that night and imagine what it would be like if all the tens lined up and brought her back for ten minutes, what I would say, or do. I think I'd just sit on a couch and be in her arms. She would be wearing a soft jumper. I would kiss her face, sniff her, but I'd want her to talk so I could hear her voice. I would just let her give me advice about being a mother. Ten minutes would be plenty.

52. Write the phone call you wish you could have.
Hi, Mum!
Hi, Jayney.
What are you doing?
Oh you know, just working with the light.
We drank champagne for you today.
Ooh, lovely!
Real stuff, not bubbly wine.
It's all the same to me.
Am I doing OK, Mum? Do you think?
Yes, but you need to go easy on that lovely man of yours.
You think?
Yep. You need to listen more. Stop talking so much.
Am I doing the mothering right?
You could use a rest. But I love that you live in Paris! What an adventure.
It's just occurred to me that I do that for you.
Why? That's strange.
I think because it feels like drinking life dry, like that thing by George Bernard Shaw that they read at your funeral and we put on the program: *I want to be thoroughly used up when I die, for the harder I work, the more I live.*
Yeah but don't use yourself up too much, you look wrecked.
Can you come and babysit next week?
Of course! Anything to get my hands on her.
Thanks, Mum.
Slow it down a bit, OK? Smell the roses. You're doing good.
OK Mum.

Sea

My favourite thing to do in the rue du Faubourg-Saint-Denis, if I have a moment alone, is to walk to the Monoprix and go upstairs, past the old-cheese smell of the downstairs supermarket, to the clothing and homewares section. I love this Monoprix because nobody really comes up here and it's downtrodden and plain and comforting and it reminds me of my first job at Target at the age of fourteen. I cried when I first got that job, in the changing room, trying on the uniform – a neat navy skirt and white button-up shirt. Mum was kind. She said, Don't worry, you don't have to do it yet. Perhaps she wasn't ready for me to be an adult either.

I will start with the kidswear and see if I can find some bargains for the Chunk. Usually there is a sale of some kind: *pastille verte -30%, pastille rouge -40%, pastille jaune -50%*. Then I'll go to the women's section and look at pyjamas, then stockings and undergarments. I imagine all the women throughout France in these undergarments, all their shapes, sizes, dreams, commonalities. I like the feeling of joining them, the sleeping women, morning women, women accepting the simple pleasure of plain cotton. Then I'll go to homewares and see if there are any bargains there, or interesting new prints on sheets I'll never buy. There's a large changing room in the back corner, full of discarded clothes and fluff and junk, where I can try things on without disturbance, throwing them on the floor after, or over a rack if there happens to be a storeperson there, which there almost never is. The clothes are unsexy, boxy, plain, but in the mirror I can try to defy them, or be them: the office clerk, the good French mum, the child-woman in a floral nightie, the not-Godard's-Angela, Angela's mum. I spend a lot of time in that changing room. It's the one public place in Paris where there are no people. Downstairs I'll look at rosewater and fleur d'oranger water and bathroom products, and, if I have to, I'll buy groceries, then leave.

Today I'm not alone. M is out rehearsing in Pantin and there was an accident at Club, so I had to bring spare pants and decided to give up on work and just take her. There is a sale on ladies' lingerie, and the Chunk gives me ten minutes in the cabine d'essayage before getting bored – the salesgirl game I made up has a short use-by date.

The Chunk doesn't have her scooter and we still don't have a pram, so the walk down the street is long, me carrying her, putting her down, carrying her, putting her down. We buy yoghurt from the Turkish épicerie and, as we are walking back up past number fifty-seven, notice the door to the theatre school is open. A rare sight. People are entering the building, and we find ourselves going in too, the Chunk dragging her stuffed flamingo along the cobblestones to the familiar doorway. The women at the reception desk are new, and I introduce myself and ask what is happening. They tell me it is a LEM presentation – Laboratoire d'Étude du Mouvement – which as an ex-student I am welcome to watch, with my little Chunk.

As we wait for the doors to open, I show her the rocking horse under the stairwell, the Marcel Carné posters, the photos of the old rue du Faubourg-Saint-Denis with horse-drawn carriages and men in suits and produce carts. The boxing ring with men's faces lit up, watching. Perhaps women were not allowed. The Chunk is more interested in wiping the wall with her flamingo.

I've never quite understood the LEM – something about freezing poetry in air. At the theatre school we used the movement of our bodies to express ideas, but the LEM students, in a practice entirely separate from ours, use structures they build from paper, cardboard, sticks, wire.

I sit the Chunk and myself down on the floor closest to the exit, in case I need to whisk her out. So far she's the perfect angel, cross-legged, back straight, listening, like she must have been shown to do at Club. It scares me a little how well behaved she is. The students come out one by one and move with their pieces, showing how they work and explaining them to us. It's quite boring and I find it hard not to flash back to all the shows we made here, to sitting in this exact spot and watching my classmates try and try and occasionally hit on something magnificent. So many flops, but also those moments, especially towards the end of the second year, when we started to find some sparks of *juste*. This one piece comes back to me, that I wrote and directed with Faye and Ravi. A couple, on a first date. I'm the waitress, and hide under the table, springing up to ask them, Apéritif pour commencer? The couple are excited, they like each other, order wine, the waitress pops up with an array of condoms: Apéritif pour commencer? The woman on the date, to the audience, expresses her desire: *I am a shoebox, I would fuck a mildewy carcass right now, my hole is aching…* The man talks to her of backgammon.

It was a weird piece, smashed together, absurd, physical. The waitress kept offering new things – an STD test, a baby – the couple fucked beneath the table, now babies were spurting from her, the waitress offered her own body, now she was a gossipy neighbour, the couple had a mortgage, a car, now they were divorcing… Apéritif pour commencer? asked the waitress. The couple remembered they had somewhere else to be, but it had been nice, real nice.

I didn't even know then what it was to be married and have a child. I'm not sure why I chose to write so negatively about it. Perhaps it was just the easier ending. I suppose I was thinking about my relationship with Adrien. I remember being plagued by my biology, feeling frustrated at my lack of uniqueness, I was just craving to fuck and spawn and die, like everyone else. It seems funny now I'm sitting here with the Chunk, as she sucks away on her flamingo's foot. I kiss her head, her focus tight on the group flying white paper structures around the space like birds.

A student comes out to show a plywood piece that bears the movement of the sea. I think that's what it is. It's not wave-shaped or anything obvious, but the angular construction, moving with his body, shows the violence of the sea, the unpredictability. The Chunk starts to wriggle and I hold her on my lap, watching the student not show the sea while all I see is the sea, the sea in Dad's village, waves that ripple then dump, the unpredictable tides, the ocean currents meeting the bay.

In class, a teacher said, *Un acteur doit être capable de voir la mer dans le métro*. An actor must be able to see the sea in the métro. I think it was something Lecoq said, or relayed from another teacher, or it was relayed through a relay, during the workshop on neutral mask. Not female, not male, no past, no future … The actor must embody the impossible, even facing a wall, they must contain vast landscapes, sea, sky, desert, river, forest. The phrase has stuck in my head all these years. I used to sit in the métro and try to see the sea. What did it mean? Back then I was all about representation. Now I think that it had nothing to do with acting or representing or showing. It had to do with being. You can't be an actor without imagination, and an actor must contain universes. The actor must *know* the sea to see it in the métro, and we were told to go and see and experience everything we could, to keep it inside of us.

I know the sea. I know its moods, its smell, its feeling. The calm beneath the water, the quiet. As a kid I would be semi-drowned in it, dumped by the summer waves. Agnès Varda says if you opened people up you'd find landscapes, and if you opened her up you'd find beaches. I think if you opened me up you'd find sea, the currents down near Dad's place, where the big ocean meets the bay, all the wreckage beneath of old ships that couldn't negotiate the reef, one of the most dangerous shipping routes in the world. Someone local has to drive the ships through, it's so specific – pilots they're called. Mum's cemetery is full of them, headstones dating back centuries, pilots who drowned performing the treacherous ladder-climb from boat to ship, the one who left *a wife and four children to deplore his loss.* A lighthouse, high on the rocks, foghorns in the night. Rough winds and surf for the crazy ones. A local guy who, after being dragged beneath the reef, always surfs with a dagger in his wetsuit in case he needs to cut himself free. The bay beaches a mix of calm and rocky and clear and murky. Seaweed sometimes, others pristine. You have to know where to dive and when you find your spot it's the greatest secret you ever kept.

On the métro with the Chunk the next day, I try again to see the sea. She sits on my lap, playing with my coat button. There is a game I normally play to keep her occupied. Can you see … a doggy? Can you see … a sac à main? Today I ask her, Can you see … la mer?
    She points at me.
    I laugh.
    Not la *mère*. La mer! The sea!
    She is confused and goes back to fiddling with a bit of loose string.
    I'm a mère. A mother in the métro.
    Perhaps that's what they meant. An actor should be able to see oneself as a mother in the métro. Or see one's own mother in the métro. I try to imagine my mother, here, in the métro. There she is, in the corner, that woman with her back to me, in the next carriage, there, getting off, brushing down her skirt. She would have loved to be in the métro, my mère, but never saw it.

I can't see the sea, or my mother, or myself as a mother, right now. All I see is flesh and clothing and sneakers and a skateboard and a backpack and two shabby suitcases, one blue, one red. A soft, sweet head, silken curls tied up in pigtails, my face in them, smell of love.

We're gonna see the sea, I say, breathing her in.

Our Stralia! She squeals.

Our Stralia.

Dad is there, at the airport gate, waving his arms, Bon-jewer! He takes the Chunk from my arms and her body relaxes into him, so safe, so calm. M and I follow him to the car, her sleepy head looking back at us from his big, sure shoulder. That feeling of her being taken from me, and still so safe. More safe. At his place, he tells us to go and sleep, and settles her on his chest on the couch in front of the TV. At 2 am, we awake with a start. He is in the same position, on the couch, colours lighting his face. She is sound asleep.

We take the train to my sister's, and her son, who is three months younger than the Chunk, comes running down the platform as we step off. They talk constantly on the computer – cuzzy onda poota – but this is the first time she's seen him in the flesh since they were babies. They run to each other and embrace like lovers in an old movie.

Christmas is hot and the kids run around the garden beneath the sprinkler as we drink and eat the traditional fare. It's all so familiar, so joyful, so like our own childhoods: house, backyard, tree, sprinkler, children running free. As we sit, boozed-up, in the shade in the afternoon heat, a feeling comes over me. A dark, insecure feeling. My sister refills my glass with rosé and bends over instinctively to hug me tight. I feel a surge of warmth and remember the fierce charge in my body when she was born: *I must take care of her forever.* My brothers here, now, grown men, seven and nine years my junior. They were my babies too. My sister and I tortured them, dressed them in girls' clothes, yes – but we also changed their nappies, bathed them, adored them. When Mum died, Dad became my baby too, I suppose. Everyone saying, Be sure to look after your dad, and the boys. Like my sister and I had an ability to cope that they didn't. We had each other, it was true, and we were women. But that pressure. To mother the family.

I tried. The boys were eighteen and twenty-one. I encouraged them to talk, to cry, I tried to think of things Mum would say. After Gran died she bought an abundance of supermarket cakes and made us all sit with her and Dad around the kitchen table and eat and drink whiskey, though we were underage. We had all seen Gran's stiff, dead body and wanted to hide beneath the covers in our rooms but Mum made us stay. It was warm, so warm, we told stories, she made the death OK. I tried to do this when she was gone. I booked us a grief counsellor, made us all go out to dinner first. But instead of opening up at the counselling session, they all sat in silence as I sobbed uncontrollably. It wasn't supposed to be like that.

When the surprise scholarship to go to the Lecoq School in Paris came I felt happy for them that I was going. It would be a relief, not to have this stand-in mum, this imposter. I couldn't be her, I knew that, but I was trying to evoke her, the comfort she brought. This was impossible, of course. And once I left, it all felt right. I could love them from afar, and they could love me too, and the gap of Mum could live in its proper distance, from earth to the beyond.

It is right, still right, this beautiful distance. We are all living our lives, Dad has his girlfriend, my sister is married and pregnant now with her second, my brothers in relationships and with proper jobs. But it is strange, as a mother, to be sitting in this yard, so simple and so joyful, having created a life for my own child so different from my own childhood. Look at her, look at M and me, relaxed and talking our language with those who know and love us, free to enjoy ourselves as she enjoys herself, not having to entertain her or take her to a gallery or shoo her in behind a door so we can enjoy our freedom.

The temperature rises and we stay indoors with the air-conditioner on and watch cricket and do crosswords as the Chunk plays with the crates of toys Dad and his girlfriend have gathered. Claire calls with news: her book of poetry is going to be published in the summer. She is ecstatic and so am I for her, as well as slightly sick in the stomach. She is being published. What must that feel like, I wonder. To have a book being made, with a cover, words printed, pages. She will launch it at the English Bookshop, upstairs, where I once did the reading of my early chapters, and where she and I and M and the Chunk first met, at M's gig. It's all perfect.

I suddenly can't stand being inside and grab the Chunk, drive her to the beach. It's still a furnace outside but the sun is setting. I strip her naked and carry her down the steps into the water, which is like a pool, the heat seeming to have flattened out all waves. There is a community of swimmers, each floating listlessly in the lake-like salt water, the sun now low, shade cast over the high tide by the gnarled moonah trees. The Chunk is delighted, and shocked, at our free mermaiding, I didn't even bring her little floaties. I hold her with just my fingers, and we glide and roll. She hasn't learned to swim yet and won't put her head under, but I place my hand beneath her back and let her feel what it is to float. Free. Freee.

Mum watches from the cemetery, a stony patch the size of a human grave, though there's just a few ashes in there. We could have just taken a small ashes spot, but for some reason Dad got the life-sized one. More room for us all later, perhaps, or to imagine she's in there, her lovely body laid out, hands to the sky. He's put an oval photo of her there, baked into the plain black plaque. Around her are marble graves, it's terrible, her mound of dirt is shadowed now.

The next day, the Chunk and I go to the local supermarket to buy plants for the grave. She wants a pansy flower that costs two bucks and has no chance of survival. That one won't work, I say, and she starts to cry so I say, OK fine, and then she wants the other colour, and the jonquils too, and I say, God, but buy them anyway. I also buy some lavender, because it's hardier, and a little bush rose.

Someone has planted a cactus on Mum's dusty rectangle, a very wise choice for the rocky, dry soil. Ha! I laugh. She's cactus! – then realise we haven't brought a shovel, so we dig with sticks and our fingers, and manage to shonkily plant the flowers. In her university robes, Mum looks pleased. We get water from the tap in my water bottle and sprinkle it on.

Later, Dad will send us a photo of the grave. Neither of my pragmatic plants have survived, but the Chunk's flowers have gone rampant.

Our flight isn't until late, so in the morning I seize a quick window while everyone's still sleeping to jump on Dad's bike and ride down to the water, though it's raining. The air has turned cool and I know the water will be cold. My skin pricks with goosebumps.

Get in, says Mum. Don't think about it!

I know there's no time to waste, I need to absorb as much nature as I can before returning to concrete. I ride along the beach path, find the spot, rest Dad's bike up against the rocks, put the towel on the sand and run in, no toe-dipping, no hand-swishing. I've never done that before. But here I am, in. And the great thing is that, though it's summer, because it's Australia, nobody is around to hear me scream. I don't have to worry about anyone watching me in my bikini composed of an old bra and fraying knickers. The beach is mine, except for a few buoys and a tanker passing in the distance. One pilot boat. Black lighthouse to my left, white lighthouse to the right. Piece of kelp around my thigh. My feet throb, I dive in again. It occurs to me that Mum must have done it this way because there wasn't any time to waste. Not just because she knew life was short, but because she had literally no time to herself.

And in the water my pelvis is new, no memory of the nine-pounder, no neck pain from copywriting, I'm free, Nijinsky in *The Rite of Spring*, hopping, dancing madly, making sounds, an idiot, it's fantastic, I'm a fish, I twirl my toes into the sand. I wonder if it's more fun to be Nijinsky alone in an impromptu bathing suit in these cold waters or to actually be Nijinsky.

When I'm in Paris my mind is in the sea. When I am here and I close my eyes and I dive deep down, I'm there, walking down Paradise Street, passing a caryatid, pushing a pram, feeling joy in intense, measured doses. Here there is a more general, softer feeling of wellbeing, not the same highs and lows. In Paris when I feel high I could burn myself on the sun. The lows are agony. The sense of generic calm here is always something I've thought to be feared, luring us into complacency, slumber, death.

Down deep is a sharp stream of coolness. I stay in it as long as I can before coming up. It feels good to hear nothing, see nothing, be completely gone for a moment.

Heart-rip at the airport, Dad and his firstborn grandchild. He never complains, is proud. He gives her a small toy dog this time, which she names Vanilla Ice Cream. She waves, in her little socks, and then the gates are shut and we are gone.

Having to move through customs and all the checks keeps me from crying, and once we're through and the Chunk is playing obsessively with Vanilla Ice Cream, M turns to smile at me.

I can't wait to get back, he says.

Me too! I say, swallowing the lump in my throat. Now he mentions it, I am excited. The life we've set up suddenly feels more solid from here than it did when we left. I have work, he has a band, the Chunk has Club, and her friends, and we have the streets and our apartment and our wonderful, wonderful office. And we've only just begun. The Chunk will start school in August, the work is mounting, soon things will feel even more secure and I will be able to think of other things. The impasse. Writing. The dream.

The Olive Grove

To get my mind into the copywriting place, first I must receive the brief. I won't take it by phone anymore, or meeting. Wherever possible I insist on it being emailed to me A) to avoid the staggering amount of time wasted sitting around a table listening to people enamoured by the sound of their own voices, huffs and sighs, and B) to avoid having to understand everything that is said between each huff and sigh, and force them to figure out exactly what the client is asking them to deliver instead of lumping it on me. Then, once the brief is written and sitting before me, I am free to attack it at my own leisure and in my own way.

My way consists of:

Reading the brief quickly.

Scrolling through a few social media sites.

Googling people I know.

Googling myself to see if in fact I've written a book yet.

Typing out a quick first draft in response to the brief.

Spending time on fonts and headings.

Browsing *VeryChic* and narrowing in on a few holidays I'll never go on.

Browsing *Say Who* and marvelling at the glossy people, their names, their complexions, their clothes, wondering how everyone looks like this, imagining what their homes look like, their sex lives, wondering if I'll see Adrien in one of the pages, wondering if I'll see myself.

Then, once I have the concept in my mind, I will write as hard and as fast as I can, to clear the job away and be done with it. The work I submit must be flawless, brilliant, in order to avoid any feedback or allers-retours. Once allers-retours start the job can go on and on. I hope for not a single piece of feedback, just a giant tick, then to invoicing. That way I can move cleanly on to the next job or, ultimately, arrive at the place where my head is clear to work on the book.

I can't work on anything creative until I've cleared the copywriting. If I have a job hanging over my head I can't concentrate. But when I get to the place where the copywriting is done, the pinnacle, I can write.

Which never happens.

Because of the rapid work at excellent level, the jobs keep coming. Our rent is being paid – just – and if I can make enough to create a small buffer we will be able to rent our very own place when Sido and Jacques get back, and maybe, just maybe, then we will have the stability for me to write, and M to keep going at his music and for the Chunk to be fed and clothed.

I say yes to every single job and deliver it yesterday. We're doing it. Getting there. M's band is getting more gigs now, mostly opening for cool bands from New Zealand and New York and Melbourne and Montréal, their name is getting around, and more support offers are coming. The dance show still pays, and there are more dates lined up, and there is talk of a corporate gig or two, which also pay, but it's all as sporadic as my work, though that is becoming more and more regular-sporadic and almost enough to rely on, but you never know what tomorrow will bring, so I still say yes to everything.

You can breathe now, says M, doing our accounts. You're doing brilliantly. A good variety of clients, you're a real Sterling Cooper.

Without Lucky Strike, I say.

You could use a Lucky Strike, he says. We all could.

What is our Lucky Strike? I ask.

Our Lucky Strike is one giant, rich, regular client, that makes us feel like the bottom isn't constantly about to fall out, even for just a small period of time. Take away this feeling of constantly rushing to show they can rely on me, I'm their bitch, will do anything, any time, all hours, even the impossible. I feel the monster stir, *you're a prostitute, he is whoring you out and he is fine with it*. Shut up, monster. I am free. I created this. Copywriting came from your desire to be free, to work in your own time, so you could act and make theatre, and though you don't do that anymore you've grown accustomed to working in your own time, in your own way. And it means you stand to make some serious coin because you can pile two or three jobs on top of each other, work faster and make more money. You can still pick up the Chunk occasionally, take her places, be available to run to her if she needs you, and you can work opposite M, listening to his new melodies, and running your copy ideas past him as he sits on his side of the room.

And what's the goal again? I ask M, my mind so busy I sometimes forget what the point of it all is.

To have balance, he says. Creative lives, parenting lives, love lives …

The impasse, I say. That's it. The ground-floor atelier in the impasse.

The impasse, he agrees.

It occurs to me that in the impasse I am not just writing all day long, nor is M making music all day. I had thought that was our dream, but when I look closer, there's more to it. Money work means we don't have to rely on our creative work to make the money, which means we can enjoy it more, push it further. There are many children in the house, our daughter and others. I know she is the only one of ours and that is how I like it. I notice there is a bit of dreaming time in there, *New Yorker* time, but that is only because we have achieved the balance, everyone's needs are met, nobody is stressed or overworked.

It doesn't seem that complicated, I think, pushing off in the thick snow to collect the Chunk from New Club, abandoning my bike at the end of the rue Ambroise-Thomas. We're moving towards that, I suppose, but sometimes it feels like we're actually moving in the opposite direction. My inbox this week has been a bit quieter, but I find instead of taking the time to breathe and recover, I fuss and stress and sit on alert waiting for the work to come, knowing the minute I switch off it will come anyway. I would like to use the time to work on the book but the shift in my mind, from the deeper place of concentration it requires, is so painful sometimes it makes me afraid to even go there, for fear of being interrupted. M doesn't understand this, he is a master compartmentaliser. If he has five minutes spare he'll put it to good use. I feel ashamed, like a time-waster, when I complain about how little time I have to write, but then have sat for ten minutes looking at *Say Who*.

In the slushy entranceway of Club I say goodbye to the ladies and zip the Chunk into her snowsuit and push her through the white, impossible streets to Julhès to buy cheese and gnocchi for her dinner. The half-stoned server asks if I'd like to try sauterelle – grasshopper – and I think it must be a type of cheese, like an escargot is a kind of pastry. Then he holds out a plastic jar of small, dried creatures, and I realise I have to eat it now, have to *dive in*, as Mum would say. The Chunk giggles when I hold one out to her, and refuses to eat it, running Vanilla Ice Cream along the ledge of the drinks cabinet. You eat snot and cardboard, I say in my head, not sure why you're so picky. I put the bug in my mouth and chew. It's revolting but I'm proud, and tell the guy, C'est délicieux, showing my girl how daring I am, how strong, how together.

M takes a night off and my work is done by 8 pm, so we huddle together in bed and watch *Before Midnight*, the new Julie Delpy and Ethan Hawke conversation thing. There's a party upstairs that makes our room vibrate, so there's no sleeping anyway. Julie says the only time she gets to think is when she takes a shit at work – she's starting to associate her thoughts with the smell of shit. And she rants at Ethan about the way he goes off each day into the olive grove to think and wonder, while she and the other women peel vegetables in the kitchen. It infuriates her, because she has such trouble dissociating herself from Ethan and their kids. She can never allow herself the time to stop and dream.

He answers by saying that, if she fucking stopped whining all the time, she'd have plenty of time to dream.

A very bad call, which causes her to walk out, slamming the door.

He can never understand the complexity of her connection to her kids, that infuriating instinctual urge – despite all her efforts to be an independent, strong feminist – to be with them at all times, or provide for them. How difficult it is for her to allow herself the time and space to separate from them, especially in her mind.

I don't go to the olive grove. M doesn't have time to either, but somehow he still manages to find moments of mind-space to read and listen and observe. He keeps his mind alive. There's a certain guilt he doesn't feel.

Do women in relationships with men have to fight harder to keep their inner worlds alive? The man does his share – huge in our case – then takes a walk in the olive grove. The woman *can* do that, but to do so she has to overcome a monstrous part of herself first, to resist going with her instinct and spending the day in Sandpit Park with the man and kids. All it takes is for her to say, I'm going off for a walk, and the man and kids will say, Great! It's always better for the family if she does. But it's anti-instinct. It's an effort to say it.

M gets it. He agrees that he doesn't have that same parent guilt.

How ripped apart we are by parenting. Before, we took it for granted we were on the same boat, rowing in the same direction. Now we're on distant shores, sending smoke signals to each other: Helloooo! Can I goooo for a walk in the olive groooove?

The olive grove is crucial to both of us. It's tempting, and easy, for me to just never go there, to get all pious, and then get angsty with M when he goes – and most especially when he comes back talking about it. Like yesterday when he read a good piece in *The New Yorker*. I don't want to know about the stories. It pains me to hear of the outside world when I can't find the ability to step outside of this nest to explore it myself. His neat, crossed ankles.

As the trees regain their leaves, and the blossoms come out in the concrete on Paradise Street, the Chunk turns three. We are gun-shy as the date rolls around, because her second birthday was a travesty: she bawled into her strawberry cake at Old Club, and cried all through the party we organised for her on the weekend, sitting there in the black dress with the white collar because she had suddenly grown out of everything else she owned. She sat next to Claire, eyes glazed, talking to nobody, eating fairy bread.

C'est normal, Maude at Old Club had said. It's a grieving. At two, they realise they're no longer babies.

Poor thing. Being not a baby anymore must be terrible. I feel like I can remember that feeling of stretching out of my baby body, growing tall, less pick-uppable, more autonomous.

That night she cried a particular deep, emotional cry. Not a baby or a protest cry. A mournful, adult cry. I may have misread it, but for the first time I felt that she was aware of the distance between herself and her relatives. Perhaps she was growing out of the narcissistic stage where she only saw herself. Perhaps she was tapping into the greater sadness. Perhaps she could sense my sadness at her not being in a room with her root kin. On Skype, Grandad had set up a little table with her favourite tea-party set from his house, and he had sent her the same set to Paris as her birthday gift, so they could have a tea party together! Though the idea was brilliant, she saw it for its absurdity, its horror, and she was right. She sobbed like someone had died.

Don't worry, I told her as I tucked her into bed. The ordeal's over.

This year we've lowered our expectations. Booked an animatrice – a party entertainer – suggested by the little music school opposite the Récollets, invited just five friends and their parents, and kept food minimal. But the excitement has kicked in. She gets it. She sits in her Elsa dress and wings, waiting for her friends to arrive. The animatrice was supposed to come early, to hide and get changed and, once all had arrived, come out from the bedroom as a surprise, but she turns up after everyone else, reeking of booze and cigarettes. As M ushers her into the bedroom past the gawking kids, she asks gruffly for a double espresso.

She was supposed to be a princess, but her arrival in the main room where the kids are playing is such a fizzer that none of the kids pay attention. She tries to lead them in games, but they are far more interested in each other and their own imaginary worlds. She gives up and sulks in the corner, looking like she might pass out.

After cake, she sets up her pantomime theatre, and we gather in the living room to watch. Traditional French guignol, violent and sad. The kids don't mind, the foreign parents raise eyebrows, the French parents watch on in glee. Jippy and Francine sigh at the shameful quality of her performance. I'm going to have nightmares, M whispers in my ear. The Chunk laps it up, face covered in cake and face paint. Before long the kids rightfully begin pushing on the tall cardboard theatre and the animatrice gives up, checks her watch, goes to the bedroom and gets back into her jeans. The kids put on the best show, making the puppets squeal and fight, then the animatrice shoos them out, packs up the show, collects her cash and leaves.

After a ceremonial bath with Marie-France's girls, the Chunk demands to sleep in her fairy wings and we let her. She goes to sleep happy. A big girl, almost.

A few days later, Claire and I are eating lunch at the dining table while the Chunk has her daytime nap. The door to the hallway is closed, as usual during sleep time, but midway through a sentence Claire notices the handle moving and cocks her head. I whip my head around. Who could be pulling that handle? The Chunk sleeps in a high barred cot. A ghost? The door swings open and out marches the Chunk, pleased with herself. How she even reached the handle is astonishing, but how did she get out of the cot? I pick her up and return to the cot. The bars are still up, nothing has broken. What the hell? She is still too small to climb over.

Bizarre, says Claire. We sing her Lassie and go back to lunch.

Five minutes later, the door handle again.

In the coming days we enter living hell. The devil has possessed her. The second we put her down, bam, she's up and out again. We consider putting a camera in to observe the athleticism. Ah! M realises. She's too big for the cot now. She wants the big-girl bed. We put her in the single bed. She lies down, we tuck her in, then she gets up.

I am growing wild. The only time in the day when M and I have a moment together is at 7 pm, after she's down. But now *BAM!* There she is at the table, smiling at us like a doll from a horror film. And the angrier we get the more she smiles. Giggles. I smack her butt one day, whack her! It feels mortifying. I lose my temper completely – want to smack that smile off her face. But she only laughs more. I want to check myself into an asylum. We take turns holding the handle of her bedroom door while she kicks and screams without tiring. I lie on the floor with my foot on the handle, telling M, You go out! Get some peace! We'll do shifts!

What is happening to us? What do we do? We can't even leave her with Bastien for five minutes to regain our sanity, it's too cruel. We are stuck with her, night and day, surveilling her like a mental patient.

I sit in her room and watch her go to sleep in the big-girl bed, not daring to move a muscle. I am Mum, watching myself. Did I do anything like this as a child? I don't remember hearing about it. But as I sit here watching her, waiting, I can feel my mother in me, watching little me in the bed. It's weird. When it looks like she is finally asleep, I get up to leave, slowly – and up she gets too, like she's tied to me with string. I honestly want to throw her out the window.

My dad's advice, so far proven to work, is to distract. When you can't snap them out of something – look! A birdie! Distraction doesn't work. Violence doesn't work. Calm parenting doesn't work. Even bribery doesn't work, she doesn't understand how it works yet.

M and I snap at each other, dispute strategies, try to calm each other down, empathise with each other. I feel unhinged. After the smacking episode I don't trust myself anymore not to do something insane. M and I are distant, sleeping badly, struggling to keep our sanity. One night, like war victims, we sit on the floor and hug. We would drink something and commiserate further if we weren't constantly interrupted by her smiling fucking head.

Always trust them and assume they are trying to do the right thing, even if things go wrong.

If punishment is needed, always be consistent and don't threaten if you don't intend to follow through or are likely to cave under pressure.

As parents, be one with discipline and don't discuss differences of opinion in front of the kids. Go into another room.

As I put her back in the bed and slump against the wall something occurs to me. Perhaps the problem is that we're going along with her. What if we did the opposite? What if, despite the crazed smile and dominant behaviour, she is actually feeling insecure? We have been meeting her with the usual disciplinary tactics that make sense. But what if we're getting the sense wrong?

The bars to the cot are down. When she first started scaling the sides, we put them down so it would be less dangerous when she got out. Then she kept getting out, so we moved her to the big bed. Could it be that it's all happening too fast for her? Could it be that she's not ready? That she thought she was, hence the first scaling, but then, when we responded and put the bars down and put her in the big-girl bed, she felt insecure?

What if we try the opposite of what we've been doing? I say to M.

He shrugs, up for anything.

She is back standing behind me, listening with her crazed smile. I pick her up and hold her for a moment, like a baby. Then, instead of taking her to the bed, we place her down in the cot, bars up. She curls over and starts to suck her thumb. In a matter of seconds she is asleep, and doesn't wake until seven the next morning.

This was some strange theatre. She needed the antithesis of what she was portraying, her body crying for help in the most aggressive and unhinged way she could muster. Pure absurdism, identifying logic and doing the opposite. It almost broke my brain, but somewhere in there my body knew what to do.

We sit in the salon, slumped on the floor against opposite walls.

Something strong. In a tumbler glass, I say.

Yes, he says, not moving.

Bride of Chucky …

Let's hope this is it.

Oh, this is it.

M nods, face vacant. She's transitioning, he says.

We all are.

M is smiling at me now. And we're laughing. And he's pulling me to bed and it's suddenly like none of it has happened, not the hellscape, not even the child. We are just us again, for a moment.

Meat

On my phone is a message from Sophie, my friend whose building the elevator accident happened in. We haven't spoken for years. Her voice, her name still feels like a strange part of my psyche I can't quite place, like it belongs or comes from somewhere else. We arrange to meet at La Marine for lunch. I almost can't get away, but buy myself an hour, M salutes me, busy in his headphones.

I'm not sure why she has asked to see me. Since I moved back to Paris, I haven't contacted her, though I think of her often. She's liked a few of my photos on social media, and I am following her jewellery boutique, but I haven't known how to see her or talk to her. I still feel so strange about what happened, guilty, like I don't want to remind her of it, or Lou. Lou was only four when it happened, when she called my name from the ground floor and I leaned over to see her precious face … that memory still so strong, of her face so bright, drawing me in, to death. The elevator stopped just above my head, I was saved from decapitation, unlike the boy in a similar building in the 17th not long after. Sweet Lou. I haven't seen her since the accident. I'm honestly not sure if I were to see her that we would not both fall to dust.

Sophie is there, at a corner table, same bouncy brown curls, same porcelain skin, face more lined, more softened. Our eyes fill with tears at the sight of each other. She asks me all about the Chunk, and M, and the music and writing and acting, and the copywriting, and teaching – which I'm suddenly filled with relief I don't have to do anymore, realising how far I've come. She now has a son, and they all live in Montreuil and are happy. Lou is eleven and in collège. Sophie is still making jewellery, she has her own shop. Her voice is still as delicate as petals.

There is something I've longed to ask her, and now we're here and I'm not sure when I'll see her again, I think I should ask it. It's a terrible question. I'm afraid of it. I feel the same way about it as when I wanted to ask Dad what it was like to watch Mum die, as if asking would destroy him, or the earth would melt. When I finally did ask he didn't implode, but he couldn't quite tell me. He choked up and said something like, She was … gone. I wanted to know the specifics: did she say anything, what did her face look like, was it awful, was she still fighting, was she in pain, did her eyes go backwards, did her breath expire, her lungs fall like in the movies, what is it like to witness the exact moment of someone passing from life into death? Silly to ask, because how could he be expected to answer, he was surely nothing in that moment but pure love. I think what I wanted was for him to put me right there, in that moment. Because I wanted to be there. I felt guilty I wasn't. Now I'm a mother, I think perhaps she had arranged it like that – waited until we'd left to get Thai takeaway because she physically couldn't leave with us there. Like how at night in our house, she could never slip fully away into sleep.

Sophie pulls out a gift for me. A bracelet she has made, in gold, with two parallel bands coming to join in the centre. That's us, she says in her sweet voice. Forever linked.

I put on the band and admire it. I wonder how my life would have panned out if it weren't for the accident, if it weren't for Sophie, if it weren't for Lou. A gruesome near-death, and yet it's what brought me to M, our child.

Can I ask you something? I say to Sophie.

Of course.

What did Lou see that night? Did I harm her for life? Is she OK?

Sophie looks down, then back up at me. No, she says. She didn't see anything.

What do you mean? When she walked up the stairs to where I was, she must have seen.

No, she repeats, taking time to speak. I knew something had happened almost straight away. I didn't hear anything, but after you called out to Lou then went silent I had a terrible feeling. My heart stopped, you know? I even sensed it when I entered the building, like something bad was going to happen, before you called to us, before you started playing the game of hide-and-seek. It was so strange. So I told Lou to stay well behind me while I walked up the stairs. She was far back.

And then what? I ask.

I saw you dead, she says softly. Je t'ai vu morte.

Morte has a sharper sound than dead, it cuts the air.

I was sure you were, she continues. You were so still.

And Lou didn't see any of this?

No. I ran back down and pulled her outside. When I came back up, Éveline the nurse was with you. And you were alive …

Far out, I say in English.

It really is a miracle you lived. But there is something else I wanted to tell you. She smiles, her eyes glistening. It's so strange, Jayne. But I had to tell you in person.

Tell me.

Well you know, on the tenth anniversary of your mother's death, you posted a picture on social media: 10.10 on the tenth of February 2003.

Yes, I say.

Well, listen to me. Lou was born on the tenth of February 2003.

Ha! We sit for a moment, smiling at each other, like we know what this means. It's so strange it's funny, and we start to giggle, an absurd sound that builds to laughter. Of all the days for Lou to born herself, she chose that one. Then, on the day I was to die, it was her sweet face, so much like Mum's with its deep, dark eyes, drawing me there. Sophie is smiling, reading my thoughts. The world seems to melt around us for a moment, leaving us alone at this table, sharers of a small, weird gem.

As I walk up the canal after, my mind goes wild. If it did mean something, what would it mean? That Lou was the reincarnation of Mum, and she had been waiting for the right moment to take me to death with her, but then when the moment came she changed her mind and pressed the button to stop the lift's descent, saving me? I remember missing her so much that night, that cold month before the accident. And they never knew what did stop that lift – even a team of experts couldn't figure it out. It had remained a mystery, the only reason I'd survived.

I pass Old Club, and peer surreptitiously in the windows to see if I can spot the Chunk, aware that if she sees me I'll have to collect her and there are three more work hours left. She is sitting in a pile of costumes, diligently brushing a doll's hair. She is alone but seems perfectly content, and I have to fight the urge to rush in and grab her. She wouldn't be here if it weren't for that lift stopping, and probably not here if the accident hadn't happened. I would never have returned to Australia and met M. I would have stayed here in my little place in the rue de la Chine, become a puppeteer, an actress, an entirely different person.

Back then I didn't mind if I died. Death was my playtoy. I measured my aliveness with it, kept it close. Now, as I watch her, I realise it is no longer allowed. My death is hers. It is owned by them now. And I must never die.

Seeing Sophie has knocked me. Something has been exposed, a raw sinew, a nerve, the flesh beneath my scars, still tender to the touch. I thought by now I had moved on from all that, was over it, grateful, happy, strong, but I feel peeled back like the orange I opened yesterday, which looked like a normal orange until I dug into the skin and opened it out to reveal blood and red flesh that jolted me back to seeing the haematoma on Mum's back for the first time, the blood inside like wings jammed up against the translucent flesh, bursting to get out.

This skinlessness, this oozing makes me want to wrap a heavy blanket around myself, us, build a fortress, watertight. Work is the answer. Work will provide the money to build the fortress, pay our rent, pay the deposit on a new place when this lease is up, and we will be happy, oh so happy, how happy we shall be.

I work harder, faster, better and more. One-hour jobs are done in ten minutes. My mind is a machine, my fingers steel rods, my back, neck, brain, head, pistons firing, nobody can know how much one person can do. I could have staff, M and I discuss it, even he could do some of the work, and we try this a few times, but by the time I have explained the brief I would have already done the job twice over. And if he does the job I have to check it anyway, and in that time I could have done it again. No, just keep it this way. M takes kid responsibility, admin, food. Jayne is the machine.

In early summer my neck seizes up and my hands clench like claws. I type through the pain, forcing my body to behave, which leads to a deep sense of panic, to breathlessness and vertigo. My hands won't stop shaking. I can't sleep. We've decided to stay in Paris for the summer so I can work and M can record his new songs, but around 14 July, when it goes quiet for a few days, we decide I should take a break, get out of the city, to rest and perhaps write, think of things other than 'big ideas' for shampoo and showerheads and pizza bases. Though it's bad financially, and risky to be suddenly unavailable, M says I can't afford not to go.

Claire suggests an artists' residency she's heard about in Carcassonne. They have one room available for a small amount of money, in an old, unpretentious hillside manor house two artists have restored.

In the train carriage I'm a new person, steam released from imaginary valves all over my head and body. But my reflection in the window, with the fields going by in the background, is a ghost I don't recognise.

At the residency the other artists are all painters, except for a young Canadian writer and an old American sexpest poet who takes a shine to me instantly. Fresh meat.

I sleep for two solid days, with interruptions to Skype with M and the Chunk, but the service is bad, and she doesn't like it anyway. On the third day I feel almost myself again, some kind of self, so I walk and read, unable to think about writing, or anything at all. The shock to my brain at stopping the furious copywriting feels like clamping on the brakes, and my body feels whiplashed, needing to unwind. The sexpest tells me about the *source* – a running stream two hours' hike away with fresh, cold water. I walk to it in the afternoon sunshine, then around the gorge, the rocks and trees, then come back and sit on a chair to read as the light dims. The artists are pleasant. The sexpest is pesty, wanting to read me his poems and stories about fucking. We eat dinner in a sombre stone room, then I sleep again, and the next day I begin. Day four. Three days left.

My draft sits on the chair, smirking through the jaws of the bulldog clip. How I loathe that clip. I dream of binding. A good, hard spine. I dream of the day I will crunch that bulldog clip under my heel, murder it, make it bleed. But what is in those pages is a bunch of air. It wouldn't stand up to a flick test, let alone the presentation we've all agreed to do tomorrow night by the fireplace. I'm ashamed of it. I will read something silly, a sexy part so the sexpest gives praise. At least he is concrete, solid. I can rely on him to be exactly who he is.

I have come to the conclusion that the first draft, which I began to write based on my notes from the theatre-school days, is better than any of the heady, cleverer stuff I've written later. So I feel like I've wasted my youth. Back then I wrote things down as they happened. It was compulsive, a curse almost, like I wanted to bottle every day in the rue du Faubourg-Saint-Denis before it was gone. But the writing was fresh, unruined. Now I don't even know what I'm writing, or how to write, or why. The bones and muscle are there, M said after he last read it. Just not the ligaments. You need to write the sinew, he said, the bits that hold it together, flesh it out. But to do that I need to know what I'm *saying*. Who I am. Barthes said we have several selves. Breton imagined living in a house of glass where who he was would eventually become *etched by a diamond*. I don't want glass sheets. I don't want many selves. I feel transparent, that's the problem, everything is slippery, what I put down slides away the next day with the new person I become. I am changing too fast, losing all I've built.

Outside the sun is sharp, my thoughts muddled. I keep thinking of something Nadine said after my reading years ago at the bookshop: Why do you feel the need to fictionalise it all? Why don't you just write the story truthfully? Non-fiction? The idea was repulsive to me. What is truth? Bataille, Francine told me, said: *Truth has only one face: that of a violent contradiction.* I have it on a Post-it. Writing the truth doesn't necessarily make it true.

I'm overthinking it. Too close to it. Perhaps I should write in French, like Beckett. Limit the affectations of my native tongue. Perhaps I can escape myself by writing in French. It should be like theatre. That feeling of danger, like anything could happen. Naughty, bad, evil. Duende. The craic. I hate the writing I do, but I hate myself more. Is that what a writer is? One who hates themselves more than the writing? Artaud said man is meat for pain. All writing is pigshit. And that no one has ever written, painted, sculpted, modelled, built or invented anything except to get out of hell.

This is hell. Perhaps I should give up. Perhaps I should read. Finish *I Love Dick*. I'm up to a part about Hannah Wilke, who used her body in her art – stuck chewing-gum vaginas all over her face, photographed in graphic detail her slow death from cancer. She was ridiculed, shamed as an exhibitionist, but her work was stark, ironic, a mirror. Chris Kraus writes: *If women have failed to make the 'universal' art because we're trapped within the 'personal', why not universalise the 'personal' and make it the subject of our art?* I don't know. I copy the phrase onto a Post-it and stick it to the wall, to think about.

The sharing soirée goes as expected. Everyone talks about themselves too long, including me, and I titillate the sexpest to the point of sweat with a passage on female masturbation inspired by Steven Berkoff's *Gross Intrusion*.

That night I dream I rewrite the book as a choose-your-own-adventure. I feel happy when I wake, like I've solved the dilemma of all these choices that have to constantly be made, all the wrong turns, the dead ends. M calls as I'm packing to leave, I tell him the idea and he asks if I'm high. He doesn't seem to understand what a brilliant idea it is. Though, as I say my goodbyes, it's already starting to fade.

At the last minute I print the thing out on the house printer and hold the hot pages in my hand on the way to the station. I force myself to read it on the train back, imagining that perhaps there's something miraculous in there I hadn't realised I'd done, but it's formless, a mess of ideas, not juste, no reason for being, and the question keeps coming to me: why, why, why.

Unstable Street

She is tired at Club, they say. On Monday when I pick her up, she wants to bring home Françoise, the black girl doll with the strikingly well-moulded vulva, and when I say no she throws a French tantrum like I've never seen.

Non non NOOOON!

J'veux PAS!

Tu es MÉCHANTE!

It reminds me of the kid I babysat when I was an au pair, same words, same knees, same – almost – kick to the shins. Little scowl.

JE VEUX PLUS TE PARLER.

I scoop her up, apologise to the ladies, and take her straight out into the freezing air, where she immediately sobers up and forgets about it.

Niflettes? She pouts.

It shoots through me how French she is. Now that she is spending more time at Old Club and New Club, and less and less with me, she is becoming culturally estranged from me. She looks Parisian now, hair pulled back all neat like it has been brushed, her buttons done up to the top, cared for by the ladies, happy, bien, fulfilled. She has forged her own selfhood, feels independent from me, just like in the dream. I feel terrible, an awful mother, for all I've missed, knowing *other people can't give the love I can, especially from the age of 0–5*, though she doesn't seem to mind at all. This is her life, it's all she knows. She holds my hand as she pushes along on her scooter. Part of the landscape.

She wants to go to Hospital Park, so we get the niflettes. We have to stop in the shops all the way back so she can say hello to the shopkeepers, and by the time we arrive in the park the sun has gone and it is freezing. I haven't brought her coat, or mine, but there is no chance I can call it off. My phone burns in my pocket. Another half an hour, I tell myself, I will be present with her for this small amount of time until we get home, when M will take over while I work.

Nobody in the park except for an older woman in a dressing gown who is hooked up to an IV drip, sitting on a bench, smoking.

Baba? The Chunk wants to play bubbas, so I take Big Bubba out of the bag, but she puts the doll back in the seat. Maman bébé bubba. OK, I'll be the bubba. My head pounds, fingers going numb, her cheeks turning pink from cold. Quick bubba, I tell her, Then we need to go home, it's getting cold. MAMA BUBBA. OK, jeez. I sit on the damp grass.

She moves around me, picking up grass and letting it fall, banging her little fist against a tree trunk, gathering leaves from the nearby gutter. I'm irritated, running combinations of words through my mind for the skincare headline, doll, parts, enter the doll, season of the doll, doll it up, doll out ... She approaches and puts her hand on my shoulder, inclining her sweet little head: Wassa orajjuss?

Ooh, yes please, Mama.

S'OK, love. She puts a leaf in my lap. Issa too 'ot?

No, it's nice and cold thank you.

OK, sweetie. OK? She gives my head a light pat and moves away to gather more leaves. The last light is dying on the old stone walls, their aged cracks casting dark shadows. IV woman is long gone.

The Chunk returns to fuss over me, brush my hair to the side, kiss my cheek, compliment me in a gentle voice – darling, sweetie, my little love – checking my temperature and the temperature of the things she is feeding me – good girl – furrowing her brow with concern, checking I'm OK.

I realise something. She's being me. Could this be how she experiences me?

Dun wuwwy, love, s'OK ... Bubba cwy? Mama's chest?

I lean into her sweet baby chest and pretend-sob but really do. Her little body rocks me back and forth. S'OK, baby. OK now? *Pocoyo*? Caca?

Thanks, Mama. I'm OK now.

I sit as still as I can as the last light fades, and though I'm worried she will die of cold I try to let go and absorb every move she makes. I lie back on the wet grass as she changes my nappy, let her wipe me with a chip packet she has found and comb my hair with a stick.

Every day I feel like the wicked witch, manoeuvring her around the city, shoving food down her throat, trying to get her to sleep so I can work, reluctantly playing her games. And despite all that, this – what she has just shown me – is what she thinks being a mother is.

God. Perhaps I'm doing better than I thought. Perhaps this constant feeling of never being good enough is normal. Perhaps that's the motherhood condition. To keep us always awake, alert to predators. Perhaps my mother felt terrible at it too. Perhaps she hid her guilt. Perhaps she was a great performer. I am a performer but it heartens me that the Chunk is experiencing something deeper than my lostness.

Bastien comes up to babysit and we take the métro to Saint-Michel and walk to Claire's book launch. It's a hot night and the English bookshop is filled with summer tourists. All the better, says Claire. She's glad most of her friends are away. She is seated in the upstairs window, wearing a forest-green dress with thick silver necklaces around her neck. Her hair is wild, her eyes alert. I can see she is sweating.

The room is half full with people on rickety chairs and a bench seat along the side wall, beneath all the dusty books. The bookseller died recently, and I wept when I found out, remembering his warm, eccentric presence, him listening to me that night when I shared my first chapters all those years ago. Our friend, his daughter, now runs the shop, and introduces Claire, smiling. She loves this book, she says, it's the best of the Irish voice, with a French sensibility and an eye on the city and its people that she's never read before.

If Claire is nervous she doesn't show it. She takes her time, relishing the moment, the audience silent, the air thick. I think back to that night here, with the newborn Chunk, when Claire and I met and we listened to M play with the cellist. The same magic is in the air, the same warmth. Claire knows how to bring the craic, and I wonder if it was her who brought it back then too, or was it the mix of the four of us, or was it just the bookshop and the feeling it casts over everyone who gets to sit up here and listen to something precious, deep, raw.

She's a real writer now. She laughed when I asked if she'd quit the agency now that she is published. I have to believe she will one day. She will be Boland, Beckett, she will drink and spout words at the Dôme, a full and proper artist, beholden to none.

By the time she reads her final poem, the room has become crowded, and we lose sight of her when people line up to talk and have their books signed. M and I slip away into the night, walking towards the métro then deciding to go instead up through the Marais, see how far we get until we're tired, talking about publishing and how hard it must be to get work over the line. But you're published, I say to him. You know what it feels like.

Writing is different.

Not necessarily.

Yeah I guess you're right.

He tells me about how his first band's first demo had gotten them signed with a label, and then the second, third and fourth albums just flowed. I can't imagine what that must be like, I say. I'll be rewriting my book until kingdom come.

You won't, he says. It will happen.

How will it happen? How? I say. I can feel my cheeks reddening. I don't deserve to go down this path, oh shut up, shut up, monster, you went away for a whole week, it's nobody's fault but your own that you haven't made advancements since you returned, shut up, just shut up.

It's a slow process, everyone says it, he says. Books take years, especially first books. You're finding your voice. You'll do it, I'm certain of it. Just keep going.

We walk in silence until my phone starts to ring. It's Claire, begging us to meet for a drink near her place. We're not far.

You go, says M. I'll relieve the babysitter.

You sure?

Course. I'll see you in the morning. He kisses me.

I meet Claire at Le Mary Celeste. Her face is flushed, glowing, her eyes bright. What did you think? she asks.

I order us champagne. What do you think I thought? I say. Incredible, Claire. To hear you read your poetry out loud, it brings it even more to life.

Poetry is for speaking.

Of course. But your voice, your Irish voice … it was the craic!

I say it was!

We drink.

Who was the guy in the black T-shirt? I ask.

Oh, that's the publisher.

Alphonse? I pictured him as some old fart.

Me too. He's quite the fox.

Oh là là.

He's married, two kids, not even flirty.

You did it. You published a book before having kids.

I don't think I'm having kids.

Are you not? I joke.

Nope. Well, if I am, I need to decide now.

And what, have your eggs frozen?

Or whatever.

We talk of eggs and sex and men, and I get drunk and my jealousy of her comes out in a torrent of passion, an inchoate mess of writerly fury and artistic envy and anger at myself and pride in her and M and resentment of this life we have built on my teetering tagline ability and I'll never publish anything and it doesn't even matter and why am I so angry, at him, at the situation, at the situation of music in the world, the end of CDs, the robbing of the artists, the going under of labels, the slog and humiliation of it, it's not M's fault, and parenting, the actual hard work, I respect him for that, his willingness to do that, but there's just no *balance* and Claire is brilliant so brilliant, can she introduce me to the publisher.

She is drunk too, so that helps, but I walk down the boulevard afterwards feeling disgusting, a disgusting person, mean, a bad woman, bad friend, the devil. She told me I should talk to M about the frustrations, that he will understand, that he isn't stupid and he will have known all this time something is up, that I should come clean, talk about it all with him, or the situation will keep festering, and that's bad in a relationship, bad bad bad, especially in a relationship like ours where we're such good friends.

But we're not friends anymore, I'd slurred. We're parents.

I wake with a hangover and get through breakfast and dressing the Chunk before dragging myself into the office. My chest is lead. I feel like a ghastly pimple has risen in me and popped last night and though I haven't said anything to him it's already all out in the open. His gear sits beside me, waiting for him, as my inbox starts to fill. The thing is I *want* him to be a musician. He *is* a musician. Like Betty Blue needs Zorg to be a writer. *How can I love you if I can't admire you?* she shouts. *We're only learning to die here!*

Would I still love M if he let that part of himself die, that part I love so much? If he became a Suit? An insurance salesman? I *need* him to be a musician. It's who he is. If he wasn't a musician I wouldn't know him. Because he wouldn't *be* him.

I remember after the recovery, when I first returned to Paris without him, he had made me a burnt CD entitled *Songs for Jayne* with three songs on it that he had composed on the guitar and asked his friends to play bass and drums on and some other tricky things, but not enough to make it sound too much, just perfect, subtle things to add to the story of the song. I listened to the songs on the crowded métro. They coloured the surroundings differently, coloured them with the sea we'd waded in together down at Dad's, with the warm air.

When we ended up in Paris together, living in the Récollets, he was there for about two seconds before he started making music. He would pull the big curtains shut and I would lie up on the mezzanine in the dark and be taken on rides through the imaginative planes he was creating – all the stories and the people and the cities and the streets – and I would feel like when I was a kid and Dad would put on *Peter and the Wolf* and my mind would go berserk.

I remember him telling me how, before he met me, he was invited to replace the guitarist in a band that later became a world-killing stadium act. They all own houses in London now. He knew at the time they would be huge, but after a few rehearsals he turned it down – he liked the music, but it would always be theirs. He was a writer, he didn't know how to play in someone else's band. I loved that about him.

All day my stomach is tight. He can tell something is wrong but thinks I'm just hungover. Once the Chunk is down in the evening I tell him there's something I need to talk with him about. He looks concerned. He sits down opposite me at the dining table. I try my best to look in his eyes, but the words won't come, so I shift my gaze to my hands.

I feel like I'm about to tell you I'm cheating on you. That's actually what it feels like. I've been cheating on you. Ever since Nanashi, when you told me you wanted to start the new band.

Oh.

I've been keeping it to myself this whole time, and I have to come clean.

OK.

I don't think the band is a good idea! I never have. I'm so sorry to say it! I'm sorry I didn't say it earlier. I didn't know how.

Oh.

I'm sorry. This feels worse actually than if I'd slept with someone.

Right.

He looks crushed. I feel disgusting. I'm sure he knew it but leaving it unsaid meant it wasn't real. Now it's real. My small words express an enormous betrayal. I can see him counting back this whole past year. I am calling for change. Which implies a level of disrespect of and mistrust in the path he has chosen, he has been living all this time with someone of mauvaise foi. Adrien would say that to me, if I got annoyed at him for something: Tu es de la mauvaise foi! I have bad faith, I am Bardot in *Le Mépris*, smouldering with resentment at a seemingly innocent decision made – in her case, her husband's leaving her to be driven by another man to a soirée, in mine, that my husband has chosen to make a band as we build a life in the city with a small child.

I guess I understand, he says.

It's not that I don't believe in it, I say. It's just – I don't think it's the right choice right now. I don't understand why you chose it.

Well I do, when you explain the logic. But I just ... don't trust that it will ever be an income-earner. Not enough to support us. It's taking too long.

OK. What do you think I should do?

I need you to have a job that's *regular* and *acceptable*, I say, hardly believing the words exiting my mouth.

Can do, he says. Let's do it.

A few days later he has secured a job interview with the Irish pub on the Grands Boulevards. We sit with his printed CV and coffee at Le Zephyr, watching traffic and looking at the green frontage a few doors down with its Celtic symbols, trying to imagine M working in there.

They say they should be able to pay him to bartend as a 'musician' somehow, so he can work legally. The mood is glum. Though it feels right for him to be making a pragmatic move like this, it also feels dumb. We discuss the pros and cons. Pro: he has a job. Cons: shit pay, late nights, more pressure on me as I'll have to be with the Chunk at nights and home earlier from the office and picking her up from Club ... Wait. Are we insane? Limiting my capacity to earn, which is high, so he can go and work long hours for terrible pay? When, if he is supporting me as he has been doing, the potential for us to get ahead faster is more probable?

This is stupid, I say. Let's just keep going as we are. What were we thinking, having him work with teenagers and backpackers? He's forty-two! He suggests he work more closely with me, in the time he has away from the Chunk, learn the job, do more admin, and of course all the invoices and income and tax. We return to the office and work out a plan before he kisses my head and goes to collect the Chunk.

It feels good. I feel sad. He will still do the music, of course. In fact, I realise, not much will change.

The next night he goes back to rehearsals. The practical side of things seems to have rectified itself, and despite the mauvaise foi I've shown in the potential of the band he keeps moving forward. I realise how relieved I am he hasn't been derailed by what I said. I'm not sure what we would have done. I'm not sure if I would have known him anymore. It would have been tragic if he had crumbled. Is that what I wanted? No, it wasn't. Then why did I do it?

I don't know. I didn't like the feeling that we weren't talking to each other. That he didn't know clearly where I stood. That had never happened to us before. It was horrible, a cold war, we had become like puppets, shadows of ourselves. Thank god he is strong enough to move past this, even with the knowledge he doesn't have my support.

Is that the person I am? The one who says, See, told you it was impossible.

The Chunk will be the one to say, Papa, you did it! I always knew you could!

He battens down the hatches. I can see he feels alone, like I don't believe in him, that his only choice is to make it happen, work harder.

I silently start to barrack for him.

Elysian Fields

They start school at three, or as soon as they're propre. Which means clean, which also means toilet-trained. We started potty-training her at home on the little red plastic thing, which she liked at first but got sick of, then one of those things on the toilet seat, then we let her run around naked in the apartment, and fairly soon, after a few oui-oui and caca incidents, she was propre. By the time she starts school, she is well over three, so she is good and solid and ready. Every time we've passed a school since she was a toddler, she's wanted to go in. École! École! Isaac is only two and a half and is not at all propre, but Charlotte Gainsbourg brings him in and he cuddles up to the Chunk. He's a baby! I think, as he pees himself. The Chunk attends to him like a little mama, and I am out the door. She is fine, but like her first day at Club, M and I go to Chez Jeannette and hold back tears for the entire practice hour. How can she be at school? Her cousin won't have even started kindergarten yet.

It's not really school, the maternelle. The Maternal. It is from ages three to five, and a kind of preparatory school, where they learn creative things, art and good times, before they enter the école primaire and all the colours disappear. Even at the Maternal, though, the school hours are strict: 8.30 am to 4.30 pm minimum, penitentiary rules, except on Wednesdays when for some reason they finish at midday. The huge steel gates shut at 8.20 am, and you're not allowed in unless you file through the courts, basically. Inside, it is lovely – they draw and paint and sing and sleep for an hour in a little dortoir with stars projected on the roof – but our hearts still feel walled off. She is off, in her own life. She has stepped right out of me and gone straight on.

The introductory hour goes fine, then the next day a few more hours, then full time the next. She skips off with her cartable on her back, her schoolish casual clothes, her little black shoes with white socks pulled high. The other parents meet before and after school at Madame Gen – cool parents of this now-cool quartier, smoking and drinking coffee in their casual jackets and sneakers. At first I'm too shy to stop and mingle, but once the school term has settled in, I occasionally go in, say hello, and sit to answer a few emails. The atmosphere is warm and convivial.

I like to watch the mothers. Most drink a quick coffee standing up, perhaps pick at a croissant and dash off, some stay, work from computers, talk. Charlotte Gainsbourg and her casual-chic friends smoke and shrug and laugh. I notice a woman speaking English with her husband – she introduces herself as Amal. Their child, Sami, is in the petite section too, but they split up the three English-speaking kids to make sure they didn't stick together. Marius's mother always sits at the same table by the door, smoking. She sees me but has no desire to talk to me, and makes no effort or excuse. She sits alone, morose but fine, thinking, drinking a coffee. She looks at no phone, no book, no computer. She just sits. I'm not sure why this intrigues me. I think it's because she is taking time to herself. I think her name is Viviane. You can see she is thinking about her own life. What is it she's thinking about? Sex, I think. There's something fleshy about her, alive. She is definitely having sex. It oozes from her. She's not a beautiful woman, but she is sexy, she is in her body.

Oh, to read her thoughts.

Smoke.

You smoke because you want to put something in your mouth.

You smoke because you don't want to eat.

You don't want to eat because you want to feel.

You want to feel because you have a lover.

You get sex but that's not what you want.

You think you want to be sexy.

But that's not what you want.

You smoke to be here.

You smoke because you're social.

You smoke to say, I'm here.

You smoke to say, I'm here, to yourself.

You smoke to say, I'm here, to yourself, and there are more important things in life than death.

You smoke to take a moment.

I am taking a moment. Smoking. Writing nothingnesses.

Bones and muscle.

Ligature.

Flesh, blood.

The Chunk loves school but gives no detail. After school, as the kids play in Pig Park, Amal tells me Sami was corrected for colouring the boots in different colours. Boots are brown, the teacher said. Colour them brown.

Tuesday is a public holiday, and M said he'd take the Chunk so I can have a full day working on the book. I still have copywriting work jammed in every pocket of my brain, and was so exhausted by the work over the past few days, few weeks, few months, few *fucking years*, I slept in until late morning. Annoyed at myself for wasting the window of time, I dropped and smashed a coffee cup. As I cleaned it up, he made me a new one and one for himself, and the Chunk watched *Pocoyo* as we drank it. The look on his face annoyed me. He was annoyed that I was annoyed at him, after all, he had tried to give me some space to write and I hadn't used it. Hadn't *walked in the olive grove*.

What was wrong with me? Why didn't I use the time? Why did I feel guilty, sleeping late, wasting the time, time I could have been spending with him or my child, if I didn't write? Why did I feel the shadow of the previous days' copywriting work over me, boxing me in, reminding me that even if I found some writing flow it would be cut off tomorrow anyway, and the pain of this would be so great it was better not to start at all?

Unfortunately for him, I got him to speak his thoughts. They were measured, kind, and enraged me beyond belief. I should go and use the time I had. Perhaps it would help to compartmentalise things better moving ahead, he could help me if I needed. It's a shame I didn't get in there sooner, but there's still a few hours, if I go now.

I storm to the office and tap out a wild message.

Consider not sending.

Sent.

When I have copywriting or translating hanging over me, it is practically impossible for me to concentrate on the book – especially at the point it is at right now, where I need to think deep. I am wrecked from overwork. I resent the insinuation that I could have gotten off my arse and into the office earlier today to write. I need space and time to think in order to work. Perhaps keep your ideas on how I can be more productive to yourself for now. Thanks.

No reply. He doesn't engage in wars by phone. I waste the whole afternoon feeling guilty and lonely and useless and missing them and scratching over old material, ruining it with overthought, fuming over M's comments and the note of resentment I detected in his voice, maintaining my rage. Tonight he will apologise. I will stand strong in my righteousness. Because I am right. I am the worker. I will not be questioned. I am the paid, the suited, the workhorse, the labourer.

What do you *want*? he asks, restless in bed. Do you want to swap? Because I would *love* to go off to work each day. Buy my coffee, sit at my desk, talk with adults. I would *love* to not be small-talking with mothers at the school gate, sitting in parks, schlepping groceries up the stairs.

I apologise, and lie there feeling sick.

He forgives me, I think.

I do not want to swap.

I lose her, in Pig Park. The park is crawling with ant children, as always, teeming with them – kids on pigs, on slides, on monkey bars, running and sprawling and clambering – and I look down at my bag and back up again and she is gone.

Nobody has seen her. Friends spread out in different directions but can't find her anywhere. I rush around the usual parts, the big pig sculpture, the little pigs ... She is nowhere to be seen.

Panic. Running around now, calling her name, kids clear out, she's not here, oh god, I run out into the side street, no sign, now I'm really panicking, finally I run out past the church though I know she'd never run out here, and into the long, narrow park full of the lost and destitute that leads to the refugee camp at the top of the rue du Faubourg-Saint-Denis. What will I even do if I can't find her? How would the police find her, how would they know it was her? Why haven't I tied a bracelet around her wrist, branded her, installed a microchip?

By some miracle I see her. A small lump with her green cardigan on, huddled beneath a tree. She is shivering. My baby! I wrap her in me and we sit for a long time, rocking back and forth. She must have gotten caught up in a wave of kids coming out the gate, or did she just run out of the park for fun? I want to shake her, ask her, What happened, but she doesn't speak, she just clings to me.

Terror. Back in the apartment she seems to have forgotten all about it. I am ill, and guilty, as I relay it to M. He will hate me, shame me, commit me. He wraps his arms around me. It's not your fault.

I teach her my phone number, as a song. Make her sing it to me every day. Hold her hand tight everywhere we go. Tighter than ever. She is confused, pulls away. I would rather stay inside with her, or know she is inside, I can relax when she's at the Maternal. She still can't be trusted to walk in the street without her hand being held, and I will never, ever, look away from her in a park again, not even for a second.

The shock of it lasts weeks this time. Her little cowering body. If she'd been picked up, even by someone caring, how would they have found me? I would have roamed the streets, the police stations, forevermore … I would have lost my mind. I think I *am* losing my mind. It goes around and around in my head. What if I lost her? What if I lost her?

The Dodger comes to town. He and his gallery-owning girlfriend have unexpectedly rolled into Paris for twenty-four hours – an opening for one of her artists. He asks us to dinner and we need to make it work, get out, be adults, have fun, brush off the cobwebs clinging to us. Bastien isn't available, but at the last minute Francine says she can do it. The Chunk is already asleep by the time she arrives. She doesn't quite know what to do with herself, looking around the apartment, a little lost in the familiar space that will soon once again house her own flesh and blood. She has brought her computer, and sits it on the coffee table with the glass of white wine I offer. We haven't seen each other much of late, and I feel guilty about asking her to come, perform a job, when I owe her a phone call, apéro, respect and dignity. She waves us off, glasses deep on her nose, Amusez-vous bien.

By the time we fly out the doorway and into the street I am definitely spiky. A badly put-together outfit, terrible eyeliner I should never have started, too late to stop for an apéro, the necessary brush-down between the world of tiny clutches to the lights and dazzle of the adult realm. I am flustered, and way too eager, rambling on to M about some random junk all the way over the canal to Parmentier. I am sure the Dodger must have booked a restaurant of the same name in a distant French suburb because you can never get a table at this joint at such notice.

They are running late.

We stand in the entranceway and an elegant hostess approaches. I feel painfully untrendy and flustered but try to pout it up a bit, be cool, be coooool. A couple has entered closely behind us – a stunning Frenchwoman and her older-looking male friend – and, just as I go to talk to the waitress, the woman steps in front of me. As if I am invisible. Usually I'd just allow it or grumble a bit. But everything accumulates in that one raging moment – every time I have been ignored, stepped on, nearly run over, cut off, denied, hung up on, overlooked. I hiss, *Excusez-moi*, and step abruptly back in front of the woman, turning my back to her in such a way as to cut her off from the hostess's view then stating audibly in English and with demon bile to M, FUCKING FRENCH. I say it deliberately so the Frenchwoman can hear. There is spittle around my top gums. How dare she.

It doesn't feel good. Especially when I see the look on M's face, and remember our tenet: She who smiles last wins. It's always you who loses if you let things get to you here. What was that Hemingway line? *No matter what the provocation, a foreigner must keep his temper in France.*

The waitress can't find our name on the list – and once I point to the Dodger's name on the sheet we realise that our table is for six. Damn. He must have invited the artist. Of course it could never be as perfect as expected.

M and I sit down at one end of the table. He is still gobsmacked by my outburst. I try to pour some honey on the mood by rubbing his knee and ordering beers. Then, to my dawning horror, I notice the rude Frenchwoman and the man moving towards our table. Oh fuck. I look down at my napkin. It's the artist and his wife. I wish the polished concrete floor would swallow me whole.

The wife sits next to me, the artist on the far seat. Should I say something? There is no doubt she heard me. And, as she introduces herself in perfect English, I realise my 'fucking French' was unlikely to have been mistaken.

I hate myself, I think as I slug back bubbled water, wanting to drown in it. The man seems put out, but he is older, Greek and may not speak English. The lady also seems uncomfortable, but that could be because we're missing the common link. That's what I tell myself. Perhaps none of us can be bothered meeting new people tonight and neither couple had been aware of the other's impending presence ... Or had they known? I wonder in my clammy sheets that night. Is it possible that the woman had not been trying to overstep me in the queue? She was simply trying to point out on the waitress's chart that the booking was for six not four, and that they were the other two?

I roll over and moan, wanting to die all over again.

M doesn't think the restaurant episode was very funny. He's tiring of my attitude, my outbursts, my stressed-out demeanour, my inability to relax, to hug or kiss him properly. I try to calm myself, be less electric, but I can't seem to slow down, like a computer running hot.

Headspins. Breathlessness.

Claire suggests I start seeing her psychologist.

The psychologist works from an office on the Champs-Élysées, across and down from the Big Agency, which must be strange as well as convenient for Claire. It's certainly strange for me. I meet Claire before my first appointment, in the downstairs café, hoping I don't bump into a client.

The Elysian Fields, I say, as we drink our coffee. Is that what the Champs-Élysées means? The ultimate paradise?

You're thinking of the Empyrean, she says, the place in the highest heaven, Beatrice's rightful place.

Oh.

The Elysian Fields is the uppermost level of hell, in Dante.

Makes more sense. It's such a strange street.

Where the heathens go. They're good people, but because they're heathens, they're stuck between hell and purgatory forevermore, unable to ascend to heaven.

That's where I will go.

Yes you will, Jayne.

You won't because you're a good Catholic.

She has, of course, read the Bible. She's read all the big books. Joyce of course, Proust, Dante. Is it an Irish thing, to be so laden with grand thought? Or just a poet thing.

You should be writing books full time, I tell her.

Fuck that, she says. Advertising is far better for the soul.

I have half an hour before my appointment, so I go and buy macarons for my family, then proceed to eat them all as I wander the street with its grand vitrines and old passageways, groups of tourists and bustling businesspeople. Something definitely hellish about the Champs-Élysées, so full of stuff yet empty. I have a habit of buying macarons every time I step out of the Big Agency, as if to cleanse myself, or perhaps punish myself. Mandarin, passionfruit, rose-petal ganache, they go too fast. The macaron has a short life, which is how I convince myself it's OK to eat them all at once, including my family's gift.

The psychologist is neat and Welsh and has a giant tissue box. It doesn't take her long to find her way to Mum and the accident. The tissue box taunts me, I refuse, this is dumb, let's sit here and cry like we did at the family counselling session, that was helpful. She is kind, this lady – Susan – with her neat hair and meaty face. She is great, says Claire, she couldn't get by without her. I try to be patient and open to it.

She asks a lot of questions about my life that go further back, and I try to focus her on now. NOW is where I need help. Help me live in the now. She asks if I feel depressed. What does that even mean? I ask. Of course I'm depressed, no I'm not depressed, I'm just very very tired. Any history of depression in the family? Yes, yes, but what has that got to do with anything. Why am I here, I am fine, but thanks, thanks for seeing me. Breaking the ice is always tough, she says, be sure to come back in a week, we've already made great progress.

Great. And I'm out the door, crying all the way down the Elysian Fields to the Monoprix, crying down to the women's section, crying flicking through the racks of PJs. The Elysian Fields Monop' doesn't have such a good changing room, and I have to wait, so I cry and look at baby clothes, crying at how quickly the Chunk has grown, crying that she is no longer a baby, that she doesn't fit into these things, that she wore that little onesie once, that she smelt like Mustela baby wash.

The psychologist is annoying, I don't have time for this, the point is to build myself up, not to cry, to fall. The idea is to gather strength, to move ahead. She insists you can't move forward without ironing out the knots. I go two more times.

The psychologist fired me because I cancelled at the last minute, and this time it wasn't even the right day. I tried to explain to her how the reason I hadn't turned up was the exact reason I need her more than ever but she didn't buy it. Now I need to see the psychologist to counsel me about feeling so bad about trying to cancel her on the wrong day and her thus firing me and me getting upset about it.

A flooring fatigue pins me to the bed. The psychologist's anger at me, I couldn't do my job, she has left me now, I am alone. I curl my body up tight and squeeze to make the thoughts stop.

Take me to the asylum. *Lazy bitch.* Take me to the white room, with the white sheets, the silence, strip me and take everything away. *What about people who are really sick.* Lock me up. *Crazy bitch.* Solitary confinement. Feed me moosh. *What about the people who are actually starving, ungrateful bitch.* I think I'm depressed. I should go on antidepressants. *They're artificial substances. They have side effects. Maybe don't even work. You have to go and see a psychiatrist to get the prescription, and you can't even show up to appointments.* Just go for a run. *It's cold outside.* Do some yoga. *Can't be bothered.* Meditate. *Can't concentrate.* Go for a walk, get yourself together. *Can't be among people.* Maybe I should kill myself. *You'd really do that to her? To them?* I think I want to leave my family. *You long for them every moment you're away from them, and also when you're with them.* Maybe if I just go away for a bit. *How dare you. Your child needs you. And remember how much you missed them?* Maybe if I straightened my hair. *Yes, cover up how ugly you are.* I think it's just men. *Yeah, it's men. Men are shit.* But he is so patient and doesn't even show his frustration at me. He is kind and loving. *Yeah but he reads* The Paris Review *when there are clothes to put away.* Maybe it's PMT. *There is no such thing as PMT. Only truth.* Is this the truth then? *Yes. This is the true you.* But I don't always feel like this. Soon I will feel alright again. *Yeah, soon you'll be all love and your husband will look at you like, Phew, that's over, and be sceptical of your affection and then finally open up just before the true you returns and bites him again. Soon he'll get tired of it, you know, not love you anymore, he'll find someone better.*

I tell Kiki about my symptoms, the neck pain, the panic attacks. She is worried. I don't tell her of the desire that comes over me sometimes to throw myself in front of the métro, but I think she can feel it. I just can't find the answers, can't see what's in front of me, all I can do is work and work and pretend and pretend and try and try.

She tells me about a guy she went to see once in London, a huge, wrestler-like man from the Balkans, a registered GP who does something called 'bioregulatory medicine', which takes everything into account – what you are in your head and your mind and your body – and practises not only medicine but massage, needles, talking; he takes every aspect of your life into his therapy. It takes a while. He helped her get over her ex-husband.

But I'm not getting over anything, I say, I'm just fucked up from too much work.

I call him anyway. He has a big warm voice, gruff and direct and I feel instantly at home. I thought we'd make an appointment or perhaps, if he was coming to Paris, I could see him then, but he spends a whole hour asking me questions about my life. Taken by surprise, I answer him. Being on the phone makes it all feel anonymous. At the end of the hour he says, Keep going, you're OK, you don't need to see me, but call me if things don't improve, and hangs up. He doesn't charge me or anything.

OK then. I'm OK. I just have to get my shit together.

Masculin Féminin

How she imagines he saw the night

Thought I'd do something different. Surprise her. She loves surprises. When we lived in Paris together in rue des Annelets, Sundays were lovers' days. That was, and still is, one of the things I like most about Paris – Sundays are Sundays, you walk, go to the markets, no work happens. If it was cold we'd put on heavy clothes and scarves and hats, and if it was hot we'd bring extra layers just in case it got cooler later. We'd hold hands and walk all day, happy in our grimy sneakers, happy just to be together.

So tonight I thought, rather than booking somewhere for dinner, I'll take her out and we'll do lovers' day, walk, talk, and see where we end up.

Big mistake. I could tell as soon as we left the flat. I said we were going to the Left Bank and she assumed I'd arranged something over there. Odd, she said, we never go over there. But her face was flushed, and she was excited to get out of the house, to put on a dress. It's been a long time, and getting out of the house is an effort. I could see us both, as we prepared to escape, thinking, Why are we doing this to ourselves, it would be much easier just to stay in. But we need this, we are distant. I thought I could close the gap.

It was a cold night. It had been mild but there'd been a cold snap and the evenings were like ice. She had a nice dress on – the gold one she bought in a sale – under her coat, without stockings, imagining I suppose, in retrospect, she'd be going for a short walk from the warm métro to a warm restaurant, eating warm food, then enjoying the burst of briskness back to the warm carriage or perhaps a taxi home.

I said, Let's get off at Odéon, and we got off and stood on the island in the middle of the street. Which way? she said, looking around, teeth chattering.

Oh god. Sometimes I think something is great all the way up to the second I realise it's not, it's the opposite of great.

She looked as though she was going to kill me. Kill me. She is a control freak. These days everything is measured, everything worked out in advance, and if something goes wrong, even a little thing, she loses it. Look at her now. Trying to act like it's OK. Right, OK then, which way? That way? Good. And we walked down the Boulevard Saint-Germain in the light but icy wind. On our lovers' walks we'd often go to l'Avant Comptoir, the little stand-up place. I didn't really want to take her there, I wanted to stumble upon something new, but it is really good and I knew it would make her happy so we walked/ stormed there, but it was stuffed to the gills. I thought we might be able to stand and have a croquette and a few bits of ham with a glass of wine, like we used to, but the dude just looked out the window at us apologetically. Au Comptoir, next door, was full too, of course. Aren't we having a great time? I asked, to try to diffuse the mood. She gave a tight grin, and her eyes looked somewhere else, that thing she does where her eyes glaze over and she is gone.

This is hell, I knew she was thinking. And I was in hell too. Does she think she's alone? In hell? I should have booked somewhere, I know that now, but couldn't she see what I was trying to do? What I'm still trying to do? Often she'll be like this about an idea of mine. She won't want to go. To a gig, say, or a show. She never wants to go to a party, but will be the last one to want to come home. I have to drag her sometimes to places, and so often she'll say to me after, Thank you so much for encouraging me to come! I absolutely loved it.

She often hates albums the first moment she hears them. Now I wait ... wait ... until a few days later when it's, Play that song for me? And I'll play it. Then she'll go around promoting it to everyone like she heard it first. It doesn't bother me. I think it's funny and kind of sweet. It's just her.

But that's the reason I am here, on the boulevard in the knife-icicle wind, the reason she is huddled and marching to nowhere, glancing occasionally at me for direction. If I get this right, even after the terrible start, she will forget all this and celebrate me and celebrate us, and we'll be back, things will come back, we'll be back there like the lovers on the lovers' days, and we'll be happy.

She loves it when I take control. She has this idea that we were always equal, even – like, genderless. That before the baby we were just two friends doing things together. But she loves being female. When we first met, the thing she loved most about me – and she says this all the time – was how I surprised her, how I took her places, how I didn't need to be looked after, the way I took charge of my own life in Paris, the way I made decisions and led things. She's always contradicting herself. She says she wants us to have no gender but then she wants so bad for me to be the big man, to earn, to take her places, to prove myself a big, worthy male, a father, a big, worthy father. She doesn't know what it is she wants. God she is ugly tonight. It is amazing how attractive she can be and how, when she is angry or in this mood, this foul mood, her face turns hard, her cheeks go kind of stiff. She looks harsh, meaty, her eyes little beads, her mouth tight. You look like you hate me, I will say sometimes, when I am telling her something. She will say, Oh god, I was just listening, that's my resting face. Resting bitch *face. I don't believe her. I know the difference between resting face and hating face.*

None of these restaurants are good enough. Now we're in the touristy part around the rue de Seine, she is giving me a look: What on earth were you thinking? Now she is on the phone to Claire, can she recommend anything on the Left Bank? Of course Claire can't. We're on the <u>Left Bank</u>. Well let's just walk back over to the Marais. Great. A word that can be said in so many ways. The way she says it – great – is dark, but not so dark as to not be pleasant, she doesn't want to be the one who ruined the party by being a bitch, yet she is a bitch, she might as well stop trying to cover it up.

I do feel sorry for her. She is exhausted. She might cry.

I am enjoying the night. It's cold over the bridge but so lovely. I grab her hand and try to stop for a second but she kisses me back with cold, tight lips and says, I'm literally freezing, can we just keep moving? So we walk to the Philosophes. Full. Same with Petit Fer à Cheval. So we go to the guy's third and dullest restaurant, L'Étoile Manquante, which is empty. It is always easy to get a table here, I don't know why, it's the same menu in all his restaurants, and it's not ugly or anything. It's one of her 'toilet restaurants' because it's never busy and they don't mind if you run in and use the bathroom without buying anything.

We sit down the back. Nobody here but a few tables of tourists. She sighs, pulling off her coat and leaning over the table to look at the menu close up like there's an ant on it. I can see the top of her head, her centre part that is innocent, not the face I can't see, squashed into the menu. It's like she's been through an ordeal. She could at least be a bit grateful. So I fucked up. I tried. I went for gold rather than a safe bronze. If I'd nailed it, I'd be her hero right now, she'd be kissing my mouth. She orders the poulet and I get a steak. She is bored, this is not a date night. This is two adults trying to be kids, this is a place we'd have sat with glee on a lovers' day, down here at the back, grateful to be able to afford two whole meals rather than share one, our whole day, our whole lives ahead of us.

Her face has softened slightly. She still can't look in my eyes.

Well, this is nice, she says. She doesn't mean it to come out sarcastic, or does she. You can see she doesn't know what to say. I don't think she's meaning to be a bitch, but she can't help it, and that is making her even more frustrated.

They have tarte tatin tonight, I say. I can reserve one.

OK, she says.

We clink glasses.

How she saw the night

I will fucking kill him. I want to take him and roll him in mud and drop him into the Seine. NO BOOKING? I am a constantly starving overworked BITCH and if I don't have FOOD in a WARM ENVIRONMENT at the GIVEN TIME OF EIGHT O'CLOCK LIMIT NINE I will murder a RAT in the SEWER and EAT IT WHOLE I am huddled in my coat and my mind is SPINNING ARE YOU SERIOUS WHAT CITY DO YOU THINK WE LIVE IN ON A THURSDAY NIGHT OR ANY NIGHT YOU HAVE TO BOOK A TABLE I BOOK FIVE DIFFERENT RESTAURANTS AND CANCEL FOUR ON THE NIGHT DEPENDING ON WHICH ONE FEELS MOST RIGHT BASED ON MOOD, WEATHER, TIME ALLOTTED, PREVIOUS MEALS, SEXUAL ENERGY what did you think we would just wander hand in hand in the FREEZING COLD I need to eat or I will die DON'T TAKE ME ON A DATE AND HAVE NOTHING PLANNED I DON'T UNDERSTAND HOW YOU COULD NOT UNDERSTAND ME IT MAKES ME WANT TO CRY CAN'T YOU SEE HOW HARD I AM WORKING AND HOW HARD IT IS TO EXTRICATE MYSELF FROM THE CHUNK AND HOW MUCH I NEED THIS TO BE PERFECT OR EVEN JUST GOOD DON'T

LOOK AT ME DON'T MAKE ME THE BAD GUY DON'T MAKE ME THE BITCH JUST LET ME DISAPPEAR INTO A HOLE
 DON'T
 LOOK AT ME

Tarte tatin does soften the mood slightly, and we do talk a little towards the end. Small talk. Neither of us will say it, dare speak it. We are fraying. I can see in his eyes that he knows it, this is not working. We are not working. He is not working, his music is not working, though it *is* working, the band is *working*, but I am tired, we are tired, and we can't speak to each other now, we can't reach each other, to speak it is to lose, or to give it all up, and neither of us is ready for that, but we don't know how to heal it.

Neither of us talk of the bad date night. We go back to our usual routine, working, looking after the Chunk, it's not important, we get into a rhythm, mechanical, but with the same outward affection and care as always, juggling time and the Chunk, eating and drinking our 7 pm wine together. Months pass. The weather eventually starts to warm up and the windows are opened and the sounds of parties and drinkers on the terrasses below start to fill the night air again.

On the night of the Fête de la Musique, M and I tag team: he goes out in the afternoon and comes back home at 10 pm with bright eyes and a sweaty face, telling me to have fun and not come home until at least dawn. I'm wearing the gold dress again that I found in a sale bin at Claire's favourite dress shop, the best dress I've ever owned. It is gold with silver stripes across it and pockets, and comes just to the right length to be both sexy and comfortable. I feel good in it, like a person I want to be. Like a Parisian that goes out at night and lives their life. M draws me to him in the doorway and we kiss, then he pulls away to send me off with an admiring look. I stroll out into the crowded streets full of sound and bodies.

Tess the magazine editor and Valentin and some friends of ours who live around the canal are at the Pointe Poulmarch, dancing to a calypso band around a street pole with a bunch of other friends I don't know. Claire has gone to find drinks, and when she arrives we dance, then squeeze our way up the canal. She's been around République and the Marais and says it was too crazy, too many people, here is better, we should stay. It's too hot to dance and my heels are stupid on the cobblestones and my gold dress itches but I drink as much as I can and move to the blend of music coming from all around me and across the city. A group of young guys in shorts are jumping off the bridge of Atmosphère and we stop to watch and take photos. I have had enough already. Claire is nowhere in sight, and I strike up a conversation with Tess's Argentinian friend, who it turns out lives in the Récollets.

You should see his studio, Tess says. Hard to believe it's the Récollets.

I made the studio mine, he says.

What did you do with it?

Wanna see?

Sure, I say.

Anything to get out of here. And I don't want to go home, it's only been an hour.

As we walk up the canal I discover he's a writer. I tell him I am too, well not a real one, a copywriter, trying to write a book. He is a real one: he's published a few books, and plays, and short stories. His English is ridiculously good.

His studio is in the artists' building, right on the corner, looking back over the park. It feels like no Récollets room I've been in, and I've lived in four now. He has taken out the cheap fittings in the kitchen, installed a proper benchtop, and put in a full-sized fridge, oven and cupboards. The standard plastic chairs and cheap tables are nowhere to be seen – the open-plan part of his space is filled with elegant, comfortable sofas around a designer coffee table. There's a beautiful worn dining table along the wall overlooking the park, and – the best thing – the other two high walls are filled with bookshelves that reach right up, with ladders. The mezzanine bedroom sits above the ladder and I wonder if you can climb all the way up and over the wall. He hears my thinking and says, Come and see the bedroom, gesturing towards the stairs. I climb up in the way I've always been accustomed, like a wildcat – the stairs are slippery and it's the safest way.

Somehow he has made that space into a real grown-up bedroom too.

This is ridiculous, I say.

I know, he says, smiling.

Do you plan to live here forever?

Maybe.

They don't let you.

Well, then it will be for someone else. Besides, there are a few who have been here for years and years.

Really?

Anyway, I don't want to stay forever.

Why not?

I don't know. It's not forever.

I would want to stay here forever.

I like your dress.

Thanks, I say. It's my golden boy.

I climb down to look at his bookshelf. He pulls out the books he's written. His arms are long and dark. He must be in his late forties, possibly older. The books are intelligent, academic. I've never heard of them.

He brings in a bottle of wine and lets me have one of his cigarettes, which I smoke at the window, though I don't have to.

Is it comfortable? he asks. The dress?

It is, but it's a bit itchy. Like it has tinsel in it or something.

You can take it off if that's more comfortable.

I smile. No thanks.

I should leave, but I don't. I know he's harmless and I'm safe in the Récollets and I'm enjoying being out and feeling like a young person again. He pours the wine into two glasses on the table and I sit down on the leather sofa and kick my shoes off, curling my legs up. I wonder if I'm leaving sweat on his couch. I don't care.

What's it like to be published?

What's it like to be sexy?

Ugh, I'm out of here.

I'm just teasing. But why don't we?

Because I don't want to.

Why not?

Because I'm not interested.

Why not?

I'm not sure. I like my husband.

He laughs. You like your husband?

Yes. I like him.

So you want to be faithful to him?

No. I don't care about being faithful. What about you? Aren't you married?

Yes, but I will still fuck you.

Do you do that a lot?

It's fine.

Does she know?

She doesn't.

And how does that make you feel?

Fine. I don't think it matters. She is working in Stockholm. I live here for now.

Do you love her still?

Yes.

But you fuck others.

Yes. And you are a good girl.

I'm not a good girl at all.

But you're being a good girl.

No I'm not.

Yes you are.

No I'm not. I actually feel rebellious.

Why did you get married?

Because I liked him. Loved him, actually. And it felt crazy to do something like that. To rebel against my own rebellion. What about you?

I just got married.

Do you feel stifled?

No. But I need affairs.

Will you break up with your wife?

No. I don't think so. I don't know.

I guess marriage doesn't fundamentally matter. I'm not *not* wanting to fuck you because I don't want to be unfaithful. I actually don't want to fuck anyone much right now. But my husband is the only one I do want to fuck.

Would you fuck me if you weren't married?

Maybe. I don't know. I would probably still rather talk about books.

(A pause.) He sounds like a great guy.

Asshole.

I just think you're more traditional than you think.

Maybe you're the one who's traditional.

How so?

Maybe it's radical not to cheat.

He laughs.

Maybe it's radical to get married. Maybe it's radical to be a housewife.

He laughs again.

At uni I worked in this bar with all these students, radical thinkers, artists. This girl started waitressing, and all she wanted was to marry her boyfriend and start having children. We were dumbfounded. Then I realised how radical she was. A radical feminist. Because she was doing exactly what she wanted. She didn't feel ashamed. It was shocking, more shocking than any slut behaviour.

So it's radical to be boring?

It's radical to do what you want even though it is something society perceives as safe.

You're just making excuses to stay in the safety of convention.

You want to think that because me making my own choice is threatening to your masculinity. You need to tell yourself that the only reason I won't fuck you is because I'm a domesticated wifeling.

Perhaps.

You're good-looking. You're a writer. Successful. If I was going to cheat on my husband or fuck someone for fun, it would be with someone like you. It's interesting to me, my lack of desire for that. Sorry if I gave you the wrong impression, but it was never going to happen. I literally came to talk about writing. I can see that's not going to happen.

Let's talk about writing then.

Do you think your wife fucks other people?

No.

How do you know?

I just know.

Do you think she knows about you?

I think she probably knows but won't admit it.

Would she be upset? Would she leave you?

Yeah.

And that doesn't bother you?

No.

I think you're not happy. I think you're trapped.

I think you're delusional. You're not alive.

So the only way to be alive is to abandon yourself to someone else's lust?

No, it's to abandon yourself to the moment and what you really want. The experience.

The experience I want is to live fully inside what I've got, inside my choices. I've made a good choice, I'm fairly sure of that. I don't believe in monogamy at all, but I do feel a sense of desire to honour what it is I have, and what I truly love. I keep thinking I'm going to leave this room, but I'm using you now, to get my thoughts straight.

I don't mind, he says, sliding back onto his couch, surrendering, finally.

I should go.

OK.

He lights a joint and hands it to me and I lie back on my couch too, both of us looking at the same wall.

Are you lonely, then? I ask.

Isn't everybody?

A long pause. He pours more wine.

It does disturb me, to feel right and good, I say. Married, a mother, faithful, Christian-like. I think I'm unique, modern, but I'm basically the same as my foremothers. Worse probably, as I don't think they liked their husbands.

You're a pure wife. A natural-born, pure wife.

Yes. Wow. I never set out to be. I told my husband from the start if he found something he wanted he should go for it.

Maybe that's why it works. The freedom.

But you don't have that.

I don't think we like each other that much.

So it's the convention that keeps it wrong and dangerous. If the convention isn't there it's not such a big deal to fuck around. You're actually more conventional than I am.

He laughs. Perhaps.

I feel like a rebel just loving my husband. Not that I'm doing a good job of that now. I'm a horrible, dissatisfied person to live with.

That's not rebelling.

I think it is. For me anyway. It would be easy for me to cut out. I don't know, I might. I give myself total freedom to leave – him too. Though we're married, I make it clear he owes me nothing. He says I owe him nothing either. So I'm free. Free to do what I like. He's not me, he doesn't own my life. It feels wilder and sexier to stay with him. To try and figure out how to love him.

You don't love him?

I love him and I like him. I like him in the way that, when you're a child, you like another boy or girl. I like him. He's my boyfriend, my friend. I like who he is and I want to know him more. My god, if he could hear me talking to you now. He thinks I don't like him at all, I think. I love him too. But at the moment it's like I *can't* love. I'm drowning. Perhaps that's it. I'm sticking with my friend for now. Not because I don't want to hurt him. Not because I'm denying myself something. Just because that's what I want.

You're not a feminist.

Yes I fucking am.

The weed softens my brain, my outline disappears into the couch. We lie in silence.

Perhaps I'm just afraid to feel anything again, I eventually say.

He doesn't reply. When I look over he has fallen asleep. I get up and leave the building, the familiar smell of the hallway and the stairwell catapulting me back to studenthood, the days I'd walk in or out like this, freshly fucked, drunk or high, lost.

I walk back down the canal like I used to when I couldn't sleep, and sit on the edge of it, watching people dance. The bridge-jumpers are gone, it's 3 am, things are winding down. Drunks and ravers and stumblers. I want to go home right now, I want to see

M, feel his sleeping body, roll it over towards me. I haven't felt this feeling in so long I want to savour it. A couple approaches and sits down next to me, laughing loudly, and I stand and walk slowly up the rue Beaurepaire to Répu, and along the rue du Château d'Eau towards home, where M rolls towards me, sensing both love and nowhereness.

Class

In the middle of a work rush my phone rings. I wouldn't normally answer while working, but it's a particularly tricky translation and I need a break, so I answer: Allô, c'est Jayne.

M is rolling up his guitar leads and I prop myself on his window ledge, kicking at him gently as he leans into me, falling back in between my knees. I sniff his scalp. Someone is rambling away, I can't hear her properly, work, a meeting, can I come out and meet the team …

Non, désolée, I say abruptly, I can't take on any more work, and coming out to the suburbs is not possible …

She keeps talking, I add perfunctory *mm-hmms* and *ouis*, more interested in watching the deliberate way M handles his equipment, lining up his pedals in the case, laying down the guitar, pulling out plugs … then as I go to hang up, something in the caller's tone makes me ask, Sorry where were you calling from again?

She is calling from the number-one luxury brand of all time. *Class*. The eponymous, the timeless.

I jump down, backtracking wildly, Ouiouioui of course I can come, sorry, I didn't hear where you were from.

It's OK, says the smooth female voice.

She lives nearby, in the Cour des Petites Écuries. We arrange to meet the following day at Chez Jeannette and I hang up, turning to M.

It's our Lucky Strike.

The next day a thin young woman in a shirt and black jeans is sitting at one of the rickety front tables at Jeannette. She has an espresso, Grég brings me un allongé, and she cuts straight to it.

As she speaks, I remember studying, at the theatre school just a few doors down, the physicality of status. The higher the status the more immobile and silent – buddha, gurus, gods… The lower the status the more gesture and sound – the drunkard, the peasant, the lunatic. Irène is the highest of high status: her olive skin seemingly bare, her clothes well-cut without flare or flounce, her brown hair loose and unfussed-over. A line of vibrant blue on her top eyelid is the only mark of fashion or creativity – and, as it's the only flourish, it stands out. She speaks in a gentle voice as though she has no need or use for passion, or to dilute what is in her by letting any of it out, to waste on me, this lively bar. Perhaps high status is acceptance that you cannot alter the dynamic of a space, or its people, or at least you shouldn't try.

The brand has a dilemma. Since it began, silence has been their way. They have simply photographed their products and clothes, and put their name to them, and the name has spoken for itself. But times have changed. Now, with social media, they are losing market share. It's not possible anymore not to speak. Their silence is reading as dusty and old-fashioned, so they need to learn their tone of voice, and create universal English copy that speaks in their way, which is, not to speak.

A few days later, I am in the office of Irène's creative director, Anne-So, a tanned fifty-something woman, stylish to a point of intimidation. She looks me up and down, approves of my minimal style – black duster jacket, black jeans, black top ... Black makes it harder to see the cheapness. She is excited, she says. She can already tell I'm going to capture their tone. It won't be easy, she says, we've never done this before.

The voice must be simple and true. *Juste*. No fancy palaver, no puns or flowery turns-of-phrase. No word plays, no cleverness, it needs to be translatable from English into a gazillion languages. Straight, elegant, a little black dress.

I try to speak as little as I can, keep my face still, like a man, nod. I am ready for this job.

To celebrate, we get Bastien to babysit and go across to tiny Vivant Cave, the new, more relaxed place next to fancy Vivant in the old art nouveau boulangerie on Petites Écuries.

Vivant means alive and living, and I feel alive tonight, facing M in his beaten-up jacket and shirt, his face fresh, eyes shining. I am wearing the golden boy. I feel alive. I feel *vivant*. M and I drink champagne and look into each other's eyes. No tears. This is living, this is it, we are arriving, we are almost there.

M has come here a few times and knows the Swedish chef and is proud to order food from him and wine from the laid-back sommelier. We laugh now about the bad date night, it has become a great source of craic. Now he delights in seeing me happily seated at a table he arranged, watching my face as I try the things that look simple but are so rich with flavour. A dish of what looks like plain spaghetti and cheese constantly opens out into new flavours, like Willy Wonka's gobstopper.

M is beaming. He says now I can cut back on the last-minute and underpaid jobs that take so much time, but I argue there's no way, what if Class pulls the pin tomorrow, or if any of the other clients do? For now I'll keep going. He looks nervous, but I say it's fine, the feeling of having this one big client will change the way I approach the others, I'll be more calm and less desperate to impress, though I know inside myself that won't happen. I've become a perfectionist. Not because I care but because, if I get it perfect the first time, there is less feedback and the job is done quicker. And the quicker the job is done, the quicker I can clear the next, and the sooner we can get to the Empyrean and be who we really want to be.

He puts his hand on mine. I feel a sense of peace come over me. A clarity. For now, it's time to bury the desire to write. Cut it out. Stab it. Drown it. Suffocate it. Set it on fire. It's brought nothing but frustration, exhaustion. It's time to grow up, be responsible. I put it in a drawer in my mind. I can't do it. I give up. I am tired of being tired and tired of being frustrated. I want to live, in harmony, with this city, with M, with the Chunk. I still love it here every day and am grateful beyond belief. We renewed M's visa a while ago for another three years and it's not long until we can apply for residency. The Chunk will get her passport after all.

We can live here in Paris, I will be a good mother, good wife, use the spare time I have to take pleasure in my family and the city, rather than jamming writing into every corner, the frustration only growing. Look, it's done, I cut it out, *snip*.

I will just take photos for now, and notes, in my phone or wherever, pieces of the city, for the day I sit down, and reflect, and write, even if it's when I'm dead.

It's better this way.

> Early summer uniform, Paris
> Man: loose blazer, slim jeans, trainers
> Woman: short jacket, loose pants, sandals
> Parisians don't walk and eat
> Walk and text
> Step in shit, you're a tourist

THE SEA IN THE METRO

                        Old people dancing in squares
                        Tango classes in République
A woman just stopped me in the street and said, My haemorrhoids hurt, it pinches
        I cut her hair at the front for the first time
        She looks like Lloyd from *Dumb and Dumber*
A man standing outside the mairie yesterday, orating passionately in a booming voice. He couldn't feel the ice-cold step beneath his bare, blackened feet
    The meal you were trying to make look nicer always somehow looks shittier than the one you were carelessly making for yourself
                Seriously wondering what life might be like on the Left Bank ... Is that a late-thirties thing?
      Testing how long one can last with dry shampoo
  I see flowers
      I washed my handbag
The favourite activity of the little girl's favourite cartoon pig was jumping up and down in muddy puddles.
The cartoon pig lived on a hill somewhere in the English countryside.
The little girl lived on one of Paris's grimier streets.
The puddle lived outside the New Morning jazz club.
The puddle was composed of many things.
The little girl was wearing little pink sneakers and little blue pants and little grey socks with tiny flowers sewn in them.
The little girl was wearing the week's piss and spit and cigarette butt and ash and perhaps some sewage and probably some old coffee and a few old chips. Not to mention the centuries-old grime and plague and dead ants and spew and grease and rat fur and beer funk.

The little girl was delighted.
The little girl's face crumbled upon perceiving the shock of passers-by.
The little girl's eyes spilled over as her mother rushed to pull her out saying I'm so sorry darling, but you mustn't jump in puddles! Puddles aren't always puddles.
The little girl tried to understand.
The smell of my own cake is making me gag. How can so many right ingredients go so wrong?
    If you stop at one child are you letting the team down?
        Betty Blue cuts her
        own eye out when she
        can't have a baby, his
        only way to set her free
        is with a pillow
    Can you live in the city and in the sea at the same time?
Sun in Paris really does change everything
Two young Parisian men, eating their burgers with knives and forks
    Can someone please lobotomise the
    Frozen songs from my head?
I can't LIVE like this anymore! says three-year-old in the rain
    She just farted and blamed the character on the iPad
    Boulevard des Italiens: one man rummaging in
    a bin, one man asleep on cardboard box
Bibimbap, so hot right now
Rue Saint-Denis: I can't tell who's a prostitute and who's here for fashion week
I buy cabbage again from the marché Saint-Martin.
White and red, to make the okonomiyaki, but a while later I throw it out.
I buy it again.
White and red.

There it sits.
M says, Oh god you bought chou again.
Yes, I'm going to make okonomiyaki.
I don't make it
and I throw it out
and a while later
I buy it again

                        Rilke wondered if Paris was somewhere
                        people came to live, or to die
      Just wrote the word disencouraged and looked at it for ten
      minutes. Losing English at rate of knots
          I used to put moisturiser on my legs
          Now I can't be bothered
          I remember Mum just getting tired of it and giving up
Getting fat ... on beurre la baratte
          Can any couple actually watch the end of *Amour* together?

Old photo used as a bookmark. A motionless merry-go-round against a clear, starless night. Streetlights in the distance, poking through the thick trees of La Villette. Summer. The streetlights illuminate the gold in the lacework around the old fairground ride. We had ridden our bikes, then stopped and chained them to a pole to walk a bit. In the middle of the park was a still, quiet manège. The babysitter cost ten euros an hour. We were running late, but we stopped for a second.

    Keep smiling when you order the same coffee from the same
    man every morning, even though he is closed off. He might
    be your age and have a nice face and it might be hard that he
    is so shut off, but keep smiling and say, Have a nice day. Don't
    let it get to you.
    Smiles are for tourists and idiots, Valentin will say.

Smile anyway. Smile again the next day and say, Bonjour, and don't say anything more than that (nothing idiotic about weather, traffic, politics, et cetera). Just enjoy the feeling of the words curling and exiting your mouth. Keep them sounding nice, but don't try too hard. Don't take it to heart that for thirty-six weeks you have come in and ordered the same coffee and his face hasn't cracked in any hint of recognition.

Keep ordering, keep being polite. You may say, Bonne journée, or, Bon week-end, depending on the occasion, but don't say, Bonne fin de journée – that's subservient, and comes off as passive aggressive or even patronising. Know your place. The precise edge upon which you sit.

Keep plugging away, day after day. Smile, speak, exit.

And then –

yesterday –

the tiny muscles in the face will start to ease a little, the faraway hint, not of a smile, but a certain warmth. And that tiny hint will feel as warm as the first hint of sun after a long Paris winter. You want to bask naked in the warmth of that sun – it engulfs you entirely.

And then –

today –

a slightly dropped shoulder, a distant echo of a hint of an invitation at friendship that will come in two centuries, when you will walk in and he will just start making your coffee and drop a comment about the idiot cool hotdog joint that just opened up across the road and how much the area is changing and how cold it's been – seems like forever! – and did you go away for the summer?

And the Wednesday siren will sound and the distant echo of a walking brass band will float through the office window,

rich, sad and serene. It's the two old men, in their tatty clothing and bare feet, walking down the rue Richer as they do each month, in solemn procession, a small amp blaring a backing track to accompany their melancholy song.
And you will open the window and listen and breathe
And think
Fuck I love this fucking city.

My phone got stolen, another one, so I spend the day at the police station on the rue de Chabrol, watching the two women behind the counter dealing with things more important than me, such as phone calls to their friends and discussions with one another. That feeling of constantly wanting to remind them that I'm here, that I exist, though I know that they know full well that I am here but they don't see me, don't care about me, don't care that this is the fourth iPhone I've had stolen, don't care that M did the 'find my iPhone' thing and found himself outside a block of flats calling out, I know you're in there FILS DE PUTE – his favourite new insult – son of a whore – and an elderly man leaned out the window and swore back before pulling his curtains tightly shut. He was in there, the fils de pute, the salopard, but there was nothing to be done, said the cops, it happens all the time – because of apartment buildings and door codes, people can't be found. Even if you get in, the tracing isn't accurate enough to show you the correct door, and even then they'd just deny it.

It was my fault anyway. I'd put it by my side, beside my hand, as I watched the Chunk play in the Récollets Park with my hawk eyes. It was there, then it wasn't. Nobody saw anything, said anything. This lonely feeling of being surrounded by people and yet so alone, like the world is mocking you.

In the late afternoon, fielding calls and emails from my laptop, I give up and walk to the office the long way, past the vintage shops of the rue Condorcet, noticing their prices have suddenly gone up.

I need winter boots, and I remember once buying some here for twenty euros that I wore for years. My old acting agent's office is around here, I wonder if she's forgotten me yet. How long ago it seems since I sat there, begging for work as an actor here, a career, her telling me to marry Adrien.

M is in the office, working away, headphones on. I tell him about the police and he clenches his jaw and breathes out. It annoys him how I lose things. He has never lost a single phone. Is it that nobody dares try it with him? Or is he just more careful? A few weeks ago, mounting the stairs at Pont Neuf, on my way to a voiceover on the Left Bank, a group of refugees asked me to sign a petition for them and as I read the sheet I felt a strange pressure on my left side and turned around: a guy's hand was in my pocket. I spun sharply and he retracted his arm, looking ashamed. He was so embarrassed that I just looked at him sadly and walked away, but I suspect he would never have tried that with M. Would M have sensed the person sneaking up to take his phone as he sat watching his child? Known the papy frotteur next to him on the métro was not just a creepy old man but a foil for his mate, already a carriage ahead with your precious device?

I find myself seething, as though being me is not enough punishment, and collapse in my chair. Just be more careful, I hear him say, is it in my head or did he say it for real? It doesn't matter, I know what he's thinking, and I hate myself, and I am also angry at the injustice. We say nothing, just work away for the rest of the afternoon. I hit a rare patch of quiet and run out to pick up the Chunk from school, tripping on the pavement on the rue des Petites Écuries and landing embarrassingly on my knees. As I brush myself off, grateful Steve Saint-John isn't passing, I look up and notice two black caryatids. A male and a female. It's the first time I've seen a man and a woman like that. They are spaced apart, on either side of the porte cochère. Neither has legs. She, to the right, has both breasts exposed, and is swathed in cloth, one arm wrapped protectively around her body, the other reaching up to her hair, which is covered in cloth and a wreath. The male is reflective, holding a long object covered in flowers, wings coming out his ears. He's an angel. He holds his opposite arm up to his head in mirror to hers. They are looking away from each other, not in a playful way. They've had a fight. They hate each other.

The Chunk is overjoyed to see me at the gate and I take her for Orangina at the window table at the Napoléon.

Is it hard being a mama? she asks randomly, after a conversation about the Barbapapas. In her favourite Barbapapas book, the blob-like creatures' beautiful, rambling home is demolished and they have to move into a tiny apartment, *but Barbapapas aren't made for apartments*, so they take off into the wild. The Chunk's favourite part is when Barbamama turns herself into a tent to protect the babies. She's been fascinated lately with mamas, asking all kinds of questions about mine and M's and about when she will become one, in Tinyland.

Yes, I say. Very hard. You're always making food, cleaning up, washing your kids, picking up their toys, trying to teach them to pick up their own toys ...

She looks down at her Orangina.

But being your mama is amazing. I love being your mama. It is the deepest, richest experience of my life.

She plays with her straw. I'm gonna be a GOOD mama, she says. I'm gonna be a best mama.

You will, I bet, I say. Do you think I'm a good mama?

No. You workin' all the time. I won't workin' all the time when I'm a mama.

I'm not working now, I say, smiling. But she's right. I am working now. I am always working. When I'm sitting with her, playing with her, reading with her, my mind is elsewhere, working, thinking of slogans, words, other things.

I try to be with her now. Forget everything else. Dinner tonight, the perfume campaign, the overdue bills, the phone notes I may now have lost. She senses my presence immediately, her being lights up. We play with coins, making patterns with the different sizes. Let it go … My mind softens.

The Natural Order

Sometimes I want to surrender to the natural order of things. Choose the simple, natural life, like François and Thérèse in *Le Bonheur*, their tiny bed, simple space, little children. Do everything to please my family, cook and clean, be a seamstress, be feminine, gentle, give that noble cause everything I am.

Folding M's T-shirts, I notice a black one with white fluff all over it. Carelessness, again. Well, not carelessness. Time-pressedness, which comes from a messy flat and Francine coming for dinner and a rogue white towel and thinking, If they went through together in this load I would have the satisfaction of getting every item of washing done today as opposed to the feeling of the never-ending load. What harm could it do?

But harm it does, again, and I get a lump in my throat because I remember a recent moment when M came up to me holding his favourite long-sleeved black top, misshapen and covered in white gunk. The look I gave him, one that reflected aeons of female repression, repression that doesn't even belong to me. *Jeanne Dielman Jeanne Dielman Jeanne Dielman*. A look entirely undeserved, he takes the lion's share of the 'woman's work'. But I still gave it to him, that look to send shivers down your spine. The look of womanhood towards manhood, fuck you, fuck all you've done to us. I don't know where I got the look from. Maybe my mother when she was feeling used by me and my three siblings as a slave. An awful, loathing look. He quickly walked away.

Putting his T-shirt back in the basket now I feel sad. Because I realise that all the nice female stuff I have inside me that was normally reserved for him and, for example, his washing, I have given entirely to the Chunk since she was born. I hang out her washing with such pride, such love, I make clucky little noises as I delicately lay out each little dress, each pair of tiny underpants. She is clean, I wish she would make more mess, I revel in a yoghurt stain, it means I get to wash it. That's how I used to feel when I hung out M's things. Love. Care. Pride. I liked my female role as the washer of the clothes. He would do it himself, but I don't trust him, he puts pegs in the wrong spots on my clothes, once destroyed a precious top.

I keep thinking back to that time during the menace when I felt the woman in me take over, how sad and confused it made me, how I didn't like it. The inability to fight it, the residue staying with me after the birth. Perhaps I resolved too hard to find that male side of myself again, defend it, never give in to the female drive.

I wonder what it would be like to accept being a woman, what that would mean. Why does it feel a fate worse than death, or death itself? Would it be that bad to take pleasure in caring and tending and washing and baking?

I don't think it's in me. I was born with the rage.

And things don't work out well for Thérèse.

The Chunk tells me there was a tarantula on the wall of the boys' toilet at school today. They all went in to look as Maîtresse Monique 'got him' with a piece of paper.

And took him outside?

Yes, she says. Took him ousside.

She goes on to tell me that the spider hissed at Maîtresse Monique. And she could see the spider's big tongue come out as he hissed.

Do spiders have tongues? Spiders don't have tongues.

Si, spider has tongs.

Well if they do, they're too small to see.

No, this tong, it was big as lapin.

As big as a rabbit's tongue?

Yeah, and the spider she say, Ssssss! wiz 'is tong as Maîtresse Monique get him down.

The bald-faced liar!

No school demain, she says, shaking her head. Spider.

Even the concept of her missing a day of school is impossible. There must be no grey area. My world will fall down if she is away from school, the Jenga tower will fall. If children don't go to school, this whole city falls apart. Tucking them away neatly each day is the only way it can work. But I can't quite feel her at the moment, her lies have been out of control. I love them, but it bothers me she knows I can't verify her outlandish statements. I have to suck them up, trust her.

Spiders in my dreams. Right now, a spider above me. A web across the bed, and the spider directly above my eyes, looking from the threads. It is a large spider, brown, there are patterns on its legs, I see hairs. It's dawn, aubade, the light is dewy on the strands of web and the spider's abdomen. My heart thumps suddenly, I reach across to M.

There is no spider.

But I could see it! I could see its every detail!

M goes back to sleep. I lie stunned. I swear I was awake when I saw the spider. I feel confused, like the guy in *The Science of Sleep*.

I remember years ago going to Louise Bourgeois's rétrospective at the Pompidou with Kiki. Bourgeois was still alive, and I was mostly captivated by the model of her childhood house with the guillotine above it, and the femme-maison models and paintings – especially the marble one of the woman lying down, her head a house. I also stood for a very long time ogling her spider – the one straddling the home-like cage, the sitting-room chair, dedicated like all her spiders to her mother. I thought she'd chosen the spider to represent her mother as a foreboding, terrifying creature, but I later read she chose it because it represented neatness, order, intelligence, patience and self-defence. Her mother was an actual tapestry weaver, it was Louise herself who was preoccupied with unravelling and re-ravelling her emotions and memories.

Her best friend was her mother. Like the filmmaker Chantal Akerman, who took her own life only a few months after her mother died. Her mother had been her muse. When I read of her suicide I understood completely.

Guess what? I say to the Chunk. On Thursday at school they're going to take your photo!

No! she says. I don't want!

I stop brushing her hair. She loves being photographed, more than anything.

Why not? I ask.

It's mine! she says.

I keep brushing. So, you'll all be in a group and they'll take your photo. We'll be able to send it to Grandmama and Grandad and your cousins …

I don't want to! she says with a desperate look. Iss my black photo!

The sun isn't up yet. She is talking nonsense, with that other-worldly edge. At least that's what I tell myself, because it's too early in the morning to acknowledge the truth, which is that there has never been a single shred of nonsense to a single word she has ever said. But a 'black' photo? Her recent string of odd, esoteric comments is also blurring the edges of my judgement. For example, last night:

Which restaurant are you going to, Mama?

Aux Deux Amis.

Oh. When I was a man I used to go there.

Maybe the black photo is something ancestral. I wonder at it for five seconds, then hustle her off to school.

Wednesday comes. She is eating pasta in a tutu. They're going to take your photo tomorrow, I say without thinking. We'd better wash your hair.

Her face crumbles and she starts to really cry. But it's mine the black one! I don wun them to have it!

I don't know what you're talking about, honey, I say. What's the black photo?

It's my black photo! Foncy gave it me!

I suddenly remember the beautiful Eisenstaedt postcard Francine gave her a few months back, of ballerinas in an old Paris studio, because she'd come to watch one day and it reminded her of the room where the Chunk's ballet class takes place, up in the rafters, with the circular windows. The Chunk had been carrying it around ever since, in the bottom of a shabby book bag, showing it to everyone she met before clutching it hard against her chest.

The black-and-white one? Of the ballerinas? I ask.

She nods, tears dripping in her bowl. It's mine!

But what's that got to do with … Oh.

She thinks they're going to take it away.

On Friday, I tell the story to Francine. She's come over to find some of Sido's old baby things, to take over to America. Sido had a boy, and Francine is going over to visit for a month. I don't like that. This family she has. Her own. She's brought champagne of course. I'm not sure why the black photo scenario has gotten to me.

She is protective of something? Francine suggests.

Perhaps it's that. That she would be so afraid that someone would want to take something off her. That she is more afraid, more fragile than I think. I've only ever seen her defiant over her things, never crushed like that.

She is fine, she's a strong little girl.

But I don't know what's going on behind those closed doors! Who she's becoming!

It's OK to worry about her, she says, pouring the champagne. We sit in silence for a moment and I suppress the urge to cry.

I don't know if I'm doing anything right, I say.

Francine smiles and in an unusual gesture, puts her hand on my knee.

It must be hard without your mother, she says, her eyes soft behind her glasses.

I can't imagine what it's like to have one anymore, I say.

I can't imagine what it will be like to lose mine, she says. Even though she's eighty-six I still can't fathom it.

It will probably be harder for you as you've had her so much longer. You'll have so much more to miss.

She looks down at her glass.

There are a lot of great women around that you don't notice as much when your mother is alive, I say, to console her. Then when they're gone, you see it. They come out for you. They form a blanket. A sort of mother figure for you, to guide you.

It's good to be a woman, she says. We get to have that. Women around us. Men don't have that in the same way we do.

No. They don't.

That night I observe M as he makes the dinner, writes in his journal, reads the Chunk Barbapapas. He strikes me as lonely. He has friends, good friends, but I don't think he has the close talk like I do with Claire and Francine. I'm that person for him, I think. I show him some affection, rub his shoulders, kiss his cheek and it ricochets through him like an attack. What's up, he asks, suspicious. Nothing, I say. He smiles, liking it, but unsure.

We've made it. We're leaving the city for a summer vacation, like Parisiens. One whole week in a nice hotel with a small alcove bedroom, with a door. This is what it's about, I realise. Escape. Pleasure. This is what we have been working so hard for.

The Île de Ré is superb. They call it the 21st arrondissement. Since I came to Paris I've dreamed of being a real summer vacationer, leaving the city with the throngs in August, the golden tan, being relaxed, a real French person, Bardot, no work calls, unavailable. Actually I'm not unavailable – I haven't told my clients I'm going away – but I'm hoping the phone won't ring, or I can put off anything that comes in for a week, keep pleasing everyone. We still need the money, I think, I try not to look at our bank balance, just keep working and trust that some day soon I'll poke my head up and, oh, we'll be free.

We hire bikes, one with a little caboose, and ride around the island, stopping at beaches and restaurants, choosing things on the menu without looking at the price first. The Chunk is delighted, she falls asleep in the caboose in the afternoons, we drink wine and eat oysters, this is living.

One day we're at the pretty townlet of Sainte-Marie-de-Ré, eating lunch at an outdoor restaurant in a pretty square. The Chunk is wearing M's sunglasses and a little short suit and we've been riffing ideas for a TV series about a couple raising a kid, filming snippets of ideas on our phones. It feels like the old days. We have time to actually talk and finish a conversation, play around. The Chunk joins a group of kids from the long table beside us and runs off to the playground, further than we've ever let her be from us. She's safe, she's free, she's a child.

M's face has colour in it and his eyes are bright. The sun pounds his forehead and he switches around to sit beside me. We kiss. I try to stay in the kiss but I've taken my eyes off the Chunk too long and though I know she's fine the terror is still there.

She runs back to the table, touches it, then runs off to play again. The other children's lunch arrives and they return to their table, interacting with the adults. They're a family – cousins and aunts and uncles and grandparents. They chatter in French, argue, wipe faces and laugh, distribute food, place napkins. We call the Chunk back to us and she stands awkwardly at our table, not wanting to sit down, her eyes on the other family, her body pointed towards them, as we wait for our own food to distract her.

An uncomfortable feeling comes over us. A certain loneliness. We make our own family wherever we go, yes, and we have such close friends, but it's not the same as that innate family feeling. Does it matter? We always say no, but in this moment something in our bodies says otherwise.

Our food arrives and the Chunk tucks merrily into her fish. She is an only child. A unique child, they say in French. That doesn't seem to bother her. But seeing her alone next to that group of kids sticks in my heart. Are we missing the point, by being here? Can that family feeling ever be replaced? Perhaps it's that we're here without friends, our friend-family here, or perhaps there is something deeper missing, that connection with her own blood. The feeling is deep and complicated, I can see M is feeling it too, and it's tied also into the savage unreconciled past of our homeland, the shame of living on stolen country. Living away gives perspective on everything, the freedom of being unattached, to culture, expectations, uncomfortable family dynamics such as grief. And yet, the undeniable satisfaction rooted in our deepest cells, of those moments she is connected to her blood relations, at a picnic table like that family, running with cousins, sitting on a grandparent's lap. Have we tricked ourselves into thinking that we can raise her effectively, beautifully, without it? In this sunlit square, having arrived at this point we've been dreaming of, striving for, why does it suddenly feel so empty?

The Chunk runs off to play. M puts my exact feelings into words, making them real, but also allowing us to justify our way out of them. Of course we feel that, we're here for the first time, and we haven't spent time like this together in years, we're getting to know each other again. This must be how all migrants feel. Who would we be if we didn't have homeland nostalgia? It's a trick to keep us from spreading our wings, *Revolutionary Road*. We will always have these pangs. It's normal, we're parents, we're human. We're going back at Christmastime.

The wine is crisp. The feeling has passed. The ride through the fields back to the hotel feels majestic. We huddle tight, a little family. We have each other.

Back in Paris it's sweltering and we juggle the Chunk so each of us can work, taking her to the new water fountains in République and letting her splash in the pool around the statue of Marianne, and to the usual spots – the creek, Sandpit Park, Hospital Park. Or we stay in the apartment, with bucket-pools, when the pollution levels are high. There's an app now that shows us when it's PM – Particulate Matter, the worst – or NO – nitrogen dioxide, the kinder pollutant.

One late afternoon we meet Claire and Marie-France and Hakim and their girls for a picnic in the square Léopold-Achille in the Marais. Francine and Jippy come later, rolling up their pants to sit on the edge of the shaded sandpit and play with the children, leaving after a small glass of rosé with us. There is chocolate and the Chunk gets sugar high and throws her clothes off. A photo of M lifting her naked body high above his head, her upside-down face flushed with laughter.

As M and Hakim play with the kids, Marie-France tells Claire and me that they're leaving Paris, moving down to Bordeaux, where her mother lives. I'm shocked, and far more emotional than I should be. Since Île de Ré I've had to work hard to get my resolve back, and until now I've succeeded in convincing myself our trajectory is the right one, that such moments of heartache are just part of the condition of living our best life.

But I thought you were an actress? I say, trying to calm my voice. An intermittente du spectacle? I thought you were living the dream!

I am living my dream, she laughs, explaining how she'll have more time to perform down there, make her own work, form a new theatre company …

But not like in Paris!

It won't be the same, she says, but she'll have a better balance. She can live on her mother's property while they find their own house, the girls will have constant care so she can work on new things, Hakim has transferred his bank job down there, soon there'll be a fast train from Paris. They'll all have a better quality of life.

Quality of *life*? I say. Soon you'll be talking about polished floorboards. Beaux volumes. Hauteur sous plafond. Luminosity. Quality of life … You say that when you're miserable and have to justify things.

Claire smiles and raises her plastic cup to Marie-France. Well, unlike Miss Poopy Pants here, I congratulate you and am sure it will be fabulous. And keep my guest room free, please.

I continue seething, head burning from too much wine in the sun. I thought Marie-France was a real Parisian. I thought she would never leave. I thought she had guts. I thought she was a feminist. Who will she call now to rage about Hakim, his stupid job, his fucking mother? Who will she cry on, saying she's had enough? Who will I call with parenting questions?

I can't believe it, Marie-France, I say. I know you love it here. I know you're doing it for Hakim.

Marie-France is such good craic audience that she doesn't respond, just turns her head to the sun and takes a swig of wine. I can see, though, her jaw tighten.

It's OK Jayne, says Claire, Marie-France is allowed to have her own life. She is French, her mother is down there, her family, it's different.

I thought *we* were family! I choke back tears. You all *leave!* First Kiki, then Nadine, now you Marie-France. Everyone from school, everyone.

To be fair, you left, says Claire. Twice.

Yes but not voluntarily!

I'm not going anywhere, Claire says.

You say that now, but I don't trust you.

Do you not? She smirks.

No, you'll go. You'll all go. Claire, you'll have a kid and go and live in county whatever and never come back.

No, she says, coolly. I'm happy where I am. In all senses.

We'll still see each other, dummy! Says Marie-France. It will be better! You can come for holidays, we'll leave the kids with my mum and go out dancing. Bordeaux is wonderful, you should think about moving there.

J'ai horreur de la province, I sulk, evoking Francine.

We leave before dark, on foot towards home. I feel drained. Stupid. M is oblivious to the argument that just went down. The Chunk is weightless on her trottinette, still naked aside from her green sandals, scooting past the loud cafés and bars, through Sandpit Park and out the other side to face the blinding sun on the rue Notre Dame de Nazareth. The strong light casts her small, cherubic shape into a long, graceful shadow along the pavement.

I think people who leave Paris are pussies, I tell M as we cross beneath the archway at the bottom of the rue du Faubourg-Saint-Denis, past where Angela's Zodiac would have been. People travel the world, adventure, go wild, go free, then they meet someone, get married, have a kid, retreat to the safest place they know. Why is becoming a family so hard that people can't uphold their dreams?

I agree, says M, they're pussies. Testicles.

Do you really?

No. It makes sense. We just want the best for our kids. And life is more complex. Joy is more complex.

I want the best for our kid and I think that's to truly live her life, and to see her parents truly living theirs.

Exactly.

We are, aren't we?

We're certainly giving it a shot.

Yes, and we're getting there.

We're getting there. Do we need bread?

In *Love in the Afternoon*, the final of Éric Rohmer's moral tales, a Paris lawyer called Frédéric is happily married to Hélène, a schoolteacher. Like Francine he hates the countryside, the banlieue. Nothing more bleak, he says, than afternoons out in the suburbs. The idea of quiet happiness depresses him. He loves the impermanence of the city, the youthfulness, how people enter and exit and never grow old. He sees the city like the sea – being carried along in the crowds, along the surface of the water, never engulfed by it, striking when the current is calm. Like the sea, the crowd is invigorating to his wandering mind. He says he wants the impossible, and he knows it. By this I think he means he wants the pretty attractions but not attachments. He loves the sea but doesn't want to be swallowed by it.

The city attracts me for the same reasons: the anonymous feeling, the solitude while feeling connected to everybody, the being part of a fabric composed by so many people. If one person is in a bad mood in the métro it spreads, and if one person smiles at me as I ascend the métro steps I've noticed how I smile at the next person, and so on. They don't know me and I don't know them, but we're alone together. All day long, connections are there to be made, and you can make them whatever you want them to be in your mind. The constant change means the possibilities are endless, and you can be, and imagine anything you want. In the countryside, the suburbs, things are fixed. What if you don't have the imagination to create more? What if it sucks you in, draws you under?

The Great Beauty

Rentrée. The Chunk is in moyenne section now at the Maternal, her teacher is a man called Maître Loïc. Things feel different in the neighbourhood – old laundromats and internet cafés in the rue des Petites Écuries are being replaced by edgy sandwich shops and pop-up bars and vintage boutiques. There's a burger place called Paris New York with a sign that reads *Cheaper than a psychiatrist*. Only just, I say in my head each time I pass, finding myself very funny. They've fixed the sign at the Château d'Eau bar and now young hipsters drink at the tables outside in the afternoons. The Napoléon has new owners and a new sign and is all shiny, they ruined it. They like it modern, buffed, but the burgers are the same at least and the lips are still in the bathroom. Night-time crowds at Chez Jeannette and the Mauri 7 spill out into the street and people moving into the apartments are the kind that complain about the noise.

The Au Bon Porc has disappeared behind boards and planning permits. The Good Pig, the old-school butcher that'd been there forever with its sign displaying the daily price of *FOIE GRAS FRAIS*, its constant rotisseries and specials, the circular thoroughfare from which to witness a stunning variety of fleshstuffs being carved and minced and chopped by men with thick, pink forearms. The first time I saw someone buy a pig's head was at the Au Bon Porc. I had a hangover, I remember, and wanted a dry saucisson for Adrien. A neat elderly lady as high as my shoulder had a shouting match with the butcher because the tongue wasn't included in the head. It's a delicacy! he said. It's sold à part! But the tongue is *part* of the head, shouted the woman. It went on for too long and I remember staring at the fromage de tête, the head cheese, holding in vomit, until she finally stormed away.

Claire and I are eager to try the restaurant that has replaced the Good Pig. From the outside, with its simple décor, brown banquettes and dim lighting, it looks like it might serve breakfasts with eggs and avocado, or simple things like toast. We could wear trackpants. But we sigh as we hold up our menus: no formule midi, straight à la carte, and all rabbit and deep-fried cheek. We choose the cheapest thing we can find to share and I tell her about the Good Pig. At the end, our coffees come without sugar or a spoon. Where is the spoon? asks Claire. Where is the sugar?

It doesn't need a spoon, says the waiter, or sugar. It's fine coffee, it can't be mixed with anything.

Sérieux? asks Claire, miffed.

What a wank, I say, sipping the bitter brew. What if I just want to stir it?

Claire can't get over it and starts a row with the waiter, which in some way appeases my anger at having lost the spirit of the Good Pig.

Then Steve Saint-John approaches our table. Is anything wrong?

So this is his new place. He seems to be taking over the entire neighbourhood. He has a kind voice, and is so warm and accommodating that he eventually calms Claire down.

It's really good coffee, he says. Perfectly balanced.

Whatever, she says. I just like it how I like it.

This place has inherited the lack, I say, once he's gone.

What do you mean?

The lack of tongue, the lack of spoon.

Oh. Yeah.

I tell her about my affair with Steve Saint-John. It's a funny story, sweet, I think, but I can see Claire's not finding it funny.

What? I ask.

Nothing. Good story, she says. She has that flat tone in her voice that reads volumes.

Did I say something wrong?

No.

I don't think she's judging me, she's been in a dark mood since we arrived. Perhaps it's about my outburst towards Marie-France, which has since been forgiven. I'm certain Claire understands the innocence of the story of Steve Saint-John.

Do you think we have it right? she finally asks. Living here, this life. You are happy, you say, but I know you're stressed to bursting. I'm happy here but I'm alone. Is it right? Are we choosing the right things?

I think so, I say, I try not to think about it too much, or I fear I'll get lost. I sometimes think I choose it because I don't want the alternative, wondering what it would be like.

See that's the thing, she says. I'm picking off the final strand of attachment to this motherhood, partnerhood thing. I know I don't want it. But how do I know now how I will feel in the future? Will I always wonder what it would be like? What if I regret it?

Her face is drained. I can see this has been plaguing her, this decision she must make right now, pressured by her biology. I flash back to all the questions she's asked me – what is it like to be a parent? What is hard? What are the advantages? How did you know when you wanted a child? Questions I've never answered properly as they seemed impossible to explain in words.

It's decided in my body, she says. It's my head that hasn't caught up. I want to write, live here, buy a place, I don't want to be attached … sorry if this is offensive to you.

Not in the slightest.

It's just that it's been ingrained in me from the start. I was always told I'd have a child. That's what happiness is. You meet someone, fall in love, you have a child.

I think people do that to convince themselves that *their* decision was right. If everybody does it, it can't be wrong.

I think if I'd met someone, like you have, I'd probably have done it. As an experiment, if nothing else. Or not, I don't know. But that hasn't happened. I felt sad about that for a long time, but I'm not sure if it's the loss of what I'm *supposed* to have wanted, or the actual thing. I actually love being alone. I like my life, this life, the life I already have. But I'm always looking ahead.

I think we're taught to second-guess ourselves. Like, what we want couldn't be as simple as that. We must want more. We must do things for fear of missing out on some magic thing that will make us happy.

And does it make you happy?

I think it makes me happy (though you know I'm struggling) because it happened in flow, and I wanted it. I may not have wanted it, and forced it, and I feel sure that would not have made me happy. It's impossible to know how you'll feel about a situation you're not in.

I'm so tired.

I know. I think this is an odd time of life, late thirties. Coming to the end of childhood, cusp of old age.

Old age!

What worries you most?

I suppose that I'll be old and sad and regretful.

We will always regret something. Not having a child, not having a second child, not travelling, not living in a foreign country, not publishing a book.

My mum had five. She wanted more.

Mine too. Four. She said she'd have kept going and going.

We're not like them.

We're not, are we.

I wonder what they would say to us.

My feeling is they'd be proud. I think your mum would find your life amazing: poet, businesswoman, soon to buy an apartment in Paris with her own money, make her own life the way she wants it.

I think yours would think you're kickass.

I don't know. I think she'd be confused at me as a parent.

I don't. I think she'd think you're just right.

I bet she'd have tried to convince me to have more.

Do you regret that?

Only for the Chunk.

The thing I've been realising, says Claire, is we're all alone. Even with siblings we are – remember our mothers' deaths? We had these big, tight-knit families, and we were each of us alone.

Even with a child you're still alone. It doesn't ease your loneliness, fill in your holes. For me anyway. You only have your life, and they have theirs, and then they leave you, and then we all die.

She smiles.

I wonder what it would be like to just choose your happiness now, I say. And live with that and see what happens.

I think that's going to be my plan.

I like it. And we have each other.

And we're a family.

And I'll end my relationship with Steve Saint-John.

You'd better, she says.

Out in the street she looks lighter than I've seen her in weeks. The sky has clouded over above the buildings as if it will rain, the last ray lighting her dark hair with strands of silver.

Tight blacks and leather boots and slick, she's slick, the things you say slide off her. Every day meetings, delivery, money money money in the bank, more money, more slick, more black, more power. She may even be mistaken for a Parisienne. Look, she's effortless, she frowns, she strides, she never gives herself away. She has no family. She is tough as nails, she knows her shit, she even drops in Australian expressions because she feels like it, she knows the French words but chooses not to use them.

She pulls her tidy balls on and clacks the porte, curls straightened, off to a préz, en team, qu'est-ce qu'elle pense, now she calls the shots, she makes her own hours, she's the CEO manbaby who comes to work for half an hour and says NON OUI NON MORE OF THAT then leaves, not quite yet, no she's not there yet but that is who she will be, she's en route. Now she charges extra for rush jobs, a lot, and when it's a job she doesn't want to do she ups the price, further, further, and they say OK and she pouts and says, Bon then, I'll do it. Huffing, sighing, touting smart things through her neat red lips. She takes Ubers now, to meetings at Class, collects her kid on the way back, the kid enjoys the bonbons.

But she has no kid. She has no attachments, no past, no future, she is present, here and now and holy fuck is she owning it. Sure, she has no time for much besides *COMMERCE* but she is happy because the more she works the more freedom they will have and yes it might not be here now but it will be SUMMERS ON ISLANDS and longer trips to Australia at Christmastime and all is going to be well, so very, very well.

The dress was in a second-hand shop. She had seen it before, a year or two earlier, in its boutique near Opéra, and stopped in front of it for quite some time. It was long and pale with delicate flowers and patterns in oranges, pinks and reds, interspersed with panels of woven lace. There were tassels at the chest, to tie up for decency or leave open for relaxation. The dress was made for wearing on long grass, on beaches, not the Boulevard Beaumarchais and most certainly not to a meeting with Class. Who would wear a dress like that in Paris?

She touched it, let it fall. So long and light and flowing.

In the second-hand shop it was ten bucks, so she bought it, with a thumbs-up from Claire, and tossed it in her bag then on the dresser before going to shower off another slick day, Patrick Bateman in her power suit, fucking the world to pieces.

One rare night in the apartment alone, she sat in the bath and turned on the shower and let the water cascade down her hair and back. She was drying herself when she saw the tassel hanging out of the bag still on the dresser. She pulled out the dress. It was a glorious dress, yet humble, simple, girlish, like nothing she'd owned before. It fell down over her naked body, drifted around her ankles, caressed her collarbone. A long wisp of soft cotton. It made her feel at once insecure and magnificent. A sense of abandonment. A softening in her body. The soles of her feet felt tender on the floor. How long since they'd known dirt, sand, earth?

The dress made her afraid. It was a dress to wear as one pegged T-shirts to a line, as one fed wet trousers through a mangle like her grandmother did, her great-grandmothers, great-great-great-great, one would tie an apron around it and call everyone to supper. Angela might have worn this dress as she padded around pregnant, Jeanne Dielman after closing the door to her gentleman caller. Thérèse would wear this dress every day of the week, floating around her ramshackle house, putting flowers in jars. Claire would, on a beach. Marie-France might, in the garden of her new place in Bordeaux. Francine wouldn't be caught dead in it. Charlotte Gainsbourg neither. Her mother Jane Birkin might, at her beach house in the later years. She would swim in the sea and throw this over her swimsuit to walk back to her house, her grandchildren, her dog, put on dinner, throw the dress over a fence to dry.

Her own mother was too busy for this dress. But she would have bought it for you, her daughter, draped it leadingly on your bed, to encourage you to embrace your female side. *We get to have the babies.*

The Chunk would wear it. She would want her to. She wouldn't impose it on her, of course. But to see her experience that full femaleness, yes, she would love to see her revel in that. To claim it, not feel oppressed by it. To dance in it.

She turned up the heat and made herself toast. She let her hair dry naturally in pouffy curls she would never show the world. She downloaded *La Grande Bellezza* because Kiki said to, and fell asleep in front of it, in the dress.

In the night she woke in the dress and quietly took it off and hid it in the bottom drawer. The next morning she smoothed the hair, pulled on the black and spent the required half-hour doing the natural make-up and power lips. She lit a cigarette as she stepped out into the street. The day was bright and the coffee strong but in the meetings she noticed she was leaking, *femaleness*. The dress had untethered some part of her, she reined it in, tightened her jock strap, fast. Lunch meeting, leakage again, gushing this time, the shame. Thai formule, a group of women from the make-up brand, six of them all young and sweet and asking too many questions, and she liked them, and out it came, the realness, the family, a photo of her daughter – oh no – the embarrassment as they kissed goodbye. She had shared too much, they didn't need to know she was a mother and had been writing a novel for ten goddamned years.

She lit two cigarettes as she hustled away down the canal, full of shame and horror. Her balls had shrunk into two pea-sized labia. She met with Claire to drink cocktails and find that perfect blend of feminine/masculine at the bar, the mojitos, the smokes, the craic. On the walk back through a music festival at République she imagined herself in the dress getting lost in it with all the other people, talking and laughing and connecting like she had as a student, open and unguarded. When had she become so boarded up?

Home again, she wriggled out of the black dress and stockings, kicked off the heavy boots, sat in the bath-shower, got out, the dress came on her body again. Her daughter saw it, threw her arms around her mother's hips, Ohlaaa Mama, so jolie! The little girl named it the Happy Dress though she didn't know why, the dress made her more unsettled than happy. There was guilt in it, like she was letting a part of herself, or the history of women, down, or was it guilt that she had not brought this side of herself to her daughter? She felt disoriented. She lay with her daughter on the queen-sized bed and combed her hair and they watched *La Grande Bellezza* though it was highly inappropriate. She rewatched a scene she had been confused about. The woman does die. She cried as she put the little girl's hair into tiny plaits, let the little girl do hers.

Mummy! said the little girl the next day when she picked her up from the tall school gate. She had never called her Mummy before.

The Happy Dress was back in the drawer. The little girl asked where it was.

Madame Lucifer

M gets a gig in Belgium.

At first I am happy for him. Then I realise what it entails. I have the entire Christmas campaign to deliver right when he will be away, so now I'll be picking up and delivering the Chunk, trying to work while she's at home. A fury rises in me from deep below. And the word that comes out is: Great.

And then, as if that isn't bad enough:

Have a good time.

Implying:

I'm not having a good time

Your work is not real work

Your life is fun

Your life is a holiday

I'm the only one who's serious here

You suck

I'm the righteous one.

In the office I ignore him, pleased with my position as the high one when he is low. Sick in my stomach at the same time about my awfulness. My disrespect. All the voices in my head, built over a lifetime of conditioning. Men change the light bulbs, women nurse the babies. Boys are blue, girls are pink. Jackie's husband makes so much money she gets to paint all day. Breadwinner. Career man. Independent woman. Artist. Liberated. Feminist.

I am furiously typing, as a mountain of shit churns in my head, when I hear him say,

Fuck.

What?

Just fuck.

Fuck what?

Fuck you?

Fuck YOU!

We laugh a bit, facing our screens. I turn to him. Sorry. I'm just overworked.

I get it. You're overworked.

He hasn't forgiven me, I can feel it in his voice. He has something more to say. We look at each other for a moment. And then a terrible thing happens. He starts to cry.

I've never seen him cry before. I don't think. Perhaps a few happy tears, around the birth, the wedding. No sad tears. No broken tears.

I don't exist just to support you, Jayne!

I sit back in my chair. I don't know what to say, how to be. I've never seen him react to me, or seem hurt by me. I know he must be, but he takes it in his stride. He turns to his computer screen.

Oh god, I say. I'm sorry.

You think it all just goes over my head, he says, but I feel it. Your anger and frustration, directed towards me.

Oh. Really.

You don't have a clue what it's like for me. How hard I've tried over these years, how hard I've worked. To support us. I know you think I'm out there having fun. I work all day long. I do all the cooking, the cleaning, the admin, everything I can possibly do to make things work. And you disrespect me. You have no regard for me or what my life is like.

As he speaks, I feel like a man. An asshole. Don Draper. The one who has no regard for the work the housewife does. I know it, I've done it, and I should know how hard it is, how much easier it is to be the one to go to work. Here you are, you got your wish. You're the man. With your big fat balls, on your computer, so important, look at you.

You say you love me, he says. But do you even like me?

Of course I love you and I like you.

We sit there in silence.

I think I'm done, he says.

Done?

I need to go to Pigalle for string. Can you organise the Chunk?

He gets up and quietly leaves.

I finish the first draft of the job, collect the Chunk from the Maternal, make some quick pasta, send M a message: *Meet me at La Buvette at 7?*

He doesn't write back.

Bastien comes up and starts immediately playing wild animals with the Chunk, who is elated. I shower, heart racing. M has never been angry at me like this. My body is a brick. I had forgotten that he could leave me. Of course he can leave me. He is leaving me.

He always makes me feel he would never leave me. I think he believes in the contract of marriage in a way I don't. He likes to feel good, right, he's the kind of person who, if we broke up, would feel he had 'failed', he has said something along those lines before. Like he needs to 'win' at marriage, at parenthood, or something. Perhaps I just assumed that. That he would never leave.

I have touched it before. I felt it before Amsterdam, nudged it a little too far. After the cheating on him by not believing in his band. But this is the worst. This could be it.

Would I want that?

No. I am not done. I am not even begun.

Still no reply to my message. I race up to the 9th on my bike, chaining it a few doors down from La Buvette.

He is there, at the bar. That he showed up is something. He is drinking a beer. Writing in his journal.

I want to rush in but stand peering from the corner of the window. Watch him in the wild. From here he looks not mine, not that I ever thought he was. Would I want to date him if I didn't know him? Yes. He has an aura around him. Battered by life, masculine, raw. His girlfriend is a nightmare. Wife. He definitely has a wife. There is that weight on his shoulders. Joy too, some. Is he a father? Yes, you can see he has a child, he's not leisurely in his note-writing. He has a lot to tell and he's not wasting a single moment.

He takes his coat off to hook it under the bar, looks around, goes back to his notes. What is he writing? His fury. No. He is not writing furiously. He is writing his mind. *His* mind. His life. He has one of his own. I forget that. I have forgotten who he is entirely. He is an appendage to my life, her life, we are all function. His writing is purposeful but calm. Paced. He hasn't given up on me. Perhaps he wants an affair. Perhaps he's having one, out at nights, 'rehearsing'. Does he wish he were free, right now. Is he about to be? Look at the beautiful Parisiennes around him. They see him.

He starts to look restless, so I go in.

Bonsoir monsieur, I say.

He shuffles on his stool to let me sit down, can't meet my eye.

Bonsoir mademoiselle.

Mademoiselle? But I'm married, you know, monsieur.

You don't seem married.

Well I am, to someone excellent, with a lot of patience.

I order a glass of wine.

Who is this patient man? he asks.

He's a musician, a Melbourne guy, you wouldn't know him.

No, I'm sure I don't. But I hear Melbourne musicians are pretty amazing, so I don't think I stand much of a chance.

No you don't, sorry. But we can still flirt.

I don't feel much like flirting.

Oh?

I think I'm breaking up with someone.

That's sad. Your girlfriend?

My wife.

Is she a good person?

She's good deep down but she's behaving quite badly.

Then leave her!

Yeah. The only thing is I know she's trying really hard.

Not hard enough?

No, she takes me for granted.

Oh, that's terrible. You don't seem like someone who would deserve that.

Nobody deserves that.

Do you take her for granted?

I don't take her for granted but I'm not perfect. I've made some bad decisions.

I bet she's sorry for taking you for granted.

She never says sorry. She is always right.

She sounds like a bitch, you should definitely leave her.

She works hard but I do too. She gives me no credit for all the hard work I do at home, keeping things going.

She told me she loves you and she's very very very sorry and she will try harder.

I'm sorry too. I've tried to make it work. I thought it was working. That we were getting there. But she is just so unhappy. I don't know what to do to make her happy and I'm tired of trying and getting nowhere and getting shit for it.

We sit in silence, then I speak: I suppose we are getting somewhere, given that we can sit here in this beautiful bar and order what we like and not have to panic, thanks to Class.

That's not enough for me, he says.

What do you want? I ask.

I want this to be over, he says. This feeling. This coldness between us. We don't talk anymore. We're like friends. No, not even friends. Colleagues. I don't know what you want from me. You want your freedom, you want to work, you want to live here, but you don't see the impossibility of what I'm trying to do for you. You're just angry at me. I got this visa, you want me to be a musician, and I've tried to do what I thought was the smartest thing and it hasn't worked, but it's not over yet and yes it's taken longer than I thought but I don't know what else to do. What else would you have me do?

I don't know! I say. I don't know I don't know.

You're impossible. You want what's not possible. You want to be looked after but you want to do it all yourself, and I'm here, trying to support you, to give you that freedom, and you're resentful of me, you hate me.

I don't hate you.

Well you don't love me. You're not loving me.

You're right, you're right.

That image you have of us living down the impasse. This dynamic sort of life, with us doing our own thing, together, with our kid, here in Paris – we're actually working towards that. It's taking time, but it's coming. We're on the same page, I'm not your opponent, I want what you want, I'm doing everything I can.

I know. I'm sorry.

You need to stop this work thing. Nobody is making you work so hard. You say it's because you feel insecure, that we're making it, we're getting there, but we're OK now, it's like you don't know it, you're obsessed, you can't stop. You need to stop, to look at me, you're gripping too tight, I don't even know what you're pushing so hard for – don't interrupt, don't answer. I can see you're going to say, But we need the deposit for the new place or we're screwed, we're still only just paying the bills. No. You need to stop this, ease off, we're doing OK. I know it's been tough on you, believe me, I feel terrible about that, but our kid is so great, we've managed to spend time with her *and* live here *and* run a business *and* make music. I know your writing has gone to the side but it's not forever, she's still little. Don't – speak. Don't answer me. I can't stand it anymore. It has to change. *You* have to change. Or I'm out, I'm done.

I'm not done. Are you done? If I promise to be better, will you stay?

I don't know. I'm so angry right now I can't see ahead. You need to do something, that's all I know. Change something. Start listening to me. Not by me speaking necessarily, but just *listen*. See what it is I'm doing here. I'm not idling by, cruising along. I'm here for you, you, you. I don't know what this is, how to find you. I'm getting to the point where I can't try anymore, I feel too sad.

He looks like he is going to cry again, it's unbearable. I don't say anything, or move.

His words sit in the air around us as we finish our drinks. Neither of us feels like eating. As we walk home down the hill, I reach for his hand. He lets me hold it, but it is limp.

The Balkans Doctor. When I call he hears something in my voice and this time there are no long chats. I simply say, I need to come. He says to come Wednesday and stay until Saturday. Once M is back from Belgium, he books me a ticket on the Eurostar and I book three nights at the cheapest place near the guy's office, which is ludicrously expensive, and when I arrive it is more like a prison cell than the neat, attractive photos online, with a tiny window that looks at a wall and no air. M and the Chunk waved me off at the Gare du Nord. Leaving them felt terrible, like I was abandoning them, unsure what I was off to find. M sent me an encouraging text: *This is your time. X*

I know he needs me to figure this out, to come back different, new, decompressed, undepressed. I tried not to think about it as the train sped through the fields to the coastline, then down beneath the sea. To be down there, beneath the sea, in the train, still astounds me. I feel like looking around and saying to everyone in the carriage, Do you realise, right now, we're *beneath the sea*? A surreal image in my mind. Us, hurtling on tracks along the seabed, so fast that all is dark around us, we can't see the fish or the sharks or the shipwrecks. I'd rather this image than the cold hard fact of the suffocating tunnel with no stops. As the snack trolley passes I lean back and try to concretely understand that, right now, I am in the sea. In the sea in the sea in the sea.

Psychological, physiological, postural, structural. The Balkans Doctor is a tall, hulking man who seems slumped so his head won't hit the ceiling. He has a deep, serious face and big hands. He could murder me easily, but I instantly feel safe and have the desire to climb into his big hands and go to sleep. He makes no platitudes, no small talk, offers me a cup of tea, which he makes himself, then leads me into his consultation room, which is more like the ground floor of a house, because this is a house, a terrace house, with carpet and high windows and moulded ceilings with plain cylindrical light shades. His windows are frosted so nobody can see in and a thin blind is drawn to make the place feel extra private. There's a massage table in one room, with benches and cushions and implements around it, and an office area, which he leads me into.

So, he says. We are going to talk.

And we talk. For two hours. First about Paris and our life right now, our intense but thrilling life – M and the music, the Chunk, work – and as I speak I hear excitement in my voice, all the joy,

THE SEA IN THE METRO

I am happy, so happy, and grateful, and everything is wonderful and the man is listening and taking notes and I am thinking, I shouldn't be here, now I've said it all out loud it's all OK, perhaps I just needed to get away, sit in some stranger's office for a minute, I shouldn't have come here, this is a waste of time.

Child, Paris, copywriting, writing, you're a writer?

Yes, no, I want to be, I mean …

But you write?

Yes I write, a book, I'm trying, but I'm not now, at all, ever, I write ads, make luxury brands talk that were previously silent.

And why don't you write?

He listens as I explain the situation, the expense of living in Paris, the fragility of both our working lives, the need for security. He doesn't say much, asking questions and writing notes, mumbling words here and there. He asks me to go back to childhood, growing up, my siblings, parents … We arrive at Mum, then Paris and the accident, and I deliver the stories with aplomb, accustomed to it now, still a performer really, inside. He listens without asking much, then we get to M, the birth, returning to Paris. I skate over it all, impressive, clear, he likes me, I can tell, my stories are good, meaty. He doesn't react but I can see that he is thinking.

After a lunch break we return. He smiles with his big, serious face and tells me there are three areas to be worked on. The neck, the heart, and the belly. He doesn't tell me what working on them means, but asks me to get up on the table, closing the curtains.

He starts with the neck. It's not too bad, a lot of work has been done there now – by Bérénice the kinesithérapeute, the chiropractors in Australia, needles, massage, the works. I don't cry, a few flashbacks, the hôpital Salpêtrière in the dark of night, forgotten and crying, S'il vous plaît? S'il vous plaît? I thought I had effaced every dark corner of it from my body – telling the story over and over, examining it from all angles, being pummelled by lawyers, having to re-enact the event in the stairwell – but the Balkans Doctor is unrelenting and I enter a sort of cave, leaving my body behind. He has softened me, I'm lost, he pushes on my shoulder, my chest, until I HOWL for Mum, like a demon expunging THE POWER OF CHRIST. Your husband needs to get a job get a job get a job, he says, though I say, Yes I know but it's way more complicated than that. Get a job get a job, work though the pains, come back tomorrow.

It's not London I'm in. Under my feet I feel the railway, the concrete trembles, I'm under the sea still, shooting below the waves, eating takeaway Mexican in the jail cell and falling asleep. S'il vous plaît? S'il vous plaît?

Back the next day. His hands on me again, his big, warm, safe, manly hands, he won't break me, he returns to the chest, to Mum, she is waiting for me to leave her room to die, oh please can't I stay, I want to come with you, Mum? Chantal Akerman went with her mum, Mum, why can't I come with you, oh Mum, oh Muuuum, a big gush bursts from me like I've burst my waters. As they rush out he soothes my body with oils, on my shoulders, heat on my chest, needles in my head, I drip over the bed and into his carpet, down through the earth to the water below.

Tonight it is pizza in the prison cell and he warned me not to drink alcohol but I have a beer and pass out, waking in the night unsure where I am, a coldness around me, the lack of M and my baby, my sweet milky baby, they are a planet away, I am gone. Impossible to reach them from here, this must be what taking mushrooms is like. This cell is perfect there are partying people my mind is full of water I am asleep.

Today is big, he says. I am still watery, oozing, I nod without asking what it is that is big, why is it big, what could be bigger than these days and how will I return to real life now that my form is no more, how will I see my family let them see me like this, no edges.

His table is the only place I want to be despite the torture of the past days. Yes, torture, it is blood not water oozing from me. The heat is on my belly, he has his hands over my belly, not quite touching. It takes a long time for me to relax, I don't like it there, I cover my belly with my hands, crouch up my legs, he works them back down: It is OK, I will not hurt you, you can trust me, you can relax. I just can't just can't he knows it without even pressing there he's a god this man I am in the face of God and we are talking and he is so so kind and I trust him do I trust him DO I TRUST ANY MAN I don't trust him he is so kind he knows there is something I am keeping and it's – even to just mention it – my body turns to steel – and he asks if we can stop talking now and he leaves me lying warm for a very long time and then hovers his hands above my head, then lower to my chest, then lower to my belly

that place where she lived

where I kept her

safe with all my care

my entire self.

There is softness now. I am not so rigid now. His warm hands are *on* my belly, he doesn't bother to ask like all the stupid doctors of today, he is confident and I like that and I trust him fully, don't I, I have to trust him fully, yes yes yes I do, no no no I don't. He can sense it and moves to my feet. He spends the rest of the afternoon leaving me to lie, feeling my pulse, needles in some places, music coming from here or somewhere else.

Why are you in Paris?

It's home.

How is it home when you're from Australia?

I don't know. It just is. I've never wanted to leave, not since drama school. It's the place I feel most at home.

But you nearly died there.

I don't think about it much.

And you are sad.

Not really.

You are sad.

Yes I'm sad.

What are you running away from? Death? Do you think you can escape it by living where you were nearly killed? Where you don't see signs of your mother every day?

I've never thought of it like that.

I think you are running away, in Paris. Does that feel true?

Yes, but it feels more alive, like I'm running towards life.

But you won't turn and face yourself. You push yourself towards things you'll never arrive at.

I don't like who I am perhaps …

Now we're getting somewhere.

Burrito this time in the prison cell. I like prison. And I'm so, so tired.

Last day. He asks if I'm staying overnight. I say, Yes I am. He says, Good.

It doesn't take him long to get there. Hands hovering around the place below my belly button again. The precious, precious place she was kept. He asks me to say what happened, lying there, in the warm, with my eyes closed, and the words come out, fall out, and he doesn't move, just holds his warm meaty hands over me.

The dungeon. The bright lights. The bald devil.

This is why the Balkans Doctor is so strong. His calm hands above me as I tear at him, kick and scream, swear, punch, howl YOU'RE HURTING ME, the hands stay warm, the hands stay near, I scratch his face off, my eyes shut tight, legs thrashing, no no no no no, it's OK, he says, his hands still warm, the bald devil retreating to black, backstage now, his face the old man's rubbery face, M's face, my baby's face, my mother's face, there is no more blood, no pain, surrender.

He places something warm over me and wraps me tight, soothes me with his big hands, it's over now, it's OK, shhh, it's OK, you're OK, it's gone now, you're here.

Time spans out. The Balkans Doctor leaves me in the blanket, the room is warm, the lights are low, I smell something faint and unfamiliar, an Indian scent, powdery. It could be any time of day, any amount of time passing, I drift in a plane between sleep and waking.

Late in the afternoon, the Balkans Doctor helps me sit up. He brings tea.

I seem to remember, I tell him, though I might have dreamed it, a nurse came in after and said to me, If you file a complaint, I was there.

This is abuse, he says. You were abused.

But this happens all the time, I tell him. I'm lucky it was the afterbirth, at least I got to bring her into the world gently.

Perhaps that intensified it. What started gentle ended with anguish. And the birth still hurt a lot, no?

Yes. I remember every second. I can feel it in me now. But before today all I could feel was him.

He pats my leg. I hadn't realised I'd held on to this so long. I didn't know you could even say it. I could never tell anyone. Because she is here. How do you share the violation, when she is here? How could a violation become entwined with the first breaths of her existence? There was no way to express it. My pain flew in the face of my gratitude, my bliss at her birth. And the feeling of it was so intense, to even think of it would make me nauseous. Like the pain was still right there.

I feel much better. A suffocating weight has been lifted from my chest, my neck, my core. I hug the Balkans Doctor. His wide chest reminds me of the safe feeling M's narrower one gives me, though I haven't allowed it to for such a long time.

I get off the Eurostar into the old world. Paris feels dirty and ancient compared to modern, shiny London with its clean station toilets. I love it. I love the streets. I love the sky.

And I love them, the two of them, sitting on the terrasse of the Napoléon with Oranginas in the sun. I feel like I'm returning from war as I run and pick up the Chunk and squeeze her tight in my arms, drinking in her hair and skin.

I smile at M.

I can't remember the last time you smiled like that, he says.

Me neither.

The feeling of panic, rage, feels like it has left my body. Got up and walked out of me. I can sense his body breathing its own sigh of relief. And I ask him. About his own experience. And he tells me how hard things have been for him too. Not just in regards to me, but in regards to this city, how being locked out of the one place he was permitted to work in, music, was terrifying, and he didn't know what to do. And he didn't feel he could show his fear because he knew how badly I wanted to make it work here, and he didn't want to let me down. To do the band had seemed like it answered all the questions, he could still be a musician, make his own work, keep impressing me with his strength of character and creativity while also making money and he knew it wasn't working either from the start, but he had no choice but to double down on it, because to accept failure would mean to crumble and he couldn't do that. Then, when I shut him out, was angry at him, it was worse than ever. The worst. He was alone, with the child, supporting me, knowing I was resentful, *and* he wasn't succeeding, *and* he didn't know what else to do.

It's heartbreaking to hear him say all this, but I know he's right, I couldn't have heard it until now. I couldn't accept he might not be able to find some way to make this impossible situation work. He had to come through with the fairytale, or else.

THE SEA IN THE METRO

And here we are.

For the first time since Nanashi, it feels like we're together.

Sitting on the couch in the moonlight.

He reaches for my hand.

I'm sorry, he says.

I'm so sorry too.

It's going to be OK, he says. Better than it's ever been. I don't know how I know that. But I know.

Impasse

Even now, after four years of solid work, tax records, money put away to use as a bond, we are still no candidate for an apartment in comparison to a Frenchperson with a normal, steady job. The fact that it is just one of us working, and freelance, makes it harder. The only person who will allow us to move in, and happily, is Madame Lavigne, the propriétaire of my friend Harry's old place on the rue de Marseille. Harry left years ago, and it's been rented by a couple who are moving out because they're having a kid. The apartment has only one bedroom but it's got a double séjour that we can split into a bedroom and a living area, as so many friends did when they were students. The makeshift bedroom will face the street, which could be loud at nights and especially through the summer as it intersects with the Canal Saint-Martin, and the kitchen and bathroom are crap, but it's just a few doors down from Du Pain et Des Idées, the canal, and only a ten-minute walk to school. Our old neighbourhood again: Chez Prune, the Récollets, Dirty Park, Clean Park, the Marché Alibert on Sundays … It's not perfect and will be tricky with the Chunk but we'll get used to it.

We go to meet Madame Lavigne in her cramped flat on the rue de Seine and she even seems amenable to doing some travaux to fix, say, the cracked bath and the tired old kitchen.

Then Didier comes over for dinner and announces he's moving to London. His job offered to send him there, and he's still sad living in that apartment without Nadine. His eyes are full of tears. The Chunk sits on his lap, and he hugs her tight, as if drawing in any remnants of Nadine she may contain. His apartment will be available soon, if we want it, his name can stay on the lease until we do a transfer, which the owner will be fine with once he knows the place is in order and the rent paid.

We haven't set foot inside the place in the rue d'Hauteville since I was pregnant. It feels different now, smaller, but it is more adult than the rue de Marseille, with sturdy walls and a proper bathroom, and it's quiet. It's closer to school, and no travaux necessary. The only thing is there's just one bedroom as well. Didier opens the sliding door to the walk-in robe. It will have to do. At least she'll be cosy in there.

Packing up Petites Écuries is sombre, and the Chunk is a sport, like it's been bred into her that she'll always be on the move. Her psyche is fluid, it seems – in language, place, though that has begun to change. She is asking more questions about Australia, her cousins, if they live there all the time, why her friends from school aren't going to their Stralia at Christmastime. We have accumulated more stuff than we could have imagined, and have to sell or get rid of a lot of it to fit ourselves into Didier's flat. Some of the toys have to come with us, for continuity, and I feel criminal, though I know Sido and Jacques and the kids won't mind or probably even remember their stuff, like the Barbapapas book and a collection of soft toys.

We move in on a Saturday, dragging our belongings around by foot and a few taxi rides. The Chunk adores her closet-bedroom, right near us, and though the place is small and corporate-banal, it feels practical and comfortable. There is no romance, it has been created like a hotel room, sparse, and empty. Even with the Chunk's toys and art supplies all through the main room, it still feels cold. There's no place for the record player, the bookshelf is too narrow and the kitchen bench and table are too small for anything else. We leave it in a box, and put the Chunk's toys in the closet, where she sets about arranging Vanilla Ice Cream and her collection of bunnies on the pillow. In Tinyland, she tells us, she had a pink and purple bedroom, which she sometimes shared with Aren't I. It had her name in shapes on the door.

We put her name in shapes on the door of the closet. We won't close it at night, for fear of suffocation, her presence in the room making it hard to switch off and sleep, let alone other bed activity. I try not to think of her in the closet as a metaphor for our lives. She adores it, we snuggle in at bedtime and read the Barbapapas, avoiding the chapter where they're squeezed up against the windows: *But Barbapapas aren't made for apartments.*

It gets hot and there's another pollution crise, and this time we have air-conditioning but it feels strange to put it on, anti-French, so we leave it off unless the pollution is so bad we can't open the windows. Our stuff stays in boxes we keep meaning to unpack, but Didier hasn't moved his books out yet. The boxes become closets, drawers, craft stations. Claire calls it Camp Chunk.

Sido and Jacques are back. They invite us around with Francine. We drink champagne and share stories as the kids play, and it's not as weird as we thought for the Chunk to come back, she just rolls with it. Francine is happy, but I can't help but feel strange, like we've been cheating on our friends for these years, like we have a secret life. I'm jealous of them. Jealous they have Francine. It feels bizarre to be back in the apartment, which had grown on us like a skin, now looking and smelling unfamiliar, like in a bad dream. Francine makes an effort to pay attention to the Chunk, though I can see she is over the moon to have her own babies back. She was never ours.

Back to school. Grande section at the Maternal. Big girl, new shoes, Maîtresse Inès this year, a few favourite friends in her class this time, including Sami. They speak French together, though we encourage them to speak in their home language of English. They look at Amal and me like we're crazy.

Back to work, collecting an exhausted Chunk at 4.30, pain-au-chocs and Oranginas at Madame Gen, work meetings, restless sleep. Stressed, knuckles curled, headaches, dark circles under the Chunk's eyes, M's, mine. Dragging her from sleep in the mornings, dressing her floppy still-sleeping body in bed, force-feeding her breakfast before dragging her I-don't-want-to-go-to-school face up the rue d'Hauteville, along Petites Écuries and down Martel, the frown of the gardienne telling her to descend from her trottinette. The maîtresse's welcoming face. The usual guilt as I march out of school straight to the office.

This year there's no more compulsory sleeping in the dortoir, she only has to lie down if she wants to, and she never does. The days shorten and soon we're hauling her zombie body to school on her trottinette in the dark.

We're eating dinner one night, talking about the December break, when she says, When we go to Our Stralia at Christmas, can we stay and live there?

I smile. Why do you want to stay in Australia?

We can live next to Grandad, she says. And do tea parties.

Knife in the heart. But Paris is her home. Why would she want to leave her home? Christmas there is all she knows. Sunshine and presents. I've been waiting for this day, I realise, but never expected it to actually come.

The idea is ludicrous, we brush it aside. Everything we've worked for, all that we've done to set ourselves up, is finally arriving. We still don't have a solid place to live, but that will come. A few more years and we'll have passports, and a demonstrated income, M will have more history to show with the music, our paperwork will be better.

Over the next few nights she is restless. Can't sleep. Itchy bum. We can't see any rash and take a strict approach, telling her to go back to bed, getting more and more stern as we try to concentrate on our work. It's just a phase. Finally M takes his mini torch to look at her butt, and to his horror sees a small white worm coming out of it. The guilt is extreme. Me especially. I hadn't believed her, I just wanted her to go away so I could get my work done.

Always trust them. Respect them. Assume they are trying their best.

Once the poor little thing is asleep, M pours us each a glass of wine. His head is on the opposite end of the couch to mine, our legs entwined.

That was terrible, he says.

Wake-up call, I say. The thing that scares me is how much I needed her to go sleep.

We always need that, he says, it's normal. It's our time. But it's definitely on another level these days.

I've forgotten what I'm working for, I say, tears coming. We don't do anything fun anymore. We don't have the craic. We just work work work so we can hopefully go away in summer and at Christmas. We work so we can get *out* of here. We're not *living* here.

I don't know what fun is anymore, he says. Escape?

Those trips feel industrialised.

We're industrialised.

How did it come to this? I say. The copywriting was supposed to liberate us, give us time to do the things we love, like spending time with her and making music, writing.

You missed something: we wanted to live in Paris, says M. What you described just now is pretty simple, standard. But we wanted to live in Paris.

Yes...

Maybe we have to give one thing up.

I shiver. Are you saying what I think you're saying?

THE SEA IN THE METRO

We should at least consider it. Try it on.

Maybe we should, I say.

But I don't believe it. I am testing the feelings of the words in my own body. They don't sit well at all.

It's a disease, this idea of Australia, spreading. Now it's out, I have trouble putting it back. It creeps all over me, into me. A new kind of exhaustion. Emotional fatigue. Tired of moving. Tired of travel. Tired of the suitcase. Tired of the Chunk in a closet. I can tell something is shifting in M too.

I don't want to leave, I state one night, wobbly in heels. This is all we know. We have a home here. We can't go back to Australia. We'll never return here. At least we can stay here in this apartment as long as we like. Everything is set up. School, friends, community, work. In Australia we haven't built anything. We have nowhere to go. I can't see the picture.

Me neither, says M, but the more I think about it, the more I wonder if the impasse is a fantasy that's impossible here, unless we're megastars. It might be better for us there. Simpler. More dynamic. Less pressure.

This makes me angry. All this work, for what? To just go home?

Her school photos come back. A happy, smiling, open girl, with dark circles under her eyes. Now I look, the kids all look pale and have the same sunken eyes, it must be because the photos were taken in October when it was getting cold and they were likely still adjusting to the rhythm of being back at school. The photo makes me sad. I'm not sure why. Is it that I don't know her? That inside those gates she has her own life already? That the photographer got to see her soul and I'm only seeing it now? I miss her, seeing the photo. Is it that she is trying so hard? Is it that she is growing up? Is it that her grandparents are missing this, missing her, that she is so young and in school for such long hours, that even at 4.30 – which is early for her to be collected – I am still not done with my workday?

Is it that the children colour the boots in brown?

The school is lovely. Inside, it is all colours. Last week they were asked to wear 'petits pois' for the day, and we didn't realise it was because they were visiting the Yayoi Kusama exhibition at the Pomp-di-dou and had been doing paintings in her style all week. The Chunk brought home polka-dot balloons and polka-dot paintings and a polka-dot sculpture. Only in France, we said.

M accompanied them on an excursion on the métro one day to La Villette, where they saw a play that began with a woman howling in pain, in the dark. An avant-garde puppet show, the kids were freaking out. M felt something warm, and sure enough one of the kids had wet themselves, a pool spreading out over the cold floor. On the way back another kid got left in the métro as they alighted at Château d'Eau, but after a quick headcount the teacher realised and, animal-like, reached her gadget arm back into the carriage to wrench the child through and onto the platform. The kids get experiences, real experiences, here. Treated like mini adults.

But every day the Chunk asks what day it is, so she knows how far it is to the weekend.

Paris doesn't want us to leave. Twice she's made it clear it's over for us, but this time she is pulling out all the stops to keep us here. Work is good, the pay from Class taking the pressure off my working day, the band now have a following and are getting regular paid gigs just like M said they would. Then, out of the blue, Viviane the mother from the Maternal overhears me talking about our tiny place and offers us her apartment to rent long term on the rue du Faubourg-Saint-Denis, as they're moving to the suburbs. In an *impasse*. The impasse of dreams. Behind a large blue door near Paradise and

Fidelity streets, a few doors up from the Monoprix. Cobblestones and quiet behind the big porte cochère, ateliers on the ground floor, apartments up above, cats and kids' scooters and plants and greenery all around. A ground-floor apartment down towards the end of the impasse, private and modest, open-plan and designed for light and space, a kitchen in the centre. It's expensive but I now have a young writer working for me and we've been thinking of forming an agency to deliver English-language copy to French clients, a real niche. I will be saying goodbye to writing anything other than copy for a very long time, but that's what it takes to live here, a real career, work, and it's worth it. Isn't it.

And how could you leave?

You can't leave the place where you fell in love twice, nearly died, where you watched so much snow falling, where you slipped on your butt so hard you cried, where you screamed on bikes and got down on a wobbly knee with a ring one night on a bridge. Where you sweated in black clothes for two years in front of a row of artists you admired so much you couldn't speak to them in social situations and who shook their heads over and over as you wriggled and writhed and tried and tried and tried and failed and failed and occasionally didn't. Where you read your first experiments with writing out loud and a lady described them as 'demeaning'. Where you always felt inspired to make and do stuff even if it wasn't finished and made you look like a dick. Where you were never afraid of someone saying, Pipe down, Jayne. Where you lived in your first apartment alone but for the cockroaches. Where you learned to pee standing up. Where you were nearly raped by a hotel desk clerk and learned not to be so Nice. Where you got your heart broken over and over, and enjoyed experimenting with how far you could push it. Where you once screamed C'EST FINIIIII on a métro step and thought you could rip out a pole and javelin it down the stairwell at the back of the disappearing head. Where you rejoiced alone at having your first story published in a newspaper. Where you watched kids in the park from your window and then became the parent looking back up at your own wistful ghost. Where you tried to remember what it was to have time to be wistful and look out windows. Where you smoked a thousand cigarettes and drank wine that made you go silent with joy. Where you learned to boil an egg and never learned how to make a tarte fine though you did once try very hard. Where you made the best friends of your life and felt a new sort of pain at every departure. Where you wheeled a squeaky trolley piled with instruments down a crazy street to a stinking studio on Thursdays and made music with a group of boys. Where you created a business by accident and got serious and figured out how to act in meetings and also got your paperwork in order (almost). Where you learned to say Go fuck yourself in French and said it one day to a magazine prick who had got you to translate two entire editions then never paid you even though you were starving and he was so shocked at being told to go fuck himself that he said he would sue you and you were so young you believed him. Where you finally learned how to pronounce phrases containing no consonants and swore at traffic and marvelled at fashion and cried well enough to secure a bank account and where the beauty of the ever-changing light never ceased to stab you in the soul and where there was a time that nothing made you happier than wandering the streets all day long with nothing but your camera. Where you always felt excruciatingly alive. Where never one single banal or average day passed you by. Where, no matter what, you always somehow felt yourself, too yourself, every characteristic and emotion exaggerated to breaking point: grief, idiocy, elation, hope, fury, wonder, melancholy. Where you revelled in solitude. Where you learned how to look out over a river alone and truly see it, just for yourself.

It's twelve years since you arrived that second time, but don't be nostalgic. Think of it like leaving the theatre school. You weren't nostalgic then because you'd put everything you had into it – and, once you left, you were surprised to notice that you never wanted to go back. You still live right around the corner and to this day you pass that painted blue door regularly and feel nothing but a sense of completion.

Where you gave birth.

Look at the kid. How happy she is no matter what. Watch her go off to school, her French world, her city world. She keeps bringing up her Stralia and her life there, which for her has already started. Rainwater puddles and that great big sea. Perhaps you can have the impossible. Perhaps it's only the imagination that limits it. I remember now, it was our Korean movement teacher that said to us, 'An actor must be able to see the sea in the métro.' I wrote it down in my class notes. 'Anyone can imagine the sea,' he said. 'But the actor must be able to see the sea.' I'm sure that applies to the writer, too. If they observe it, live it, with precision and focus, they will no longer need it in front of them, to see it. It's there.

Amour

At the end of *Amour*, the old woman calls from her bed:
Mal
Mal
Mal
Pain pain pain
It drives the old man crazy.
This is not a life.
The old lady dies the same way as Betty Blue.

M and I watch the credits roll, clutching hands. We don't turn to face each other but I know we're both crying.

We want to grow old together. And go to the theatre. And die. We want to have lived and be at peace like this couple. He can suffocate me with a pillow.

When Marie-France's very old grandfather was diagnosed with terminal cancer, his very old wife and him drove their car into the forest, put the pipe in the car, held hands and turned on the gas.

I would like this with M more than I'd like to stay in Paris. I'd like to see my child with her close family more than I'd like to stay in Paris. I'd like to write a book more than I'd like to stay in Paris. I want to say I'd like to swim in the ocean more than I'd like to stay in Paris, but I'm not sure that's true. Those two are equal. They are two halves of two very different things, and both exact halves of me.

After a meeting at the Big Agency I take the long way home, along the river, past the English bookshop. Memories of Kiki and Nadine and Adrien and Sophie and the Dodger playing boules and the accident and the kid I was the au pair for who I took to the Tuileries once and he stole another kid's boat. I feel giddy from pedalling too hard and decide to loop back over the Île Saint-Louis, and stop for a moment. Then I see it. The spot where I sat when, at twenty-two, I first saw a view for myself. I was so lonely, god, I hated Paris then, couldn't wait to get back to Australia and hook up again with my boyfriend – couldn't see the point of all this wandering alone, the long days of sightseeing and babysitting and feeling lost and bored. Then I sat on the river bank and ate a réligieuse next to a fisherman and suddenly I got it. The view was in me. That feeling of joy in the aloneness shaped the next two decades of my life. I longed for it, lived for it. All these years I've looked for this spot. Now it's presented itself to me, like it was always right there.

I walk my bike down and sit in the spot I sat in at twenty-two. Soon I'll be forty-two. There is no fisherman. Nobody calling *mademoiselle?*

I am not alone anymore. I thought you always were alone, no matter what. After Mum died, even with my close family, I felt so incredibly alone, and I know they did too, so I thought that was it, we were born alone, live alone, die alone. I learned to treasure that. It was my independence.

But now I'm a mother. A wife. We are connected, the three of us, for life. If they are not well, I am not well. If they are not happy, I am not happy.

A feeling shoots through me. I need to see her as happy as I can make her.

I can give her family, love, sea, sky. More of me, more childhood. It doesn't have to mean giving up, relenting. It doesn't even have to be forever.

Night is falling as I push back off on my bike. I gather the city inside my body with each turn of the wheel. Drink it in. The pavement, the birds, the golden lights, the darkening sky. This place is my home. But I'm not me anymore, I'm a family.

Back at the flat, M can see something has shifted. His entire being seems to relax and open out. It's like he's been waiting for permission to release all he's been thinking, feeling, wondering, afraid of the reaction it would provoke. He reveals he's been looking online, at a tiny school in Dad's seaside town that overlooks the bay. She could even start in February. There are so many trees.

I might be able to keep up my work from there, I say.

I would get a job, he says. Start a café or something. Play my new songs with the old band. You would have time to write the book. Even if you keep doing copywriting, they'd be asleep during our days …

Where would we live?

We'd find somewhere … There are old army houses down near your Dad's, cheap. There's one around the corner from his place that's been sitting there a while, plain brown brick, but with a backyard and a pomegranate tree. Imagine, a little place of our own, a bedroom for her, you're writing, I'm working and making music, there's family around, no more visas and paperwork, no more Paradise City …

Maybe Australia is our impasse, I say.

He smiles. I have a very good feeling about it, he says. Like moving forward, not back.

So we wouldn't move back to Melbourne?

When I close my eyes, he says, It's not the city I see.

THE SEA IN THE METRO

    You really see the sea?
    Yeah.
    So you *are* a beach person?
    Not at all.
    I don't know if I can do it. If this can be the end.
    It's not the end.

You can't leave but you know you already have, you knew the moment she asked for it. Not because you're pandering to her, but because you know she knows where the bonheur lies. You can't leave Francine, but she is with her own family now, and though you love her you know you were never quite inside her world as she was in yours, and that you leaving won't cause the same pain for her as it does to you, or imagining life in Paris without her. You can't leave Claire, but she understands, and cries, and calls you a pussy, and though you know you'll never truly leave her you also know it's never the same when someone is gone, and that you could hardly bear the pain if it was her that left.

You will leave.
    And you will also never leave.
    And that will be the state of not just you, but your whole, small family.
    And, eventually, that will be fine.

Photos:
    Francine and her family waving from the window of Little Stables Street
    Claire and the Chunk beaming with small dog on worn velvet couch
    The Chunk on Marie-France's lawn, doing a dance routine with her girls

M and the Chunk playing guitar together, at a table in the Récollets courtyard

M singing with the band at the Grand Rex

A book, published

Girl's first photo:

Woman standing barefoot on grass in front of pomegranate tree, in Happy Dress

ACKNOWLEDGEMENTS

This book was written on the unceded land of the Wadawurrung people. I acknowledge their deep and enduring connection to the land, waterways and skies and pay my respects to Elders past and present.

I am deeply grateful for the grants and residencies that allowed me the bursts of focus required to write this book: the La Napoule Art Foundation, La Ville de Paris, Centre les Récollets, Regional Arts Victoria, Varuna the National Writers House, Eastern Beach Art House and Bundanon Trust. Thank you in particular to Nelcy Mercier and Mathilde Château at La Napoule (and to Claire Messud for her recommendation), Isabelle Mallez at La Ville de Paris, Chrystel Dozias at Les Récollets (mon ange guardien), Amelia Kingston at RAV, Jaala Hallett and Veechi Stuart at Varuna, Alacoque Dash and the Boyd family at Bundanon.

Thank you to Hardie Grant, for believing in these books, even before they were written. To Robert Watkins, Claire and Kimberley Davis and Lauren Carta for their dedicated work on this book. Thank you to my agent, Jane Novak, for her guidance and care.

Thank you to Tegan Bennett-Daylight, for her passionate creative support and belief in this book, from its first scrawlings to every step along the way.

Thank you to the Lecoq friends and teachers who accompanied me on my mad journey to discover who the hell said *la mer dans le métro*: Paola Rizza, Ravi Jain, Philippe Peychaud ... leading finally to master of movement studies Jinwoo Yoo. Of course it was you. I am so grateful, Jinwoo, for your teaching, then and now. *Les artistes doivent être des gens qui fouillent l'essence.*

Thank you to Dany Laferrière, family member of Les Récollets, who reminded me that joy is as valuable in writing as pain, and that wonder, if you let it, only brightens with age. To Helen Garner, for this same reason, and for her incredible generosity, curiosity and honesty.

To Professor A. James Arnold, translator of Artaud, for the excellent discussion over slut v whore, and for confirming my feeling that slut was likely more Artaud's intention than whore – a state of mind rather than profession. And to Antoine Quint, Hélène, and Laurent Prost the Artaud psycho-fan who helped me locate the slut quote in Artaud's tome *Oeuvres* (Edition Quarto Gallimard p. 1366). Merciii.

The creative assignments on page 70 are from Miranda July's early 2000s *Learning to Love You More* web page (learningtoloveyoumore. com). *Write a conversation you wish you could have* opened a world to me. Thank you to Chris Kraus for her personal blessing to use the quote on page 171, forever on a Post-it.

Thank you to the town of Point Lonsdale/Queenscliff, with its wild, unpredictable sea and sky, and to our beautiful bookshop community, especially Pauline Parker, Yasmin Mobayad and Charlee Brooks. To the 10th arrondissement: even in the water here, I'm there.

Thank you to my dad, whose enthusiasm and support constantly blows me away. Thank you to my sister/rock, Anna, and my dear brothers, Rod and Andy. Thank you to my treasured friends and creative family for their thoughts, inspiration and guidance: Martine Murray, Alice Retif, Leigh Whannell, Corbett Tuck, Jemma Birrell,

Rachael Coopes, Linda Jaivin, Claire Thomas, Katrin Koenning, Kate Van den Boogert, Lauren Elkin, Misha Honcharenko. Thank you to Marisa Purcell, my confidant and forever muse.

Thank you to my chosen sisters, Libby Little and Mary Kelly, to whom I dedicate this book.

To my mother, Lyn, who I'm probably trying to awaken through all this writing. Thank you for the notes you left. And for all you showed me.

And lastly, most preciously, to my little family.

To Patch, my office chum, all night long till the sun comes up.

To Matt Davis, co-author of everything I do, and am. Thank you for sharing your mind with me, your music, your strength, your Michael-Jordan parenting ... for your belief in this writing above and beyond yourself and also me. Thank you for working so closely with me on this book, though it hurts. For trusting me. For your editorial genius, your brilliant ideas, your pulling me from my routine darknesses. The joy of my life is being your best friend. Je t'aime.

And finally, to the wise, hilarious and magnificent Frankie Davis. My chunk of *life*. Your patience is astonishing. Your grace. When I announced I would miss your twelfth birthday if I accepted the La Napoule residency, a single tear slipped down your cheek, as you told me to go, with a smile. You've always seemed to understand it, intrinsically – is that because you're such an artist yourself? Or just because you're you. Oh Frankie, every day I can't believe I get to be your mother, your friend. You make me want to drink every second of this life dry.

What a ride.

Jayne Tuttle is a writer, actor and bookseller.

Raised in Melbourne, Jayne moved to Paris in 2004 to take up a French Government Enseignement Supérieur scholarship to attend the Jacques Lecoq Theatre School. After graduating, she remained in France to work in theatre, and as a translator and bilingual copywriter. In 2021, Jayne and fellow Lecoq alumnus John Bolton developed her first book *Paris or Die* into a solo stage play, touring Melbourne, regional Victoria and France. She is also the author of *My Sweet Guillotine*.

Jayne has received fellowships from the Ville de Paris, La Napoule Art Foundation and Bundanon Trust, and is a long-term artist-in-residence at the Centre les Récollets in Paris. In 2021, she was awarded the Eric Dark Flagship Fellowship at Varuna National Writers House. Her writing has been published in *The Age, The Sydney Morning Herald* and *The Guardian,* among other international outlets and journals.

Jayne co-owns The Bookshop at Queenscliff.